In praise of *Intoxicating* ...

'Break out the adjectives. A book about grog that's not only an appealing, invigorating, exhilarating and heady brew but a valuable and uniquely informative national history.'
—Robert Drewe

'Max Allen sucks you into this book by promising lots of grog stories but what he does, the sly dog, is teach you about your country.'
—Bruce Pascoe

'A history as potent as the devil's own firewater, and writing as beautiful as that final drop of Grange Hermitage. Pour a few chapters out for yourself.'
—John Birmingham

Intoxicating

Ten drinks that shaped Australia

Max Allen

'The natives had also a method, at the proper season, of grinding holes in the tree, from which the sweet juice flowed plentifully ... When allowed to remain any length of time, it ferments and settles into a coarse sort of wine or cider, rather intoxicating if drank to excess.'

—Daniel Bunce, *Australasiatic Reminiscences of Twenty-Three Years' Wanderings in Tasmania and the Australias*, 1857

First published in Australia in 2020
by Thames & Hudson Australia Pty Ltd
11 Central Boulevard, Portside Business Park
Port Melbourne, Victoria 3207
ABN: 72 004 751 964

thamesandhudson.com.au

Thames & Hudson Australia wishes to acknowledge that Aboriginal and Torres Strait Islander people are the first storytellers of this nation and the traditional custodians of the land on which we live and work. We acknowledge their continuing culture and pay respect to Elders past, present and future.

This book contains references to Indigenous knowledge and cultural practices. This information belongs to those Indigenous peoples. This should be respected, and not be appropriated.

978 1 760 76100 4 (paperback)
978 1 760 76137 0 (ebook)

A catalogue record for this book is available from the National Library of Australia

Every effort has been made to trace accurate ownership of copyrighted text and visual materials used in this book. Errors or omissions will be corrected in subsequent editions, provided notification is sent to the publisher.

Cover Design: Josh Durham
Typesetting: Cannon Typesetting
Editing: Katie Purvis
Printed and bound in Australia by McPherson's.

FSC® is dedicated to the promotion of responsible forest management worldwide. This book is made of material from FSC®-certified forests and other controlled sources.

Contents

My introduction

The wine looked like liquid sunshine in the glass. Golden, glinting, beautiful. It smelled and tasted even better. Sweet, grapey, like honey on my tongue. I gulped it down greedily.

It was the mid-1980s. I was fifteen or sixteen. Maybe a little older. All these years later, I can still remember what that wine tasted like, what the bottle felt like in my hand, the sensations of smell and flavour and vision fused in the memory. I can see the buttercup-yellow label: Brown Brothers Spatlese Lexia.

It came in a mixed case of Brown Brothers wines that a family friend had given us for Christmas. Mum wasn't that interested in the red wines or sweeter wines, and my little sister was too young to drink, so I got to try them instead. Like most teenagers, I had been experimenting enthusiastically with alcohol for years. Furtive tastes of my grandparents' sherry. A sip of Mum's vermouth from the fridge. Cans of beer or quarter-bottles of vodka shared with mates in the park, bought by the oldest-looking one of us from the wine shop where we knew they didn't care we were underage.

But this Spatlese Lexia was different. It was *delicious*. It made me stop, it made me pay attention, it made me think about what I was drinking. And it made me curious to see what the other wines in the Brown Brothers box tasted like.

I was already fascinated by flavour. Always had been, since I was a kid. A couple of years earlier, I'd even conducted my own lemonade

taste test. I'd seen one of those newspaper articles where they
assemble a group of chefs and get them to taste and rate different
brands of baked beans, or chocolate, or hot cross buns. It inspired me
to go out and buy all the different kinds of lemonade I could find – I
really liked lemonade – and taste them to see which one I preferred.[*]

This perhaps helps explain why, a decade later, I would start
writing about wine and other drinks. And why still, today, every day,
I'm driven by the same impulse to ask the same questions. What
does this drink taste like? Why does it taste that way? And what's
the story behind it?

'Have you ever tried an older one?' asked Ross Brown. 'They age
remarkably well. I've got bottles going back at least thirty years in
the cellar. Let's have lunch and I'll bring a couple to try. I might even
have a bottle of the same wine you tasted in the 80s.'

I had phoned the executive director of Brown Brothers to talk to
him about the history of Spatlese Lexia. Here was a chance to revisit
my epiphany wine, more than thirty-five years later. We agreed to
meet at Jimmy Watson's, one of Melbourne's – Australia's – most
historic wine bars.

Jimmy Watson started selling wine from his bar in Lygon Street,
Carlton, in 1935. My father-in-law remembers going there in the late
1950s. He and a mate used to con Jimmy into letting them stay after
six o'clock closing. 'We'd say, "We don't know anything about wine,
Mr Watson – can you teach us?" He'd pour us two glasses of red
and tell us: that one's younger, that one's two years older, can you

----

* It was Schweppes.

taste the difference? We got away with it a couple of times before he rumbled us.'

When I first went to Watson's in the mid-1990s, Jimmy's grandsons Simon and Nigel had started working in the bar. The day my daughter was born in 1995 at the Royal Women's Hospital around the corner, I slipped out for a quick celebratory drink: Simon poured me a sherry. I've spent many hours there since. And now here I was at Watson's again, tucking into a plate of chicken schnitzel, chips and salad as Ross Brown gently eased the cork from a bottle of 1981 Spatlese Lexia and poured us both a glass.

Ross was right. The wine had aged remarkably well. It was still fresh and luscious. Not bad for a wine that originally sold for around $2.50. Brown Brothers started making this wine in 1974, using a grape variety called muscat of Alexandria, grown in the big irrigated vineyards along the Murray River in Victoria's north-west. For most of the 20th century, the grapes were used to make sweet sherry. Ross explained that 'lexia' is a uniquely Australian name for the variety – a bastardisation, probably, of 'Alexandria': it's easy to imagine an old, weather-beaten Aussie grower delivering a truckload to the winery on a hot day and describing the grapes as 'bloody lexias'. And the other word on the label, 'spatlese', is German for 'late-harvest', a legacy of colonial Australian wine history, when white wines were often labelled generically using names of German origin such as 'hock' and 'moselle'.

As he pulled the corks from a couple of other old wines from the cellar – including a remarkable sweet muscat made in 1973 – Ross told me how the Spatlese Lexia was very much a product of its time. Innovations in viticulture and winemaking in the early 1970s – irrigation and machine-harvesting in the vineyard, cold-fermentation and sterile filtration in the winery – meant that fresh, clean, sweet white wines could be made cheaply and consistently. Consumers, particularly female drinkers, embraced the style: Brown Brothers was soon producing more than half a million bottles of Spatlese Lexia each vintage to satisfy demand. It became by far the company's biggest-selling brand. And it wasn't the only one to profit from 'lexia' in the 70s and 80s. This was the era of many other popular sweet white wines based on the grape, such as Berri Estates' Fruity Gordo Moselle – in 2-litre glass flagon and 4-litre bag-in-box – and Kaiser Stuhl's sparkling Summer Wine.

Like me, a lot of Australian drinkers look back on these now-unfashionable wines with great affection – in the same way younger drinkers will no doubt be similarly nostalgic one day about a currently fashionable wine made from the same grape: Brown Brothers Moscato.

Brown Brothers produced its first Moscato in 2000, using the same grape variety grown in the vineyards that had supplied fruit for the Spatlese Lexia, but picked earlier, lower in alcohol and residual sugar, fresh, spritzy, zesty. The wine was exactly the right style at exactly the right time: people were increasingly interested in Italian food and drink and were looking for lighter, less sugary, more sophisticated wines. Ross showed me a graph charting the decline in sales of Spatlese Lexia and the growth of Moscato. They cross over around the year 2005. The production of the former has since dwindled to almost nothing; the production of Moscato continues to grow, exceeding even Lexia in its heyday.

As Ross and I were finishing our schnitzels, an elderly gentleman who had been having lunch with his wife at a nearby table got up and came over, curious about all the dusty bottles.

'Ah,' he said, smiling, when he saw the Spatlese Lexia label. 'That was my mother's favourite drink. Twenty-five years ago. Can

I just say it's been a pleasure to watch you blokes obviously enjoying those wines so much.'

———————

There's something I haven't mentioned. It changes the story a bit. My first taste of Brown Brothers wine took place in the mid-1980s in London. I'm not from Australia.

I was born in England and lived there until 1992, when I moved to Melbourne and got married. But my family did have lots of connections to Australia. My English mum, Trixie, had lived and worked in Melbourne for a few years in the mid-1960s, and my stepfather, Bob, was Australian, so when I was growing up we took family holidays to Australia. In 1977, I spent a couple of months at a primary school in Sydney. I have clear flavour memories from that time; food and drink that was so different to what I was used to at home. Meat pies and tinned pineapple juice under a gum tree in the playground at lunchtime. Lime icy poles on Coogee beach. McDonald's fries after seeing *Star Wars* at the Hoyts on George Street. This is one of the reasons, I think, that the Spatlese Lexia made such an impression when I drank it on a cold London Christmas Day: it tasted like Australia.

Except it wasn't labelled Spatlese Lexia in England. When Brown Brothers started shipping the wine overseas in the early 80s, they sensibly decided that using a German word and a made-up Australian word for a wine destined for sale in Europe probably wasn't a good idea, so called it Late Picked Muscat Blanc instead.

I was quite lucky to even come across a bottle. Throughout the 70s hardly any Australian winemakers bothered sending wine to the UK because English people thought Australian wine was a joke – like the Chateau Chunder and Hobart Muddy in Monty Python's 1972 'Australian Table Wines' sketch. Brown Brothers was one of only a handful of Australian companies braving the English market in the early 80s. Not only that, but there were also European trade restrictions at the time on selling sweet wines over a certain alcohol level. Luckily, the Late Picked Muscat Blanc, with an alcohol content of only 10 per cent, just scraped under, giving the Australians an opportunity to compete.

Exports of Australian wine to the UK and around the world have boomed since then. But the market today is not an easy one: most of the Australian wine sold in the UK now is in the form of cheap, generic supermarket brands made by giant multinational companies – not high-quality, high-value wine made by smaller family-owned companies. The market has become *so* difficult in recent years that a month after my lunch with Ross Brown at Jimmy Watson's, his company announced it was pulling out of the UK and would stop selling wine there.

All these stories, all this history, from just one bottle.

———————

After I moved to Melbourne I married Sophie, whom I'd known all my life as a family friend. Soph's parents, Jim and Philippa, had worked with my mum in the 1960s: Mum appears in super-8 film of their wedding, clutching a bottle of Yalumba 'champagne'; Jim is the man who sent us that case of Brown Brothers wine in the 1980s. I worked in bottle shops across Melbourne and wineries in the Yarra Valley, picked grapes, lugged hoses, started writing about drinks for a small start-up magazine called *Divine* and had my first article published in *The Age* in 1993. Since then I have made a living writing about booze, travelling and tasting across Australia, visiting wineries, breweries and distilleries, restaurants, hotels and bars, from Darwin to Hobart, from Byron Bay to Margaret River.

I've had many more life-changing drinking experiences since that first taste of Spatlese Lexia. My first glass of Penfolds Grange in a restaurant overlooking the Sydney Opera House. Watching my first batch of homemade cider start to ferment. My first sip of dark, brooding medicinal bitters bottled a century ago. All of these moments have altered how I see Australia and my place in it. I have also met many of the people who have helped shape Australia's complex web of drinking cultures, through what they've made or what they've sold or what they've written. One of the most important was the late Len Evans, who emerged in the 1960s as a champion of Australian wine and influenced the drinking habits of a nation.

One of the ways Evans convinced people to put down their pots of beer and glasses of sherry and try a nice riesling or claret instead was to take the pomposity and mystery and jargon out of wine. His oft-repeated mantra, delivered with a cheeky smile and glass in hand, was 'Don't forget that wine is just a drink. It's just a bloody *drink*.'

And it worked. People lapped up Evans's no-bullshit, democratising approach. They embraced wine and have loved it ever since.

But the more I've travelled and the more I've tasted, and the more I've learned about the history of drinking in this country, the more I've come to disagree profoundly with Evans's statement. Whether it's wine or whisky, beer or cider, gin or liqueur, it's never *just* a bloody drink. There's always much, much more to it than that.

Way-a-linah:
Indigenous drinks

The gum tree stands apart from the forest on the edge of a boggy
Tasmanian frost plain. It looks like it has left the mass of other tall
and spindly gum trees behind it to brave the cold, wide-open space.
This tree is different. The branches start closer to the ground and
spread wide as they grow, stretching to breathe. Its bark is darker,
covered in sooty mould; the ground beneath it is a damp blanket
of green moss.

I spot the tree as soon as I emerge from the forest on the opposite
edge of the flat marshland. As I squelch towards it across the bog,
I see it's weeping. Small trickles of what looks like light sugar
syrup ooze from holes in the bark. Some of the holes are ragged
cracks: signs of age and the harsh weather. Some of them are small
and sawdusty, bored out by insects. But some are clearly incisions,
deliberately made by human hands, the bark around them grown
back thick and callused.

I drag my finger along one glinting drip line and bring it to my
lips, the breeze whisking away delicate threads of syrup, catching
sunlight. The liquid tastes clean and fresh, gently sweet, bright,

lemony. Delicious. Startling. Not a hint of the eucalyptus flavour you might expect to be weeping from a gum tree. I try another, darker trail of syrup, and it tastes different. Woody, herbal, the viscous liquid has taken on the character of the tree as it makes its way down the trunk. And a third, a trickle that looks like it has been flowing for a while: transformed over time, it tastes like a tart, mildly alcoholic cider.

The frost plain is as wide and open as a large suburban park. There are quite a few of these unusual trees standing around the perimeter. Some have very little of the syrup seeping from their trunks, others have more. Some of them are young, some are hundreds of years old. With damp moss below and branches gangly and twisted above, it feels peaceful standing under these trees, like I'm in a grotto or spirit glade. And then, at the foot of one of them, I see a few flat stones, overgrown with moss and grass. They look like they have been placed there to cover a hollow in the trunk where the liquid pools.

For a moment, it feels as though the people who put these stones here, who stood under this tree and enjoyed the wispy fermented cider syrup that flows from it, have only just left, and might return any second.

———

In late November 1831, English settler and government-appointed conciliator George Augustus Robinson travelled through this part of Tasmania, the Central Highlands, with a search party, looking for Aboriginal people, hoping to convince them to join others who had come under his 'protection' – which, in reality, meant transportation to Flinders Island and separation from their traditional lands. Senior tribal men were Robinson's guides on this trip, and they led him to an extensive frost plain. In his journal, Robinson wrote

that the plain was skirted by numerous 'mellifluent' trees that had
'planted themselves in the foreground of the forest':

> Most of the trees had been tapped by the natives. This they had
> effected by perforating a hole in the tree a short distance above
> the ground by means of sharp stone and then making a hole at
> the bottom of the tree into which the liquid is conveyed and from
> which they extract it, sometimes if the hole is small by sucking it
> through a reed or twisted bark. In some of these holes I observed
> upwards of a quart of this juice and which my people greedily
> partook of. It is exceedingly sweet and well flavoured and in this
> respect resembles the flavour of cider … The natives are very fond
> of the juice and I am told it frequently makes them drunk.

A few days later, Robinson was shown more cider trees on the
fringe of another marsh, and he described how the 'natives … have
made incisions in the tree and dug [a] hole at the bottom for the
liquid to drain into'. And a few miles away, he saw trees growing
'most luxuriantly, some of them twelve feet [3.6 metres] in diameter,
and the liquid was oozing out in tolerable quantities. Holes at the
bottom of the trees had been made to receive the juice and which
served the purpose of a tank … It was amusing to see the natives run
from tree to tree to suck this juice, of which they are very fond.'

In 1843 the South African–born botanist Ronald Gunn visited a
stand of cider trees in the Tasmanian highlands near Miena, not far
from the trees I saw, and wrote a detailed report on the species that
was published the following year in the *London Journal of Botany*.
The cider gum tree subsequently received its botanical name of
Eucalyptus gunnii.

In his report, Gunn also observed firsthand the cider-gum sugar's
propensity to spontaneously change into alcohol: 'I brought a bottle

of it with me,' he wrote, 'but two or three days after reaching home it fermented, blew out the cork and a large portion of it was lost.'

Another early account of Aboriginal people tapping the trees is found in botanist Daniel Bunce's *Australasiatic Reminiscences*, a memoir of his travels across Tasmania and the mainland in the 1840s, published in 1857. As Bunce described it, the Tasmanian 'natives had … a method, at the proper season, of grinding holes in the tree, from which the sweet juice flowed plentifully, and was collected in a hole at the bottom, near the root of the tree. These holes were kept covered over with a flat stone, apparently for the purpose of preventing birds and animals coming to drink it. When allowed to remain any length of time, it ferments and settles into a coarse sort of wine or cider, rather intoxicating if drank to excess.'

As with Robinson's account, what's notable about Bunce's description is the act of deliberate collection followed by delayed consumption. It's not just the sugary liquid that Aboriginal people wanted to enjoy: they also protected the sap from birds and animals for long enough to allow the yeasts naturally present in the environment to ferment it, resulting in a different kind of drink altogether.

There is a name for this fermented drink. In his two-volume work on Indigenous practices in Victoria and Tasmania, *The Aborigines of Victoria*, published in 1878, chairman of the Board for the Protection of Aborigines and recorder of Indigenous culture Robert Brough Smyth listed many Tasmanian Aboriginal words, including the word for what he described as the 'saccharine sap of Eucalyptus Gunnii (turning soon into a kind of cider)'.

Its name is *way-a-linah*.

———

Mick Quilliam has drunk way-a-linah, and his evocative paintings of cider gum trees have helped him become recognised as one of Tasmania's best-known Aboriginal artists. One square canvas in particular is striking: a bird's-eye view of the spreading branches of the way-a-linah tree, represented by a honey-yellow spiral, surrounded by a wide circle made up of dozens and dozens of footsteps.

'The painting tells the story of people gathering once a year when the trees flow, in early summer, for ceremony,' Mick tells me. 'They'd have their weddings and things up there, in the good weather, when it's just getting nice and warm, when there's lots of kangaroo around.'

Mick hasn't been to the lake country to see the trees or taste the way-a-linah for a while – too busy with his painting – but he says he used to go up with a local Elder, who'd know which trees to visit. He has seen very old trees that still bear the scars of where they've been tapped with a tomahawk. Others that show signs of early European settlers copying the Aboriginal practice and collecting the cider-gum syrup in a billy can. And he's seen trees where the earth is worn away in a groove around the base, from countless footsteps and ceremonies.

'But then you also see the dead trees,' says Mick. 'A lot of them are dying.'

Eucalyptus gunnii is very sensitive to climate. It grows in country that is just that little bit too frost-prone for other species. That's why it can survive where it does, apart from the rest of the forest, braving the cold of the bog. But the climate is changing. What was once very cold country is less cold now – not a lot, but just enough to threaten these trees. And as Mick points out, they can't just uproot themselves and move to frostier ground. They're stuck, destined to succumb to imperceptible but deadly change.

The healthy trees I visited on the edge of the frost plain are in a place called *trawtha makuminya* (the name means 'tracks through

Big River country') – 6878 hectares of land adjoining the state's Wilderness World Heritage Area, bought in 2012 by the Aboriginal Land Council of Tasmania. This part of the Central Highlands is high enough and cold enough for the trees to still prosper. But on the way up here, driving through the tiny town of Miena by Great Lake, a popular tourist and fishing spot, I saw plenty of dead cider gums stark against the grey sky, leafless branches wet from drizzle, victims of a changing world, of more extreme frosts in winter, and warmer, drier summers.

'I lived and worked around here in the 1980s,' said Steve Cronin, the *trawtha makuminya* ranger, as we drove past. 'All these trees were alive back then. Not sure exactly why they've died. But they live on the climate edge. And if that climate's changing, then this is what happens. And that's a bloody shame. Imagine what an incredible resource this stand of trees would have been for Aboriginal people.'

As well as the trees being threatened by climate change, the knowledge of way-a-linah has been in danger of disappearing. Some people, like Mick Quilliam, are lucky enough to have been shown the right trees and introduced to the taste of the drink. But most modern Tasmanians are unaware of its existence.

'Not many people had been to *trawtha makuminya* in recent times,' says Andry Sculthorpe of the Tasmanian Aboriginal Centre, which manages the property. 'We knew there were some cider-gum trees around but we only found out exactly where they were after the property was purchased.'

And even when they were located, it wasn't clear at first what to do with them.

'We could see that there were marks all over them,' Andry says. 'But it was hard to tell what's natural and what's been manmade.'

Andry says Aboriginal people are now tapping the cider gums successfully again, adding to knowledge they've gleaned about the trees through the historical record.

'They know the history,' he says. 'They know the importance, they know how they feel about it, and they know what happened to the people who should have been passing on this knowledge directly.'

When I was growing up, I was told that Aboriginal people had no experience of alcohol before Europeans arrived in 1788. No knowledge of drinking. That this whole huge continent was bereft of booze. Nothing but water, scooped from billabongs in cupped hands.

This probably sounds familiar. Almost everyone I've told about way-a-linah is surprised to learn that Aboriginal people not only enjoyed fermented drinks in pre-colonial days but also continued to do so after Europeans arrived. (A few people I've told were even still shamefully harbouring the misconception that all Aboriginal people in Tasmania had been 'wiped out'.) 'Oh!' they'll say. 'I thought Aborigines didn't *make* alcohol.' This has been the conventional, accepted wisdom in Australia – and around the world – for a very long time.

Patrick McGovern is the acknowledged global expert on historical early drinking. A biomolecular archaeologist at the University of Pennsylvania, McGovern has made a career out of unearthing ancient evidence of alcohol production and consumption – and, in some cases, re-creating those drinks for tasting and even for sale. Notably, he's the person who helped identify the earliest known example of an alcoholic beverage from residues found in a 9000-year-old Neolithic earthenware pot in the Yellow River valley in China: the drink was made from fermented rice, honey, and either grapes or hawthorn berries (both fruits leave a similar chemical trace).

In a discussion on the global prevalence of alcoholic drinks in his 2003 book, *Ancient Wine*, McGovern wrote: 'only the Eskimos, the peoples from Tierra del Fuego ... and the Australian aborigines [sic] apparently lived out their lives without the solace and medical benefits of alcohol.' In 2009's *Uncorking the Past: The Quest for Wine, Beer, and Other Alcoholic Beverages*, he qualified that opinion: 'Signs of indigenous fermented drinks are also so far noticeably absent from Australia, perhaps owing to limited excavation there.' Even as recently as 2017, in *Ancient Brews: Rediscovered and Re-created*, he was still yet to include any mention of Aboriginal fermentation – although he did acknowledge he hadn't been to Australia, and a trip here may yield more knowledge.

If the 'dry continent' myth of Aboriginal Australia has persisted even in the scholarly writings of someone as experienced as McGovern, it's no wonder some people find it hard to accept anything to the contrary.

––––––––––

The myth started to dissolve for me in the autumn of 2013, when I visited a small cider orchard in southern Tasmania planted on a hill sloping down to the cold, choppy waters of the D'Entrecasteaux Channel. Orchardist and cider maker Clive Crossley showed me dozens of heritage English and French trees he had planted there – cultivars with evocative names such as Yarlington Mill and Kingston Black and Frequin Rouge, originally grown in the cider-producing regions of Somerset and Herefordshire and Normandy. The apples grown on these trees are more bitter and mouth-puckering than eating apples such as Pink Lady or Granny Smith. We strolled from tree to tree in the orchard, crunching into the red and green and yellow fruit, experiencing their kaleidoscope of different flavours.

As we walked, Clive mentioned he'd also planted a few different species of eucalypts around the property, including one he referred to as a 'cider gum'. The two words hung in the air. I'd never heard of it. Cider gum? It was obvious why he'd wanted to plant this particular tree. But how did it get that name?

'I'd noticed a mention of the Aboriginal use of the cider gum in an old book,' he said. 'It sounds as though the sap can be drawn and fermented. It may be a myth, but I thought we'd give it a go. Haven't seen any sap yet, though.'

Cider gum. Fermented sap. Having seen the tree, I couldn't shake the image. And I began to imagine what its fermented sap would taste like. I started researching the history of the tree, looking for references to fermentation, and found the work of Dr Maggie Brady, a social anthropologist at the Australian National University.

Brady has worked for many years with Aboriginal communities across Australia, and has extensively researched the social history of alcohol and other drugs. In *The Grog Book* (1998) and *First Taste* (2008), she lists a number of examples of Aboriginal fermentation, including way-a-linah. Reading about them opened my eyes. The landscape came to life. Plants turned into flavours. As well as the cider gums and way-a-linah in Tasmania, I learned about *kambuda*, made from the pounded nuts of the spiral pandanus in the Northern Territory; *mangaitch*, made from steeping banksia flowers in water in Western Australia; and *tuba*, made from the fermented juice of palm-tree buds in the Torres Strait.

Then I read *Dark Emu*, Bruce Pascoe's groundbreaking book about Aboriginal agriculture as revealed through the journals of early white explorers and settlers: firsthand early-19th-century written accounts of Indigenous people sowing and harvesting and preserving food – a history that none of us were taught at school. I learned about the cultivation of staples such as *murnong* (yam daisies). I learned about the development of extensive aquaculture such as the eel traps at Budj Bim in western Victoria. I learned about the production of bread and cake from kangaroo grass and native millet.

And I realised that I *had* come across a few fleeting references to Aboriginal fermentation in a couple of books before standing under Clive Crossley's cider gum in that Tasmanian apple orchard in 2013. But I had overlooked them, not registered their importance, just not made the connections. I was, back then, still seeing through the dust of the 'dry continent' myth. Reading and talking to Maggie and Bruce changed that. Their work fundamentally shifted the way I think about, look at, listen to – and, importantly, smell and taste – the country where I live.

————————

I have travelled to Margaret River on the south-west coast of Western Australia many times over the last quarter of a century to visit wineries and taste wine. Often, I'm lucky enough to be there when the magnificent tall forests are in bloom: gum trees dusted with white and orange and red blossoms, spiky banksia trees daubed with upstrokes of yellow flowering cones.

One evening recently in spring, at dusk, after a day of winery visits, I followed a path into a thicket of trees fringing a vineyard. As I walked into the forest the violet light slipped away behind me. Ahead in the gloom I could make out the distinctive zigzag banksia leaves sharp against the dark. And glowing faintly, perched on the branches, the big fat candles of giant banksia flowers. A decade ago this scene would have barely registered: I would have been too preoccupied thinking about the European vines I'd just walked past, introduced plants trellised in neat long rows, trained to produce reliable crops of sugar-rich grapes for winemaking.

Now, when I saw those beautiful glowing banksia cones in the quiet forest, I thought of anthropologist Walter Roth's 1904 description of Aboriginal Noongar people using the nectar-rich flowers to make a fermented drink:

> Large quantities of the flower-bearing cones were taken to the side of some swamp, in the close proximity of which several holes were dug into the ground, each in the form of a trough about a yard [1 metre] long and 18in. [46 cm] deep. Particularly sound sheets of ti-tree bark were next stripped from the trees, each piece of bark being tied up at the ends with fibre into a sort of boat-shaped vat, the sides of which were kept apart by sticks stretched across; the shape of the vat lent itself to that of the trough, and there was one vat for each trough. The Vat was next filled with these cones and water, in which they were left to soak. The cones were subsequently removed and replaced by others until such time as the liquid was strongly impregnated with the honey, when it was allowed to ferment for several days. The effect of drinking this 'mead' in quantity was exhilarating, producing excessive volubility. The aboriginals called the cones and the fermented liquor produced therefrom both by the same – the man-gaitch.

This is not the only reference to mangaitch. In *First Taste*, Brady writes about a party of Dutch sailors sailing up the Swan River in 1697 to where the city of Perth is now: 'At one point they found what they thought were "herbs" soaking in a shallow trench, with the footprints of many people around it; it's thought that this might have been mangaitch.'

More recently, in a series of radio programs produced by the Aboriginal Alcohol Service in Perth in the 1990s, Aboriginal author Doris Pilkington spoke about mangaitch. 'Our people knew about fermentation and used alcohol on special occasions,' she said. 'We made it by soaking blossom of banksias and eucalyptus, and by dissolving the nectar and allowing it to stand. But the alcoholic content was slight and the use of these drinks was limited to special occasions and certain times of the year. In other words, we exercised our own restraints.'

And in a 2011 publication on the uses of traditional plants in the country north of Perth, Noongar (also written 'Nyungar') Elder Neville Collard described the process in a similar way, not only placing it in the present rather than portraying it as past practice, but also giving the drink a different name: 'Banksia flowers produce an abundance of honey-like nectar, which is why the early colonists called this plant the Honeysuckle. Nyungar people drink the honey straight out of the flower cone, or soak the flower in water to produce a sweet drink. This beverage is either drunk fresh or fermented to produce Gep, an intoxicating liquor.'

There are numerous historical references to sweet drinks being made by steeping various nectar-rich flowers in water across Australia. In most cases, the drinks were consumed straight away, but some-times, as with mangaitch and gep, they were also left to ferment. And not just in Western Australia. In 1878, Robert Brough Smyth wrote of similar drinks produced by Aboriginal people in western Victoria:

The natives used also to compound liquors – perhaps after a slight fermentation to some extent intoxicating – from various flowers ...

The liquor was usually prepared in the large wooden bowls (*tarnuks*) which were to be seen at every encampment. In the flowers of the dwarf species of *Banksia* (*B. ornata*) there is a good deal of honey, and this was got out of the flowers by immersing them in water. The water thus sweetened was greedily swallowed by the natives. This drink was named *Beal* by the natives of the west of Victoria, and was much esteemed.

After reading *Dark Emu*, I visited Bruce Pascoe at his home at Gipsy Point, near Mallacoota in East Gippsland. I travelled there to learn about – and taste – the murnong Bruce was growing and studying. In passing, he told me about the enormous quantity of nectar that flowed from the large banksia cones that flower every three years in this part of the world: each bloom, he said, yielded enough delicious 'honey' to fill a small Vegemite jar.

I had just read Maggie Brady's description of mangaitch, and I have a one-track mind, so I suddenly yearned to taste this 'honey' drink. I asked Bruce if he knew whether anyone has ever fermented this banksia honey.

'Aboriginal people,' he said, matter-of-factly. 'A lot of plants were used like that, across the country. Many flowers were used to make slightly fermented drinks.'

The particular banksia Bruce was referring to wasn't flowering at that time. But when I got home to Melbourne, I noticed for the first time (after living there for fifteen years) that my next-door neighbour has a banksia tree growing in his front yard. And it was covered in emerging, rather than fully 'ripe', cones. This was *Banksia integrifolia*, not the *Banksia grandis* of Margaret River, or the *Banksia ornata* of western Victoria, or the *Banksia serrata* of East Gippsland. But I was keen to try it out. I pilfered a few cones off my neighbour's tree (he's a vicar, he'll forgive me) to see what would happen if I steeped them in water.

The results were disappointing. After a day, the water began to smell and taste faintly of banana bread, and it reminded me of the taste of a honey-flavoured breakfast cereal I ate as a child. But it wasn't all that sweet, and there was no sign of fermentation. The cones obviously weren't ripe enough, there wasn't enough nectar in them, and it's probably not the best type of banksia to use.

Other attempts to make mangaitch have been more successful. Perth anthropologists Ken Macintyre and Barb Dobson, who have written about the use of banksias in traditional Noongar culture, once tried soaking ripe cones in water for two days; it resulted in what they described as a 'crude concoction with a honey-scented odour, which tasted something like a light mead'.

'It was not unpleasant to drink and gave a mild feeling of euphoria,' they wrote. 'When we discussed our experiment with some Noongar Elders, one of them explained that they already knew about this and that they called the fermented concoction *geber* (or *giber*).'

The knowledge was there. It was simply a matter of asking the right questions.

————

Why don't we know more about this? Why has the myth persisted for so long that Aboriginal people had no experience of fermented, alcoholic drinks before the arrival of the First Fleet? Why haven't we been asking the right questions?

Much of the knowledge was eradicated early on by colonisation, dispossession and the frontier wars. Killing people, moving the survivors off their land to live in unfamiliar country, and banning traditional practices in the new forced communities were all dreadfully effective ways of erasing a culture.

'In the early 1900s, anthropologist Daisy Bates wrote of annual feasts of mangaitch [before the arrival of Europeans],' writes Brady. 'She [also] described the terrible impact of white settlement on Western Australian Aborigines ... how the fences, the sheep, horses and cattle all affected their sources of food. She told how the "mungaitch honey-groves" were cut down to make way for flocks and herds.'

Even where the practices or knowledge did survive and were recorded, those records have often been wilfully ignored by the dominant culture over the last 200 years. As Pascoe writes in *Dark Emu*, accounts of organised agriculture detailed by the explorers and early settlers challenge white Australia's deep-seated precon-ception of Aboriginal people as 'mere hunter-gatherers ... simply wandering from plant to plant, kangaroo to kangaroo in hapless opportunism'. Accounts of the organised, seasonal ceremonial pro-duction and enjoyment of fermented drinks is equally challenging to this preconception. In both cases, ignoring or actively supress-ing acknowledgement of Aboriginal agency has been used as a political tool to justify dispossession. 'No grog' is another form of 'terra nullius'.

Brady argues that the idea of Aboriginal people having no previous experience of alcohol prior to European colonisation has become an easy, sweeping way of explaining that Aboriginal drinking is wrong. She says that the 'dry continent' myth has been used as an explanation for the 'scourge' of alcohol abuse in Aboriginal communities – 'that because there was no alcohol before, Aboriginal people must have some biological "weakness" that makes them more vulnerable to its effects, and to addiction itself' – and as justification for the repressive prohibition and control that has been imposed on Aboriginal people's drinking over many decades.

Reading the old accounts of Aboriginal fermented drinks, it's clear that these drinks were perceived as having little to no exploitable commercial value to Europeans, and that they were, therefore, unworthy of being studied in detail. It's the same for many Indigenous foods and farming practices. The explorers and early settlers looked at the country through a European lens: cultural ignorance and a deep lack of understanding of the landscape and climate blinded them to the potential or importance of the resources and ceremonies being observed.

In his 1843 account of the cider gums, for example, Ronald Gunn said, unequivocally, that '[the sap] has never been obtained in any quantity or applied to any useful purpose' – despite describing in detail how shepherds and stockmen had learned how to tap the trees and harvest the liquid, and despite being aware that it produces an alcoholic drink. Contrast this with how white settlers and explorers responded to *pituri*, the 'native tobacco' common across central and eastern Australia.

When Joseph Banks first saw Aboriginal people chewing 'the leaves of an herb' in 1770, he drew easy comparisons with how a European person might chew 'tobacco' or 'East Indian' betel leaves. The sight was familiar to him and he could place it in a global cultural context. A century later, when stories emerged of Central Australian Aboriginal people helping exhausted explorers on the Burke and Wills expedition by feeding them fish, bread and a 'stuff they call *bedgery* or *pedgery* [which] has a highly intoxicating effect when chewed even in small quantities', it inspired a flurry of scientific investigation.

Intrepid explorers soon set out to brave the mysterious outback in search of this intoxicating plant and recorded all sorts of remarkable claims about its effects, from enabling old men to act as seers to allowing Aboriginal people to walk hundreds of kilometres without food or water, and giving them courage in warfare.

The heroic lore surrounding pituri has survived to the present day and is familiar to many Australians – unlike the historical stories of ceremony surrounding fermented drinks, which have mostly faded into obscurity.

If the way-a-linah trees hadn't been so remote, if the mangaitch forests hadn't been razed to make way for stock, if the drinks observed by Gunn and Bunce and Roth had been more abundant, less seasonal, less tied to ceremony and place – and if they'd been stronger, more alcoholic, more like the tradeable, transportable commodities of wine and port and spirits the colonists had brought with them – then perhaps they would have attracted more attention and acknowledgement. And appropriation.

———————

One of the centres of pituri culture is the Channel Country of south-west Queensland, between Birdsville and Windorah, traditional land of the Karuwali/Mithaka people. This wide-open red-dirt landscape was scarred by waves of violent frontier warfare in the 1870s and 1880s, as Aboriginal people fiercely resisted the arrival of white pastoralists and their herds of cattle. By the end of the century, an uneasy truce hung over the country as it became clear to the Aboriginal people that the Europeans weren't going away, and to the pastoralists that they had come to rely on the local people for knowledge of country and as workers on their stations, mustering stock, looking after children.

One pastoralist who had a more enlightened view of Aboriginal culture than most was William Duncan, who arrived to manage Mooraberrie station, near the present-day infamous Betoota Hotel, in 1891, and became the owner in 1900. Historian Tom Griffiths writes that Duncan 'respected Aboriginal ownership and traditions, and Mooraberrie became a refuge for the remaining Aboriginal people of the region'. The station had also been the site of a 'peace ceremony' conducted in 1889, attended by more than 500 Aboriginal people from across the Channel Country, that helped to bring about an end to the more violent period of frontier conflict in this part of the world.

Alice Duncan was born one of four children at Mooraberrie in 1901, and grew up immersed in the Aboriginal world. The children's Aboriginal nurse, Mary Ann, and her stockman brother, Moses Yoolpee – who himself had been educated by a previous station owner, at Scotch College in Melbourne – taught Alice Karuwali culture. The young girl spent many years travelling through the country with 'the blacks', learning their bushcraft and stories and spirituality. Later, as an adult, when she was married and running a station of her own, Alice Duncan-Kemp wrote four books: rich, detailed memoirs of her early life at Mooraberrie. And in the first of the series, *Our Sandhill Country*, she described what she observed on one trip through country:

A familiar sight is the bauhinia (tree) with its twin leaves and red-tipped blossoms resembling honeysuckle ... From the honey-filled blossoms the blacks make a semi-intoxicating drink. When the bauhinias for miles round come into bloom the gins pick the blossoms off in coolamonfuls. These are pounded, and the sweet golden liquid drained off into a larger, deeper coolamon, then mixed with sugar-bag or ant honey and set aside to ferment, a process which takes eight or ten days.

Although Duncan-Kemp's memoirs have been dismissed by some in the past as romantic 'tall stories' – her own mother described Alice as being 'fairly "cracked" on the blacks' – anthropologists and historians increasingly regard them as reliable accounts of traditional Aboriginal culture.

Pearl Eatts is a descendant of the Karuwali people of the Channel Country. She now lives in Winton, a day's drive north on the other side of the Diamantina Lakes, and works on preserving – and educating people about – her culture and ancestry.

'Alice Duncan-Kemp is a trusted source,' says Pearl when I ask her about the bauhinia sugarbag drink. 'Our family's history with theirs has been one of respect and admiration. She is buried here in the Winton cemetery and some of her sources [for her books] are our ancestors.'

Pearl tells me her great-great-grandfather was Moses Yoolpee, Alice's teacher and guide, and that her mother, Joslin, now in her eighties, knew Alice. And she says she knows about the production of a drink made from bauhinia flowers and sugarbag (honey from native bees).

'Yes, that practice did occur in my mother's and grandmother's lives,' she says.

But then she hesitates.

'I'm reluctant to give too much away,' she says. 'I've had food companies, pharmaceutical companies in the past ring me up asking about plants, looking for secrets, wanting our intellectual property. So one thing I won't tell you is the method of how to make it. I'm worried people will look at your book and think, hey, let's give this a bit of a squiz, and run off with it.'

She sighs. There is a long pause.

'There are predators out there,' says Pearl. 'The alcohol industry is big-money business. But this isn't just a drink, it's not just a beverage, it's medicine. It needs to be written up at the right time, in the right way and for the right purposes. It's not some top-shelf liquor.'

———————

The vivid flavour image painted by Duncan-Kemp of honey being mixed with pounded blossoms and allowed to ferment isn't the only example of Aboriginal people using sugarbag to produce a 'semi-intoxicating drink'.

In *The Aborigines of Victoria*, Robert Brough Smyth repeated an account from the 1840s of wild honey, produced by the small stingless native bee, being collected and consumed by Aboriginal people in New South Wales.

'The honey', he wrote, 'is of delicious flavor, after it has been carefully separated from the comb, the cells of which are generally filled with small flies. The natives, however, devour it just as they find it, and are very fond even of the refuse comb, with which they make their favorite beverage called *Bull*, and of this they drink till they become quite intoxicated.'

After spending years researching the history of Aboriginal drinking culture, Maggie Brady says we need to be careful jumping to conclusions about such references. As with Brough Smyth's report of the banksia drink, beal, we can't be absolutely sure that the 'intoxication' mentioned here refers to the effects of alcohol or whether it's a description of people enjoying an energetic sugar hit.

Michael Bock, a botanist who has written about Indigenous fermentation, also points out the difficulty of ascertaining exactly how far back the process of making fermented drinks goes in Australia. 'It is not proved, although it is highly likely, that some tribes such as the Tasmanian Aborigines discovered this process before the European invasion,' he writes. 'Other tribes are more likely to have developed the techniques for converting sugar-rich, sweet drinks into alcoholic drinks after the Europeans had introduced alcohol to the Aborigines.'

But it's equally possible that it *is* alcoholic inebriation being described when writers across three centuries, from Brough Smyth to Duncan-Kemp to Neville Collard, use the word 'intoxication'. There's no doubt, for example, that these drinks could have contained alcohol. I have mixed sugarbag with water and watched it spontaneously start to ferment after a couple of days. I have tasted fermented way-a-linah collected from a hollow in a cider-gum tree. It's impossible to believe that people could live for millennia in an environment where sugary liquids come naturally into contact with wild yeasts and *not* have experienced some form of even mildly alcoholic drinks – and then thought about how they could repeat the experience.

We need to do more research in this area. We need to keep asking questions, to stop blindly accepting the 'dry continent' myth. We also need to consider the tantalising possibility that the Karuwali practice of fermenting honey with other local ingredients – and the other practices – may well date back at least as far as other examples of ancient honey fermentation around the globe, such as the 9000-year-old Neolithic Chinese rice/honey/fruit drink analysed by Patrick McGovern. We need to consider, too, that this bauhinia sugarbag drink – and mangaitch and kambuda and beal and way-a-linah – may well be some of the oldest fermented drinks known to humanity.

Firewater:
Rum and other ardent spirits

The English sailor brought the cup to his lips and took a sip. The alcohol was warm as it trickled down his throat. He gestured to the two Aboriginal men standing a few feet away from him on the beach at Botany Bay, held out the cup, signalled for them to drink too.

The Dharawal men were wary. They were suspicious of the big white bird that had sailed in to Gamay, their bay, suspicious of the men with ghostly white skin that clambered about the giant bird like possums, suspicious of the boat full of strangers that had landed on their shore. The women of the tribe had told the two men not to drink anything the white men were handing out to them. It could be poison, they said.

The sailor took out a tomahawk and showed the men how it could be used to cut down bushes. Then he indicated he would give them the tomahawk if they would have a drink with him.

The Dharawal men knew the women were right to be cautious. But the drink didn't appear to be having any bad effect on the white man. He hadn't fallen down dead. In fact, the drink seemed to be making him merry. So, they signed for him to pour more in his cup, drink some himself and they would drink the rest.

The sailor did as he was directed, handing over the tomahawk and the cup to one of the men, who brought the grog to his lips and took a sip.

The man felt his face go up in flames. '*Guwiya*!' he shouted. 'Fire!' He spat out the liquid in shock and disgust, yelling, in language – 'Fire in eyes, fire in nose and fire all over!' – as he ran into the water to stop the burning.

———————

There are two accounts of this pivotal moment in 1788, when the English introduced strong drinks to Aboriginal people at Botany Bay. Anthropologist Maggie Brady puts them side-by-side in her book *First Taste* to show how the same historical event can be remembered in different ways by different people.

The first account was written by Philip Gidley King, second lieutenant on the *Sirius*. It takes up only a few words in King's long journal entry for 20 January, describing how he and a party of marines met a group of Aboriginal men on the southern shore of Botany Bay. The men were armed with spears and made a 'vociferous' display of their displeasure at being invaded. King appeased them by offering gifts, including 'a glass of Wine which they had no sooner tasted then they spit it out'. Just like that. Matter-of-fact.

The Aboriginal version of the story was recorded in 1833 by a Catholic priest in Sydney. It was told to him by 'a Botany Bay man' whose father had told it to him. This was the detailed, evocative story of the big white bird, of the sailors 'like possums', of the tomahawk and of the drink that tasted like fire. Much more dramatic, burned into the memory.

This event has become part of our national legend: the moment when a huge wave of potent alcohol that had kept much of Europe intoxicated for centuries – rum and brandy and gin, port and sherry and wine – inundated the great dry southern land.

But we know that legend is flawed. Clearly, in many parts of the country, Aboriginal people were already familiar with fermented drinks. The difference was that these drinks were rare, mild, seasonal and ceremonial, unlike the huge quantities of strong, constantly available alcohol that the invaders brought with them. It's also not true that, when the Dharawal man spat out King's wine in 1788, this was the first time people living on this continent had encountered strong drinks. Spirits had arrived in other parts of Australia long before the First Fleet sailed into Botany Bay.

Macassan sailors had been visiting the northern Australian coast since at least the mid–17th century. Every December they left their homes in Sulawesi in Indonesia and sailed on the monsoon winds to the Kimberley and Arnhem Land. Here they harvested and processed *trepang* – *bêche-de-mer*, sea slug, sea cucumber – which they then sold to Chinese merchants. The Macassans brought goods to trade with the local Aboriginal people, who in turn welcomed the visitors for their six-month annual stay, helping them collect and dry the trepang. Among the many things the Macassans brought with them was a strong spirit from Java called *arrack*.

Drinks historian David Wondrich says this spirit was made in Chinese-run distilleries in Java, using traditional Chinese distillation techniques and ingredients such as fermented rice – much as the Chinese white spirit, *baijiu*, is made today. Over time, other ingredients – palm wine, introduced from India, and molasses, introduced by the Dutch – were also incorporated into the process. This, says Wondrich, gave arrack a 'true hybrid' flavour, combining the fire of baijiu, the softness of Indian palm spirit and the sweetness of rum.

The arrack the Macassans brought with them also tasted of something else: *anisi*, pronounced 'aahnich'. Aniseed. Maggie Brady says this refers to the aniseed often used by distillers in Java to flavour the spirit. And she says that the Yolŋu people of Arnhem Land borrowed the word, transliterated as *nganitji*, and have applied it to all strong drink ever since: '*Nganitji*', she says, 'means "grog" now.'

The word for alcohol wasn't the only thing adopted by the Yolŋu over centuries of interaction with the Macassans. As well as incorporating lots of other words into their language – *rrupiya* for money, *buthulu* for bottle – Yolŋu also made paintings of the visitors' sailing vessels, learned skills that changed the way they made tools and built their canoes, composed songs that echoed Macassan melodies and created dances that told the history of *nganitji*, including the 'drunken Macassan' dance.

In the mid–19th century, Filipino sailors also brought their own version of arrack, a distilled palm wine they called *tuba*, when they visited the Torres Strait Islands in search of shells and trepang. Islanders learned how to make the drink from the Filipinos: they called the juice of the coconut-palm buds tuba and drank it fresh like a soft drink, or fermented it to about 4 per cent alcohol, or distilled it to make a stronger drink called steamed tuba.

Brady writes that Islanders used the fresh tuba like a sauce, dipping slices of mango into it. The fermented tuba was more like a yeasty beer; Islander women used it as a raising agent in breadmaking. And the steamed tuba was often drunk, according to accounts from Elders, 'like white people drink wine at dinner', in moderation.

The way the Macassans and Filipinos introduced alcohol in northern Australia and the Torres Strait influenced the way people responded to it and how they incorporated it into their own culture. These visitors were also temporary, not interested in occupation. They gave alcohol in a 'good manners', respectful way, and it was given to reinforce 'trading friendships'.

The ways of drinking that the English brought with them in 1788 were very different.

———————

A crowd of convicts, settlers and marines gathers in the heart of the new colony to watch the latest flogging. A convict has been caught stealing a bottle of illicit rum, a serious breach of public order. It is a hot, harsh morning. Clear blue sky, burning sun, the crack of musket fire in the distance. Red-coated soldiers nursing hard hangovers tie the convict in his grubby rags to a wooden frame and the lashing begins, much to the delight of the hordes of assembled schoolchildren.

It's 1977, and I'm one of those kids, visiting Old Sydney Town, a colonial theme park that had just opened near Gosford on the New South Wales Central Coast. The place was populated with actors in period costume, all embracing their part by swigging from thick glass bottles and stoneware jars, singing sea shanties in the town's tavern, carousing through the streets in a mock-drunken swagger. We were told these bottles and jugs and tankards were filled with rum. It was an experience that burned its way into my memory. Even now, I can't help thinking of rum whenever I think of that time in the early years of the colony.

When the First Fleet arrived, it was carrying 12,000 gallons – 54,000 litres – of rum on board. That's almost 9 gallons or 40 litres of rum for each of the 1373 men, women and children who had survived the journey. Considering 1000 of these people were convicts – and convicts were officially prohibited from drinking – it's more like 12 gallons or 54 litres of rum per head.

All the First Fleeters, whether labourer or landed gentry, came from a culture where strong drinks like gin, brandy and rum were easily accessible, constantly available and almost universally consumed. Binge drinking was common and communal.

From the beginning of the settlement there was an official imbalance between those who had access to grog and those who didn't. But as author Tom Gilling puts it in *Grog*, his history of colonial Sydney, this disparity didn't last: by the end of 1788, he writes, 'smuggled and stolen liquor was already rippling through the colony's cashless economy', with the free settlers bartering with the convicts and the convicts trading among themselves.

The Second Fleet brought both more spirits and a specially commissioned unit of soldiers called the New South Wales Corps. From then on, a steady stream of ships arrived at Port Jackson, each carrying more and more barrels of booze. This new 'influx of liquor', writes Gilling, kicked off a flourishing trade in alcohol – and 'the most avaricious exponents of this trade would turn out to be the officers of the New South Wales Corps themselves.'

The officers of the Corps bought the bulk of the spirits as it arrived, and then onsold it or bartered it with the rest of the colony. Within a couple of years, liquor had become, Gilling says, 'an indispensable cog in the colonial economy'. Labourers were paid in rum, a ship could be bought for £50 and 150 gallons of rum, and land was swapped for spirits, with 4 gallons being worth 25 acres. The settlement of 400 or so people on the Hawkesbury River, out of the constant purview of the authorities, was described as 'one continued scene of drunkenness ... the Settlers selling their crops for Liquor'. And illicit stills started popping up everywhere, with the distillers often operating their sly-grog operations in cahoots with the local constables.

At first, Aboriginal people were wary of the invaders' alcohol. Some found its taste repulsive – but some enjoyed it. When Governor Arthur Phillip decided to kidnap some Aboriginal people both to learn about their culture and to introduce them to English customs such as 'civilised' drinking, they reacted very differently to the wine offered to them. Some refused. Some, including the most famous of those Aboriginal captives, Bennelong, not only accepted the drinks but soon participated in toasts.

'[Bennelong] became at once fond of our viands,' wrote Watkin Tench, one of the most candid chroniclers of the early years of the settlement, 'and would drink the strongest liquors, not simply without reluctance, but with eager marks of delight and enjoyment ... Nor was the effect of wine or brandy upon him more perceptible than an equal quantity would have produced upon one of us, although fermented liquor was new to him.'

Despite enjoying the governor's hospitality, Bennelong soon returned to his own people. After that, relations between black and white deteriorated and, writes Maggie Brady, the Aboriginal population were 'left to themselves to interpret the meaning of alcohol, and what happens after imbibing it. They "learned" by looking around at the motley collection of Europeans and were often puzzled by what they saw.' As disease and dispossession took their toll on the Aboriginal population and they moved closer to the settlement, they 'acquired a taste for the firewater of the whites'.

'Alcohol usually had a devastating effect on those who drank it, and rendered them susceptible to racist caricature,' writes

Marcia Langton in her influential study of this period, *Rum, Seduction and Death*. Langton highlights the 'role of the British men who deliberately provided the alcohol to trick and debilitate those Aborigines who had survived the smallpox and the destitution into which they were forced', despite the fact that 'their addiction to liquor was in no way out of character with the general mores of the settlement'.

A succession of governors tried to crack down on the drunkenness taking hold of the colony. In the late 1790s Governor John Hunter introduced hotel licensing, tried turning away speculative grog ships and proposed taking over the purchase and supply of alcohol to keep the price down and make it less attractive to trade. It didn't work. Hunter put his finger on the problem when he wrote: 'Since 1792 ... the Public Interest & that of private individuals [have] been ... in direct opposition to each other.' 'As usual,' writes Gilling, 'where grog was concerned, the profits outweighed the deterrents.'

Things came to a head in 1808, with the arrival of William Bligh as governor. Bligh was appalled by how the New South Wales Corps had developed such a stranglehold on the supply of alcohol. But when he started attempting to dismantle the trade, the Corps responded by mounting a rebellion and arresting him. Rum wasn't the only factor behind the rebellion, but, as Gilling writes, 'Bligh had stirred up some of the most vengeful men in the colony by clamping down on the traffic in spirits.'

Bligh's successor, Lachlan Macquarie, had more success at breaking the Corps' near monopoly – by replacing it with another one. In 1810, he granted a group of entrepreneurs, including the principal surgeon D'Arcy Wentworth, the 'Exclusive Privilege' of being the colony's sole importers of rum for a period of three years. In return, the group agreed to use some of the profits to build a major hospital in the heart of the fledgling city. This irony set the tone for much of Australia's regulatory history with booze: a hospital that treated many patients for their alcohol-related problems, funded by the sale of alcohol.

The Rum Hospital, as it became known, opened in 1816, and much of the building still stands. Its rooms can be hired out for functions, and 200 years after it was built, I hosted a wine-tasting there. I'm kicking myself now that I didn't start – or end – the night by raising a glass of rum to toast its history.

———

'Rum' was the first word that leapt to the lips of most people when I told them I was working on a history of drinking in Australia. 'You'll definitely be writing about rum,' they told me. 'The Rum Corps, the Rum Rebellion, the Rum Hospital. I learned about all that at school.' They're right, of course. I am writing about rum. It's a very important component of the history of drinking in this country.

Late one evening a couple of years ago, after a day in Sydney's Mitchell Library researching the history of rum, I walked into a bar at Circular Quay, the place where Governor Phillip famously raised the British flag in January 1788 to establish the new colony. This time, I decided a toast was in order, and I asked for a shot of the best rum they had. It turned out to be from Jamaica: deep bronze in colour, full of the warm smell and mellow taste of molasses and oak. How appropriate, I thought, to be sitting in such a historic spot, sharing the same flavour the very earliest settlers had experienced right here, 230 years previously.

Except I discovered that it didn't taste like that back then. The rum that arrived in 1788 was from Brazil, taken on board when the First Fleet stopped at Rio de Janeiro in August the previous year en route to the new colony. This wasn't sweet, golden rum made from molasses. It was a pale-coloured, rough-tasting spirit called *aguardente* – 'burning water' in Portuguese – distilled from sugar-cane juice. This aguardente was similar to modern-day Brazilian *cachaça*, but it tasted bad. Really bad.

James Campbell, captain of marines on the First Fleet, complained that the drinks ration given to the officers was 'half a Pint [per day] of vile Rio Spirits, so offensive both in Taste and Smell, that he must be fond of drinking indeed, that can use it'. Tench agreed: 'The staple commodity of [Brazil] is sugar,' he wrote. 'That they have not, however, learnt the art of making palatable rum, the English troops in New South Wales can bear testimony; a large quantity, very ill flavoured, having been bought and shipped here for the use of the garrison of Port Jackson.'

In the first few decades of the new colony, rum was imported in huge quantities along with other wines, beers and spirits, such as brandy and gin. But again, most of this rum wasn't the sweet golden stuff we're used to drinking today. It was 'Bengal rum', which was a different drink altogether.

During the period in which most of the famous rum-related events occurred in Australia, many of the ships arriving in Port Jackson came from India, and most were laden with spirits. In early 1800, for example, a ship chartered by officers of the New South Wales Corps arrived bearing moderate quantities of essentials such as cloth, tea and coffee – and a whopping 9000 gallons (41,000 litres) of Bengal rum. At that time, distilleries in Calcutta were using both sugar cane to make rum and the juice of the more widely planted date palm to make arrack. Maritime archaeologist Mark Staniforth argues that it's likely the terms 'spirits' and 'Bengal rum' were 'applied indiscriminately to any alcohol' made from either cane or date palm.

This changes things a bit. The Arrack Corps, the Arrack Rebellion and the Arrack Hospital don't quite have the same ring, do they? It also brings the taste of the grog of Port Jackson to life in a different way when you imagine rough arrack in your mouth instead of rich rum. It's certainly a better fit with contemporary descriptions of the stuff.

In 1800, Philip Gidley King – who, twelve years before, had given the Dharawal men their first taste of grog at Botany Bay – replaced John Hunter as governor. King, who had been away from Port Jackson for many years, was scathing about the damage that spirits had done to the young colony. 'Vice, dissipation, and a strange relaxation seems to pervade every class and order of people,' he wrote, complaining there was so much alcohol available that everyone, 'from the better sort of people in the colony to the blackest characters among the convicts, are full of that fiery poison'.

———————

Burning water. Fiery poison. There are good reasons why strong, distilled alcoholic spirits are described this way.

The process of distillation entails heating a fermented liquid until the alcohol in it evaporates, and then condensing the vapour to capture the alcohol in concentrated form. For centuries, the simplest way to heat a liquid was to place a container over an open fire. The aguardente on the First Fleet, the Macassans' arrack, the tuba in the Torres Strait, the rum from Bengal – all were made this way. European spirits were also made this way: the word 'brandy' comes from the Dutch *brandewijn* – burnt wine.

Ethyl alcohol – ethanol – is what spirits makers want to capture when they distil a fermented liquid. It's the 'good' alcohol, the one that our bodies can process if we drink it slowly (although, yes, if we drink too much of it, it can kill us). But it's not the only thing captured by distillation: a whole bunch of less desirable and even dangerous compounds, such as nasty-tasting acetone, highly toxic methanol and bitter fusel oils, are produced at the beginning and end of the process. Careful distillers will ensure none of these compounds make it into the bottle. But much of the booze shipped to – or made in – the new colony in its early years was anything but carefully distilled.

Firewater also got its name because strong alcohol can taste exactly like it's scorching your nostrils and your lips and your tongue when you take a sip, especially if you have no experience of tasting anything like it before.

In the Meriam language of the eastern Torres Strait Islands, writes Maggie Brady, alcohol is *kaomal nguki*, or *uweri ni* – 'hot water'. On Mornington Island in the Gulf of Carpentaria, the Lardil people call spirits 'hot stuff' and beer 'sea water' or *mela*. 'Anyone who drinks a lot of beer', writes anthropologist David McKnight, who spent many years on Mornington Island, 'is known as *melamerr*, i.e. crazy or mad for beer, just as drinking large quantities of sea water will cause craziness.' Other coastal groups reached similar conclusions, from the Wadjiginy people in the Northern Territory who chose *ngatjur* – 'salty, sour' – to describe grog to the Kaurna people of the Adelaide Plains whose word for alcohol is *kurpula*, 'sea water': something that doesn't taste pleasant.

Maggie Brady says the words Aboriginal people historically chose to describe alcohol also reflect the community's response to its introduction and attitudes to it over time. Some groups, she says, use warning words: the Kuninjku people in Kakadu, for example, called alcohol *kun-bang*, which means 'dangerous, poisonous, sleek, deadly one'. And in the Pitjantjatjara Western Desert language, one term for alcohol is *kapi kura*, 'bad water'.

But there's another word for alcohol in Pitjantjatjara that tells a different story. *Wama*. It means 'sweet'. There are similar words for alcohol in other desert languages: *ngkwarle* in Kaytetye means 'honey or nectar', and *pama* in Warlpiri means 'sweet delicacy'.

This is the heart of the difficult relationship we can have with alcohol. On one hand, we know about the pain that often comes with intoxication – and on the other, we crave the pleasure. The pleasure usually wins. In the same way, we know the perils of alcohol, the problems it brings to people, communities and society. But we also know there are profits to be made from the business of selling grog. So we sanction, we legislate, we license.

In 1812, Governor Macquarie put forward another plan to stem the tide of spirits flowing into Sydney. Acknowledging that 'The Nature of the Inhabitants of this Country is such that Spirits Must be had' – in other words, people are going to drink no matter how hard you try to control it, so you might as well get in on the action yourself – he suggested the *government* should build a large distillery. Not only would this provide a market for the colony's grain farmers, but also, writes Tom Gilling, 'it would keep wealth from being sucked out of the colony to pay for imported grog'.

It took another decade of arguing, but in 1822 it finally became legal to make spirits in the colony, in distilleries licensed by the government.

'I'm really excited that we finally get a chance to taste these old bottles,' says bar owner Seb Costello. 'We're drinking history. Because when you open a bottle of whisky and share it with people, it's not a product, it's a moment in time.'

Costello's bar, Bad Frankie, is up a side street behind a kebab shop in the inner Melbourne suburb of Fitzroy. When it opened in 2014, it was one of the first places in the country to specialise in the emerging new wave of Australian craft spirits. Back then, Seb found eighty gins, whiskies, rums and other drinks to fill his shelves. Now there are well over 500, and he doesn't have enough space in his tiny bar to stock everything that's out there.

A group of Seb's customers and a smattering of drinks-industry people – distillers, media, hospitality – have gathered in the bar on this fine Saturday afternoon to taste a couple of rare bottles of historic Australian whisky. They're from the long-defunct Corio distillery north of Geelong. One of the bottles is from the 1960s, the other from the 1980s. Luke McCarthy, author of *The Australian Spirits Guide*, has come along to guide us through the whiskies as we taste: he has spent a lot of time researching Corio, because the rise and fall of the big distillery tells a broader boom-bust-boom story of Australia's postcolonial spirits production.

After distilling was made legal in the 1820s, new stills popped up all over the country. Most were small operations, and they often struggled to survive. Distillers realised that to succeed, you needed scale, and from the 1860s – helped by a rapidly growing post–gold rush population – a number of very large operations opened. Robert Dunn's Mount Warrenheip distillery near Ballarat, for example, was turning out 2000 gallons (9000 litres) of gin a year by 1864.

By the turn of the 20th century, Australian distilling was being conducted on an even larger scale. A few operations from that era still exist. South Australia's St Agnes brandy distillery, established by winemaker William Angove in 1910 to make spirit for fortifying his port and sherry, is enjoying a renewed interest in its brandies. And the Bundaberg distillery in south-east Queensland still produces 3 million litres of rum a year.

Bundaberg was established in 1888, when a group of local cane growers decided the best thing to do with the enormous quantities of thick molasses left over from sugar refining was to ferment and distill it. When I visited the home of Bundy rum in 2017, curious to see why 70,000 tourists make the pilgrimage each year, I was struck by how '19th century' the place looked. Huge wads of steam billowed from the chimneys of a sugar-cane mill next door. The warm air was thick with a sweet, vegetal smell of silage and treacle. Soot and bagasse – the fibres left after sugar milling – lay in a fine layer over all the old distillery buildings, including the molasses well: a huge rectangular covered concrete pit, like a sunken warehouse, its low corrugated-iron roof supported by Oregon-pine beams.

The distillery manager took me inside the dark molasses warehouse. During the six-month sugar-cane harvest, from June to December, thousands of tonnes of rich, gloopy 'blackstrap' molasses are pumped over from the mill into this well, so that the distillery can draw on the raw material throughout the year to make rum. It was warm and muggy inside. Gloomy, too, apart from a shaft of skylight sunshine being sucked into the molasses and humming back out into the room as a dark golden glow. It was a close, unforgettable atmosphere; all that energy embodied in the pit. I felt I could easily topple off the wooden walkway that stretches out over the molasses only to sink into the ooze, never to be seen again. The perils of being a drinks journalist.

Bundaberg and St Agnes may be thriving, but most of Australia's other large early-20th-century distilleries have either disappeared or are now shells of their former selves.

The Federal Distillery overlooking the bay in Port Melbourne was established in the 1880s. In its heyday, it was one of the biggest spirits manufacturers in the world, producing over 4 million litres of whisky, brandy and gin a year, not going out of production until the 1970s. The refurbished building is now home to luxury apartments, the only remnant of its former life being large murals on the outside wall of the various brands of spirits once made there.

The huge Corio distillery outside Geelong hasn't had such a lucky second life. Opened with great fanfare in 1929, the big four-storey brick building closed down in the 1980s and is now mostly empty.

I have travelled from Melbourne to Geelong countless times over the last twenty-five years on the way to wineries or the Great Ocean Road on holiday. And as the car or train I'm in has sped through the suburb of Corio, north of the city, I've glanced at that big brick building and been intrigued by the words 'Distillers Corporation Ltd' emblazoned on it. One day, I decided to turn off the main road and have a closer look.

This part of Corio is flat and industrial, with wide roads for big trucks and tankers. I pulled up outside what were once the main gates to the distillery compound; the company's initials, DCL, can be seen in cracked and fading red paint on the gateposts. I wanted to get closer, to take a photo of the old distillery, and as I walked through the gap where the fence once was and crossed the lawn towards the building, I saw that one of its doors had been left open. So, feeling more like an investigative journalist than a booze hack, I went inside.

There have been various attempts since Corio closed down in the 80s to utilise the huge spaces inside, with parts of it turned at various times into an arts centre, and offices. Luckily, there was no-one there the day I sneaked in. Just silence, the smell of dust, and, sitting facing each other in the atrium, two huge copper pot stills that had once churned out vast quantities of spirit. A few empty Corio-branded barrels had been stacked around the stills for show. Behind them, the empty warehouse floors, where millions of litres of whisky once sat maturing, stretched away into the gloom.

As the scale of the building shows, whisky was hugely popular in Australia in the 1920s. Not only was this country the world's biggest market for Scotch, but – thanks in part to high tariffs on the imported product introduced in 1925 – we also developed a thirst for the locally made spirit, particularly in Victoria, where 40 per cent of the whisky consumed was Australian. That's why the huge Scottish firm DCL decided to build an ambitious operation on this flat stretch of land north of Geelong, on the rail line, close to ports. The first product, Corio Old Special Whisky, was launched in 1934, and by the 1956 Olympics, when the distillery released its 5 Star Extra Matured Old Whisky brand, aimed at the international market, it was selling millions of bottles a year.

———————

The first whisky we try at Bad Frankie is a bottle of Corio 5 Star that dates from the 1960s. It's very good: punchy, almost sherry-like, nutty, smoky aromas, and a bright, warm, linseed-oil-like richness on the tongue. It has a time-travel quality to it: smells and flavours that make you feel like you're not here and now but somewhere else, in another era.

The second Corio bottle we try, the one from the 1980s, is nowhere near as good. It's lighter, simpler, less interesting. A nice sipping whisky, but nothing more. Its mediocre flavour tells the second half of the Corio story: by the 1970s, the whisky wasn't being made with as much care and had developed a terrible reputation. Luke McCarthy explains this was done deliberately: 'After high tariffs on imported spirits were removed in the 1960s, DCL decided that the [Corio] distillery should be producing whisky as quickly and as cheaply as possible so as not to compete with the premium imports.'

There's another reason for Corio's decline. In the early 1950s, the Shell oil company began constructing a huge refinery right next door. The refinery is still there, a sprawling complex of pipes and tanks and chimneys, spewing flames and steam into the sky, dwarfing the old red-brick distillery.

'Just imagine,' says Seb. 'When the distillery was first built, it was surrounded by paddocks. Big flat areas of long grass, the buildings looking out across the bay, a train line that brought barley in and carried whisky away. It must have been so impressive. A mythical place. And then, by the 1960s and 70s, after the refinery was built, people thought they were just drinking petrol.'

This is the image of Australian whisky, the legacy of Corio, the grand dream turned sour, that Bill Lark was up against when in 1989 he famously became the first person in Tasmania to obtain a distilling licence since spirits production had been banned 150 years before. Lark wasn't the only person who established a small distillery in Australia at the time, but the quality of his whiskies and his support for other emerging producers – his rec-ognition that there is strength in numbers – helped kickstart a craft spirits renaissance.

For the first couple of decades of that renaissance, most of the distilleries that opened were smaller, family-run businesses, selling direct to bars and restaurants and through cellar doors. Since around 2015, though, the industry has grown rapidly, and there are now some bigger distilleries that, if not yet quite at the production level of a Federal or Corio, certainly have grand ambitions.

One of those is Starward, based in Port Melbourne. Founded in 2008, for the first few years, like most other Australian whisky makers, it specialised in single malt, which is a costly style to produce. Then in 2018 the distillery launched a much more competitively priced, larger-volume whisky called Two-Fold that is a blend of cheaper grain spirit made from wheat and more expensive malt spirit made from barley, matured in wine barrels. It was the first time since Corio closed that an Australian blended whisky had hit the market.

We finish the tasting at Bad Frankie with a glass of Two-Fold, and it's delicious: aromas of fresh toast, some dried fig, a hint of ripe banana, then a soft, pretty, creamy vanilla texture on the tongue, finishing with a little tannic grip and savoury complexity. A whisky that anchors you in the here-and-now. As good as it is, though, Seb is still buzzing from finally getting to open the old Corio bottles after all these years, and tasting them alongside the next generation of Australian whisky:

> What I love about tasting side-by-side like this is that you get to see the evolution of the industry. You can see the cultural differences. You taste that 1960s Corio and you can imagine old men in a pub, smoking a thousand darts while drinking it. Then you taste the 1980s Corio and you know the distillery was just smashing it out in huge volume, didn't care about quality – and everyone was busy doing aerobics anyway. And now, with the Two-Fold, we've come back to people wanting to drink spirits with heaps of flavour and character. It's really exciting.

———

Seb's right. There has never been a better time to be a spirit drinker in Australia. In the last ten years, hundreds of small, new distillers have emerged, with many producing outstanding gin, vodka, rum and liqueurs, as well as excellent small-batch whisky. Some are even producing *baijiu,* modelled on China's strong white spirit.

Baijiu (pronounced 'bye-j'yoh') is traditionally made from grains such as rice and sorghum fermented using a starter-culture mix of yeast and bacteria called *qū* (pronounced 'chew'), then distilled. It is the most widely drunk spirit in China. But it is almost completely unfamiliar to most Australians – unless they have spent time in China, on business. And those who have come across the drink there invariably shudder when recalling their first encounter: epic late-night drinking sessions in restaurant after restaurant, endless toasts, downing shots of baijiu, one after another. They warn me about how strong the drink is, 50 per cent alcohol or more, and how rough it tastes. Firewater. Something to be endured, not enjoyed. So why would any Australian distiller want to make it?

'It's my passion,' says James Mylne when I catch up with him at his tiny East Coast Baijiu distillery in Brisbane. 'When I die, I want to be known as the white guy who makes awesome baijiu.'

The young distiller learned how to make the spirit, and how to appreciate its finer points, working for a distillery in Taiwan. This inspired him to return to Australia in 2017 and set up his own brand. Like the Chinese distillers making arrack in Java in the 17th and 18th century, James uses a combination of techniques from various different cultures to produce his baijiu. When he started, he tried making a super-clean, fruity style of spirit to appeal to Australian drinkers, but his Taiwanese and Chinese friends and colleagues weren't impressed. So now he sources *qū* culture from China to ensure his baijiu has an *authentic* flavour profile.

'I want to appeal to Chinese palates,' he says. 'China and the West are so different, culturally, when it comes to food and alcohol. I see my market as mainly China and Chinese-Australian people. I'm sure there is a small market for white guys drinking baijiu. But it's not something I'd bet my house on.'

I can see why. My first taste of James's 52 per cent alcohol baijiu is unforgettable – and almost incomprehensible.

It looks so innocent in the glass. Like vodka, or gin. But as soon as I bring it to my nose and take a sip, I'm thrown into the unknown. My senses scramble. My nasal hairs burn and bristle, my tongue tingles. I flail around, trying to latch on to a flavour I recognise. Dairy cellar? Incense? Wax? Nothing in this pungent burning water is familiar.

It's as though I'm tasting alcohol for the very first time.

Blow My Skull

Van Diemen's Land, 1815

Colonel Thomas Davey, lieutenant governor of Van Diemen's Land, was a notorious pisspot.

Davey had sailed as a young marine with the First Fleet in 1787, staying in Port Jackson for a few years before returning to England. Rising through the ranks, he arrived back in the colony in 1813 to take up the position of lieutenant governor in Hobart. He was described as 'dissipated and profligate' by New South Wales governor Lachlan Macquarie, who wrote to his superiors in England regularly about Davey's 'drinking and depravity'. Davey developed a formidable reputation among the colonists, too, when it came to the grog, as one particularly colourful account written years later by cookbook author Edward Abbott makes clear.

Fourteen-year-old Abbott had arrived in Hobart just after Davey, in 1815. The Sydney-born son of the colony's deputy judge advocate, Abbott became a clerk before rising to prominence in Tasmanian society as a pastoralist, publisher and politician. In 1864 he wrote what is considered to be the first cookbook compiled by an Australian, *The English and Australian Cookery Book: Cookery for the Many, as Well as for the 'Upper Ten Thousand'*. It's a remarkable insight into mid-19th-century attitudes to eating, and includes thirteen pages devoted to mixed drinks – recipes for the 'punches' and 'cups', the 'juleps' and 'cobblers' then fashionable in Australia. To put this into context, Jerry Thomas, the American 'father of the cocktail', had written his *Bar-Tender's Guide*, the first drinks manual to be published in the US and today seen as the 'blueprint' for cocktail culture, only two years before.

In his book, Abbott depicts the 'eccentric' Colonel Davey hosting epic drinking sessions in a 'wattle hut … improvised within a mile of the capital'. Davey would install himself at the head of a makeshift table in this dingy grog den, a 'barbecued pig' for sustenance laid out before him and a barrel filled with a punch of his own invention off to one side, ready to be tapped.

Davey's concoction was a blend of beer, rum and brandy, sugar syrup and lime juice. He called it 'Blow My Skull'. The lieutenant governor would welcome visitors into his shack and hand them a tin mug filled with a generous pour of his punch. 'A challenge to liquor from the representative of majesty in a roomy pannikin', Abbott wrote, 'could not be declined.' Especially when Colonel Davey then bellowed, 'No heeltaps!' (meaning 'Drink it all; don't leave any dregs'), and you both sculled the brimming cupful of the potent brew in one gulp. Abbott wrote that the unfortunate visitor would immediately be '*hors de combat*' – out of action – while the lieutenant governor, 'having an impenetrable cranium, and an iron frame, could take several goblets of the alcoholic fluid, and walk away as lithe and happy as possible'.

Blow My Skull. It sounds lethal. I just *had* to make some.

Abbott gives us a recipe: dissolve loaf sugar in two pints of boiling water, add some lime or lemon juice, a pint of ale or porter, a pint of rum and half a pint of brandy. My 21-year-old son Riley was particularly keen to help: it has become a tradition in our house for him to try out new cocktails on Sophie and me at the end of the day, as we get dinner ready. So while I barbecued some pork chops (Colonel Davey's choice of accompaniment for his Blow My Skull), Riley found a big jug and started blending. The result was ... surprisingly palatable. The sugar and lime help to mask the boozy hit of the rum and brandy, and the beer (we used porter) brought a malty, almost cola-like flavour.

Then Soph suggested adding some sparkling water to dilute the alcohol content even further. This wasn't very 'authentic' – there was no SodaStream in that wattle hut in 1815 – but it was a revelation: the now-fizzy sweet brown drink tasted just like rum and Coke. And it was delicious with the barbecued chops.

So, if it actually tastes good, how did Davey's drink get its fearsome reputation?

By the time Abbott was writing about the original Blow My Skull in the 1860s, a bastardised version of the drink, called Blow My Skull Off, had become notorious on Victoria's goldfields. It was sold at sly-grog shops and varied in its composition. One account lists the ingredients as methylated spirits, rum, cayenne pepper and opium, while another says the 'devil's potion' also included *Cocculus indicus*, or Levant nut, an Indian plant used by unscrupulous brewers in mid-19th-century beers to enhance the effects of intoxication – and used by everyone else as a pesticide and poison.

Cocktail historian and distiller Sebastian Reaburn has found mentions of Blow My Skull Off in police gazettes of the era, where officers are warned: 'If you find a group of men up in the goldfields of Ballarat drinking this, don't try to arrest them. In fact, don't even get off your horse. You just need to club them into unconsciousness because they're mad. There's no reasoning with them.'

I didn't try re-creating this later version of the drink. I do have *some* limits.

Peach cyder: Home brew

Friday night in Footscray and Ras Dashen Ethiopian restaurant is full. All sorts of people are here. Groups of international students from the university around the corner, young Chinese, Indonesian, German people, navigating new friendships using stilted English. A middle-aged, middle-class white couple from the eastern suburbs, excited to be on a foodie adventure, pretending to be cool, pretending to be local. And lots of African families and young men in flat caps, tearing off pieces of *injera* sourdough flatbread and scooping up mouthfuls of spicy beef *wat* and lamb *tibs*.

Waves of incense roll through the air, mingling with the perfume of cardamom and clove, and Afrobeat pulsing from the speakers. The walls are decorated with traditional African paintings. A small toy koala sits in a colourful basket on a shelf. Young women in bright scarves carry platters of food while the owner, Wondimu Alameo, known to everyone as Wondi, looks on from his usual spot, hovering at the bar at the back of the room, directing proceedings with a smile and greeting regulars by name.

Most people here are drinking Coke or Sprite or Ethiopian beer (except the eastern suburbs couple, who have brought their own bottle of nice pinot noir as a talisman for the trip across the

Maribyrnong). But occasionally Wondi ducks behind the bar and emerges a moment later with a small glass flask, such as you'd find in an apothecary – round-bodied, with a long, narrow neck – full of cloudy yellow liquid. He takes the flask to a table and, with a proud twinkle in his eye, pours the liquid into Duralex glass tumblers for the diners. This one, he says, is on the house.

The drink is *t'ej*, a kind of mead, or fermented honey, that has been enjoyed in Ethiopia for thousands of years. Wondi's wife, Alemitu Aberra, makes it here at Ras Dashen, where she is the chef. Behind the bar is a big 20-litre glass container – a demijohn – of fermenting t'ej, gently bubbling, the top covered in a tea towel, a siphon hose poking out from underneath. Wondi draws me off a glass to try. Despite its pale-gold, muddy-rice-water appearance it smells fresh, a little lemony, slightly woody, and it tastes lively, like floral yellow honey, softly sweet, with a herbal tang and a little tingling spritz on the tongue from the carbon dioxide of fermentation.

My son and I have made mead a few times. We took raw honey, mixed it with water, put the resulting golden liquid into a 5-litre demijohn and waited for the wild yeasts in the honey and in the air to get to work on the sugar, slowly converting it to alcohol. Most of the meads we've made this way have tasted quite plain and simple, though. Pleasant but not exciting. Nothing like this vibrant, intriguing yellow t'ej at Ras Dashen. I ask Wondi how it's produced, why it tastes so different.

'I'm not the one who is making it,' he says. 'That is my wife's skill. It is one of these things that is kept as a family secret.'

In Ethiopia, t'ej is traditionally made by women. Wondi and Alemitu have carried the tradition with them from the time they fled their homeland during the Ethiopian Civil War in the late 1980s, through the years they spent in a camp in Sudan and their time as refugees in New Zealand in the 1990s, until they arrived in Australia at the turn of the millennium. It's a tradition they continue to uphold.

Wondi can see I'm keen to know more, so he takes me to the storeroom behind the bar and shows me the boxes of honey he buys from a fifth-generation beekeeper in central Victoria. He tells me about the *gesho*, a shrub native to Ethiopia that he and Alemitu grow in their backyard: the bark and leaves are added to the t'ej during fermentation to give it the complex herbal flavours and astringency. And he explains that the t'ej he's serving at the moment is only halfway through fermenting – which is why it's spritzy and still sweet and light – but if the demijohn was in a cooler spot and he let it ferment fully, the t'ej would be stronger and drier, and you could keep it for six months. But he doesn't go into any more detail than that.

'We will keep our core secrets,' he says, smiling. 'It's a culture thing.'

———————

Every group of migrants who have a tradition of drinking alcohol have brought their culture of fermentation and/or distillation with them when they travelled to Australia. Not the official, sanctioned commercial manufacture of booze that can be scaled up and regulated and traded and taxed, but the unofficial production that takes place on a domestic level for home consumption, beyond the gaze of the authorities, behind closed doors, in backyards. For many migrants, like Wondi and Alemitu, making home brew reminds them of the place they have left: the process of making it, the rituals associated with its production and consumption, the flavour that floods the senses when they drink it. It's as important as keeping food traditions alive in this new country on the other side of the world.

When I arrived in Melbourne in the early 1990s, I laid down
a mental map of my new home partly through food and flavour.
Crunchy spring rolls wrapped in iceberg lettuce and dipped in
tangy sauce in a cheap Vietnamese restaurant in Victoria Street,
Richmond; sweet Eastern European cakes and bitter coffee in old
brown cafes in St Kilda's Acland Street; garlic-smothered pizza and
pasta on Lygon Street in Carlton. I also discovered distinct corners
of the city through booze. Trendy cool-climate pinot noir served in
Duralex tumblers in the Dogs Bar in St Kilda; small glasses of old
Australian sherry at Jimmy Watson's in Carlton; pots of ice-cold
Melbourne Bitter at the Great Britain Hotel in Richmond. But
some of the most grounding experiences, moments that made me
feel as though I was really connecting to the city, came when I tasted
drinks made by friends – or by parents of friends – from European
migrant families.

My friend Magda's mum and dad came out from Greece in the
1960s and worked to save to buy a comfortable home in the south-
eastern suburbs, surrounded by tomato plants and lettuces. Magda's
family home was one of the first places I visited after arriving in
Melbourne. After a lunch of charcoal lamb and salad in the cool
kitchen, Magda's father slipped out to his shed and brought back a
bottle of homemade *tsipouro*, the Greek version of grappa, that he
helped a mate make every year in his backyard. He poured us a small
shot glass and we drank it quickly, managing to smile gratefully
even though it was burning our nostrils, the knowledge of its illicit
production adding to the pleasure.

My friend Vincenzo's parents are also postwar migrants, from
Sicily. They lived in the sprawling northern suburbs, with tomatoes
and broccoli in the backyard and an old grape crusher and wine
press and demijohns in the shed. Throughout his teen years and

early twenties, Vince helped his father make wine every autumn in
his parents' garage using grapes trucked down by Italian growers on
the Murray River, and would bring bottles to parties and dinners,
proudly pouring his rustic red.

These moments were formative in my introduction to and understanding of Melbourne. They were a firsthand taste of the postwar
migrant culture, and an insight into how the children of those
migrants, both university-educated, both lawyers, still felt strongly
connected to their European heritage through food and drink.

Each of the many other examples of homemade booze I've drunk
since then has been fixed to a place and the people who produced
it. Dark and mysterious and intensely sweet walnut liqueur made
by a Croatian butcher in a shed down a dirt road near Daylesford.
Crystal-clear grappa poured into a very short black coffee by an old
Italian tobacco grower in the shadow of Mount Buffalo. Light, tangy,
pale red wine made from an ancient Slovenian grapevine variety,
brought in as cuttings and planted in the Yarra Ranges on the green
fringe of Melbourne, by the grandson of a Slovenian farmer.

In every case, the drink was poured with great ritual and great
pride – which couldn't be more different from my own haphazard
and dismal first attempts at home winemaking. Then again, this
is hardly surprising as I have no family cultural heritage of booze
production to tap into. Well, none to speak of.

Growing up in London, I'd watched my parents – Trixie, the
daughter of factory workers in the Midlands, and Bob, the son of
suburban Anglo-Australians – try to make their own wine during
a particularly lean financial period in our family's life. They bought
cans of thick, syrupy grape-juice concentrate (boiled down from
fruit grown in Italy or Spain), diluted the contents with water in a
glass demijohn, added various powders and tablets, stuck an airlock

in the top and shoved it away in the dark under the stairs for a few weeks. I must have been quite young because I can't recall tasting the resulting wine – either that, or it was so dire I've erased it from my memory.

Later, when I was twenty and living in a share house in Brighton on the south coast of England, with a small underfloor space that you could call a cellar if you were feeling imaginative, I decided to repeat the exercise for myself. Can of concentrate, glass demijohn, powders from a packet, airlock. This time, I remember all too clearly how bloody awful and muddy and flat the wine tasted.

After moving to Australia and tasting all these wonderful homemade drinks from different cultures, I started wondering what I could make myself that might give me a connection to the home I'd left, something I could call my own. I found that connection in cider.

———————————

I was born and spent the first few years of my life in Bristol, in the heart of England's West Country, epicentre of traditional cider production. As a teenager living in London, some of my first experiences of alcohol came in the form of big plastic bottles of cheap Woodpecker Medium Dry cider bought underage at the local off-licence. Then, travelling around the West Country in the late 1980s, I discovered the real thing: farmhouse scrumpy, stuff of legend.

The revelation came in a crumbling 16th-century pub called the Three Tuns in Hay-on-Wye, a little town famous for its bookshops and literary festival, just over the Welsh border from Herefordshire. Saggy wooden benches by the smoke-blackened inglenook, an ancient shillings-and-pence slot machine in one corner, and an even older landlady tending the tiny bar.

When I asked for cider, instead of reaching for the hand pump on the bar or a bottle from the fridge, she rummaged around in the gloom and hauled out a plastic gallon container of cloudy golden liquid. This was scrumpy, made by a local farmer using nothing but freshly pressed apple juice and wild yeasts and time.

'Be careful,' she warned, as she poured out a pint. And she was right: with its huge, sharp aromas of pulpy windfall fruit and its furry taste of tough, brown apple cores strewn across a barnyard, this was a deeply challenging explosion of agricultural flavour. I think it might also have had mild hallucinogenic properties. I was hooked.

Australians drank hardly any cider in the early 1990s when I arrived in Melbourne. If they did, it was either Mercury, a diehard Tasmanian brand established at the beginning of the 20th century in Hobart, or Strongbow, a brand introduced by the English cider company Bulmers in the 1970s and produced under licence by Fosters. You'd be lucky to find a bottle of either lurking in the bottom corner of the fridge at your local drive-through. To this new arrival, it looked like cider had never established a proper foothold here.

At the time, one of the only small cider producers in the country was Kellybrook on the edge of the Yarra Valley. When I heard about them, I headed out to taste their ciders. I discovered the Kelly family's orchard was full of old English heritage apples – Bulmer's Norman, Yarlington Mill and Kingston Black – the same varieties used to make the traditional West Country ciders that I'd fallen in love with in the UK. Darren Kelly told me he had started making cider in the 1960s because the drink was all the rage back then. He was one of many producers, including the notorious Cider Barrel at Pakenham on Melbourne's south-eastern fringe, and Mac's, a major producer that had started just up the road from Kellybrook in Lilydale in the 1930s.

What I'd perceived as a lack of interest in cider in Australia in the early 1990s, then, turned out to be a blip: the low ebb of a long, fluctuating cycle of taste – a cycle that has flowed the other way since the late 2000s, with the cider market booming once again.

The first English cider to arrive in Australia probably came on the *Endeavour* when Lieutenant James Cook sailed into Botany Bay in 1770. Like most ships of the time, the *Endeavour* would have been stocked with barrels of cider, which was given to the crew to help combat scurvy during long voyages. But cider wasn't just medicinal: it had also been a familiar daily drink to the farm labourers who'd joined Cook as sailors on the voyage, as it was traditional for many employers at the time to pay wages in cider.

Thanks to Australia's British farming heritage, apple orchards and cider making became a common sight in many settlement farms in the colony throughout the 19th century. Woolmers Estate, an unusually well-preserved colonial farm south of Launceston in Tasmania, was established by Thomas Archer in 1817 and boasts an impressive cider house located in a weatherboard barn on the property that was built by convicts in the 1840s. Entering the gloom of the barn feels like stepping back through time to the Old Country: into an ancient cider shed in deepest, darkest Somerset, perhaps. In the middle of the large room is a traditional stone cider mill, a huge, carved, circular sandstone trough holding a massive stone wheel. It's easy to picture a draught horse plodding endlessly around the trough, rolling the heavy wheel as workers tip sacks of apples into its relentless pulping path, to produce enough cider for the farm's eighty servants.

English settlers brought a large number of different apple-tree cultivars here in the 19th century, providing a diverse pool of genetic material that still exists today in a few commercial orchards and heritage nurseries around the country. In some rare cases, the original trees themselves are still growing.

Gary Watkins-Sully's family emigrated to Australia from Chepstow, just across the Severn Estuary from Bristol, about an hour's drive from Hay-on-Wye. In 2007, the family bought a defunct 1920s cheese factory at Reidsdale, near Braidwood in southern New South Wales, with the intention of making cider. Gary had discovered that the area was a hub of cider production in the late 19th century, with some of the notable early settlers, such as Dr Thomas Braidwood Wilson – after whom the district was named – planting apple trees in the 1830s, and settlers Charles and Hannah Wilton building a stone cider factory a few decades later, modelled on those they'd seen in their native Somerset. Remarkably, not only is the Wiltons' cidery still standing – albeit in a fairly decrepit state – but a couple of their trees, and trees that Thomas Wilson's gardener Farquhar Aberdeen planted, have also survived.

When I visited the old cheese factory in Reidsdale in late autumn, Gary was still processing the last of the season's apples the old-fashioned way by pressing the pulp, wrapped up in cloth, between wooden racks, and making his cider much as the Wiltons would have done, by allowing the wild yeasts on the fruit and in the atmosphere to ferment the golden juice spontaneously. He'd saved me an apple to taste from one of the gnarly, windblown 180-year-old Wilson trees.

Gary believes the variety is a Golden Pippin. He has compared the physical appearance, growth habit and flavour of apples from the tree that Aberdeen planted in Wilson's garden in the 1830s with descriptions in Robert Hogg's *Fruit Manual* of 1860, regarded by orchardists as an authoritative text, and it matches. This is a very old cultivar that dates back to at least the 1600s. Crucially, it was described by English writer John Evelyn in 1706 in *Pomona*, his seminal treatise on apples and cider, as 'esteemed for the making of the most delicious of that Liquor, most wholesome, and most restorative'.

Biting into the apple's rough-textured russet skin released a rich, dense flood of sweet golden flavour. It was a ravishing, moving experience: I felt for a moment as though I was travelling through time and space, from now, back through colonial Australia, all the way to Elizabethan England.

Apples are propagated by taking cuttings from one tree and either planting those cuttings directly into the ground or grafting them onto rootstocks. The fruit from the new tree will stay true to variety and taste the same as the fruit grown on the parent tree. So, someone biting into a Golden Pippin apple grown in Australia in the early 21st century has the same experience as someone eating a Golden Pippin apple grown in England in the 17th century – as though we are biting into the same apple at the same time, sharing the same rough texture on our teeth and lips, sensing the same flood of golden juice on our tongues, feeling the same enjoyment in our hearts.

You don't have to travel to Reidsdale to time-travel, of course. You can just pop into your local supermarket or fruit shop, pick up a Granny Smith, and take a bite: you'll experience the same tart, juicy crunch that orchardist Maria Ann Smith experienced when she first tasted the bright-green apples growing on a chance seedling tree that had sprung up on her property outside Sydney in the 1860s.

———

I first made cider in my backyard in Melbourne in 2011. I'd found a small orchard full of old apple varieties just a few blocks from my house, in the grounds of Rippon Lea, the National Trust–owned mansion built by merchant and politician Frederick Sargood in 1868. Like many grand estates established on the outskirts of Australia's emerging capital cities in the late 19th century, Rippon Lea was originally surrounded by farmland. Much of that country is now covered in suburban houses, schools, cinemas and the ABC's old Gordon Street studios where my mum worked with my wife's parents in the 1960s. But in the 1980s, one corner of the estate near the original 1860s stables was converted to an orchard that now boasts over 130 varieties of heritage apples and pears, including Golden Pippin and the classic cider variety Kingston Black.

I'd heard that the gardeners at Rippon Lea had harvested enough fruit to make cider by netting some of the trees to stop the local flocks of lorikeets munching the crop. So I contacted the head gardener and asked if I could gather enough of what was left over – those few apples still clinging unscathed to higher branches, the unbruised windfalls lurking in the grass below – to make a demijohn of cider myself.

Not owning any cider-making equipment at that time, I crushed the apples in the most rudimentary way by bashing them to a pulp with a block of wood in a bucket. Then I borrowed a winemaker friend's old basket press, wrapped the apple pulp up in parcels of shade cloth, put them in the press, slowly squeezed them and filled a glass demijohn with golden-brown sticky syrupy juice.

At this stage, according to all the modern cider-making manuals I'd read, I should have added some safe, reliable cultured yeast from a packet. Instead, I did nothing. I walked away and waited for nature to take its course. I wanted to do what the farmer who made that scrumpy in Hay-on-Wye had done and just let the wild yeasts on the apple skins and flesh and stalks and pips, in the air, on the press, do what yeasts do naturally: turn sugar into alcohol.

Nothing happened at first. The juice just sat there. But then, after a few hours, up from the depths of the murk emerged tiny pinprick bubbles of carbon dioxide: a definite sign of microbial activity. Fermentation had started. The wild yeasts were getting to work.

As I watched those little bubbles slowly rise, I felt another strange and profound feeling of connection with the generations of people before me who have marvelled at this seemingly miraculous process. And not just the cider makers: the winemakers and brewers, all those innumerable human beings who, for thousands of years, long before scientists identified yeasts and bacteria as the living organisms responsible for fermentation, have simply trusted in the *mystery* to produce a delicious drink.

———————

I've made my own cider each autumn almost every year since that first fermentation epiphany. I've bought my own small-scale cider-making equipment. I've crawled around on my hands and knees in the mud and damp grass under apple trees foraging for wind-falls in the Goulburn Valley. I've scrambled over gates and fences to reach fat ripe apples on wild roadside trees in Coonawarra. I've made friends with orchardists on the Mornington Peninsula who have old heritage varieties: proper cider apples like Kingston Black, almost-forgotten English apples like Sturmer Pippin, unfashionable Australian apples like Sundowner.

Each year I've brought my motley harvest back home and dragged my crusher and press out of the garage and invited friends and family, reluctant teenagers and eager neighbours, to help me make cider. And after the crushing and pressing, we've all sat down for a meal and opened bottles of last year's batch and celebrated the season.

I now take bottles of my cider with me when I travel, to share with friends or to pour for winemakers or brewers or other, professional cidermakers. Sometimes people even say they like it, which makes me feel proud – and connected, as though the annual autumn rituals at Woolmers and Braidwood are echoing in my own creaking basket press.

––––––––––

Making my own also turned me into a terrible cider snob. Well, more of a snob than I was already.

The more I explored traditional natural cider-making methods, the more I developed an irritating holier-than-thou attitude to the rising tide of sweet, carbonated commercial ciders produced using reconstituted imported apple juice concentrate. As Australia's latest cider boom progressed throughout the 2010s, I scoffed at all the new wannabe brands designed to appeal to younger drinkers. I heaped scorn on the lolly-water ciders flavoured with berries, ginger and passionfruit. But I saved my most pompous ire for cynical beverages calling themselves 'cider' that weren't even made from apples: grape-based 'ciders', kiwifruit 'ciders', etc. They *really* infuriated me. But then I found out that calling non-apple drinks 'cider' is nothing new in this country. Australians were making cider – or *cyder* as they called it, using the 18th-century spelling – from fruit other than apples 200 years ago. And the fruit of choice was peaches.

When I picture Sydney in the summer of 1803 I don't immediately conjure images of peach trees laden with yellow fruit. But the peach had established itself as one of the new colony's more successful crops at this time. Indeed, the trees were growing so well that in 1803 the settlers were facing a glut of unwanted fruit. So a few enterprising souls decided to crush, press and ferment the excess peaches to make cyder.

The first results of these experimental ferments were promising enough to encourage others to have a go, and by early 1805, the *Sydney Gazette* reported that 'several of the settlers at Kissing Point [near Parramatta] have devoted much attention to the praise-worthy object; one of whom informs us, that he has already put up about 200 gallons [900 litres]; which with a few months fermentation, he doubts not will be found equal to the apple-cyder in strength, and not inferior to the taste'.

The authorities were keen to promote the consumption of lower-alcohol drinks such as beer and cider rather than the 'ardent spirits' that had caused so much social strife in the colony in its early years. So they actively encouraged settlers to make their own peach cyder. In the lead-up to the 1806 harvest, newly installed Governor Bligh even offered a prize: 'The person who will produce, in the next Peach Season, Two Hogsheads of Peach Cyder, which when One Year old is judged by him to be the best, shall receive a Cow from Government as a Reward.'

Intrigued by these stories, I decided to make some peach cyder using 19th-century principles and techniques, as a way of understanding what it was like.

According to heritage fruit experts I consulted, the peaches grown in Sydney at that time were likely to have been a white-fleshed freestone variety, now long-forgotten, and probably grown from kernels brought over from Europe. I found detailed instructions on how to make peach 'cider' in an 1874 issue of the *Australian Town and Country Journal*. And in the middle of summer, at the height of peach season, I went to the bustling Queen Victoria Market in the heart of Melbourne and bought 20 kilograms of seconds.

Following the instructions in the *Journal*, I separated the peach flesh from the kernels, crushed the flesh into pulp and macerated it overnight, smashing the kernels into coarse meal to be added to the pulp later. The next day, I put the peach pulp and kernels in shade-cloth bags and pressed them in my small basket press. The juice was very thick and gloopy and tasted, not surprisingly, like peach nectar.

I managed to squeeze just over 10 litres of this thick juice from the fruit, so rather than pouring it into an open wooden cask as the instructions called for, I used two 5-litre glass demijohns as my fermenting vessels.

'The fermentation is the most critical part of the business,' the *Town and Country Journal* told me. 'It should be in our warm climate conducted in as cool an atmosphere as can be secured.' Good advice. So, with a forecast of a few days over 30°C, I took the demijohns inside.

'Shortly after it has been placed in the vat,' said the *Journal*, 'the juice will begin to throw up bubbles, and a scum or spongy crust will form on the surface.' And indeed, by that evening some brown gel had coalesced on the surface of the juice, and the telltale tiny pinpricks of gas had started to gather. A couple of days later and fermentation was vigorously underway: I'd put airlocks in the demijohns by that point (a nod to modernity) and a steady insistent blup blup blup of CO_2 was forcing its way through.

A week later fermentation had stopped. No more bubbles were being produced and the cider was beginning to clear and settle, throwing a heavy sediment. At this point, according to the 1874 instructions, it was important to siphon the cider into another vessel, separating the clearer juice from the 'settlings'.

But when I tasted the liquid in both demijohns, I realised not all the sugar had been converted into alcohol. Fermentation had 'stuck'. The wild yeasts had given up, run out of nutrients or simply died off. What's more, all sorts of other microbes – less desirable strains of wild yeast, and acetic-acid-producing bacteria – had also been having their wicked way with the juice, resulting in some deeply unappealing flavours. The cider in one demijohn tasted like it was halfway to bad vinegar; the other was even more feral, with a lingering, gag-inducing aftertaste of mouse piss on rancid pork fat.

Rather than being disappointed, I was rather pleased with myself. In a letter to Sir Joseph Banks from Sydney in 1808, naturalist George Caley described the abundance of peaches then being harvested in the colony and the 'great quantity of cider' being made. But, he said, the cider 'may in great respect be compared to hogwash'. Suddenly, disgustingly, I could see exactly what he was talking about. I too had made authentic 19th-century peach hogwash.

The settlers, of course, knew what to do with low-alcohol cyder rapidly spoiling in the Sydney heat: distil it. Turn it into high-strength cyder brandy. Only problem was, the authorities took a very dim view of people operating stills. Indeed, no sooner had the newspapers started advocating for the production of 'wholesome' peach cyder than they ran reports of raids on illegal distilling operations.

———————

Today, home distilling is still subject to strict government control. I can make as much cider or beer or wine for home consumption as I want without needing to have any interaction with the authorities. I don't need a licence, I don't need to pay tax. But distilling that cider or beer or wine into a strong spirit – any quantity, even just a couple of litres – is illegal without a licence. And even once I have obtained a licence, the alcohol I produce attracts excise duty, which means I pay the Australian Taxation Office for the privilege of making my own spirits. And if I don't get a licence and pay the tax, I can end up in prison.

One of the official reasons for this tight regulation is that home distillation can be dangerous. It's true that the first distillate to trickle from the condenser during a distilling run contains toxic methanol and unpleasant compounds, such as acetone, that need to be discarded or re-distilled rather than drunk. It's true, too, that every couple of years someone gets very sick or even dies from methanol poisoning after ignoring this advice and drinking their dodgy homemade grappa. But the historical basis for the regulation and imposition of duty on all distillation, including for home consumption – which dates back to the Commonwealth Excise Act of 1901 – also lies in the government not wanting to miss out on the revenue it has been raising from the sale of 'pernicious' spirits since 1788.

Not that any of this stops people distilling spirits at home, of course. It didn't back then and it doesn't now. I can buy a still from a home-brew shop because, despite telling us we can't make spirits without a licence, the ATO also allows us to own a small still – 5-litre capacity or less – without needing its permission, as long as we only use it to distil water or herbal tinctures and *definitely not alcohol*. Which is a lot like selling bongs to people on the condition that they're *definitely not used for smoking weed*.

I could have easily distilled my putrid peach cyder myself. But the nagging fear of methanol poisoning led me to take my demijohns of fetid brew to a professional, someone who is well versed in the dark arts of distillation – and has a licence.

———————

The Craft & Co is a hub of artisan food and drink manufacture in Collingwood. The business, in an old warehouse site on Smith Street, comprises a brewery, dairy, smallgoods cellar and – in a corner of the main restaurant, behind a metal grille delineating the excise-licensed area – a small distillery, complete with gleaming copper still and stainless-steel tanks. The whole place harks back to the 19th century when the inner suburbs of Australia's emerging cities were full of small-scale operations like this: dairies and breweries, butchers and distilleries, servicing local markets.

Sebastian Reaburn was the distiller there at the time, and because he has extensively researched the history of spirits in Australia and is fascinated by flavour, he agreed to help me with my peach cyder experiment. As well as using the equipment to make a gin with his partner, Dervilla McGowan, which they sold under their own Anther label, Sebastian also produced spirits for Craft & Co and other businesses, from small commercial runs to even smaller experimental runs. For his littlest batches, he used a 5-litre copper alembic that is essentially the same as the stills that would have been used in Sydney in the early 19th century – except he used an electric hotplate to 'fire' his, rather than the more authentic but dangerous open flames.

After valiantly tasting my attempt to re-create colonial peach cyder and agreeing that it was utterly hideous, Sebastian poured some of the rank fluid into the still and turned on the hotplate. As the temperature began to reach 100°C, various alcohols and flavour compounds in the liquid – which are more volatile than water – started to evaporate, rising up into the copper dome of the still and from there into a thin, coiled copper tube submerged in iced water. As the vapour cooled inside the tube, it condensed, emerging as a trickle of clear liquid.

Sebastian held a small glass in the stream as it first started to drip from the still and handed it to me. It smelled strongly of acetone, which Sebastian told me was an indication of the presence of methanol. This first unpleasant-tasting and toxic fraction of the distillate is called the heads, and is either discarded or added back to future batches to be re-distilled; Sebastian chose to discard the heads in this run. The last trickle of the distillate, called the tails, was treated the same way as it contained a lot of the coarse, feral flavours of the cyder. What he was after, he said, in this first distillation – the 'wash-run' – was the ethanol and the hopefully more appealing flavour compounds in the middle.

By the end of the wash-run a couple of hours later, from 10 litres of cloudy brown liquid with a low alcohol content of between 3 and 4 per cent, Sebastian had extracted just over a litre of clear colourless liquid with an alcohol content of just over 31 per cent. What's more, this clear colourless liquid didn't smell or taste half as bad as the cloudy brown liquid had. While not entirely delicious, it was certainly drinkable. And unlike the cyder, which was spoiling in front of our eyes, the distillate was strong and stable. It wasn't going to go off. It had almost achieved immortality.

Before this point, I thought I knew all about distillation. I'd visited distilleries, drunk lots and lots of spirits, read heaps of books. But now I'd experienced the process for myself, using a liquid I'd made myself, I really understood for the first time why human beings developed the culture of distillation and have been in its thrall ever since. Through distillation, you can take the liquid equivalent of a sow's ear (or, in my case, liquid that *tastes* like a sow's ear) and transform it into the liquid equivalent of a silk purse. You can turn something perishable into something impervious to decay. You can confer eternal life on something that is dying. That's magic. Alchemy. No wonder we call the product of distillation not just 'firewater' but also 'spirit'. *Aqua vitae. Eau de vie.* The water of life.

There was more magic to come. Sebastian cleaned out the still, put the clear wash-run spirit back in, and turned on the heat for a second distillation: the spirit run. While the illicit distillers in Sydney would undoubtedly have been happy with what had come out of the still after the first run, he told me, they would have probably distilled it a second time, for two reasons: it increases the alcohol content while reducing the overall volume of liquid, making the spirit stronger and easier to store, transport and hide from the authorities; and it makes the spirit *taste* better. It's a fallacy to presume, he said, that people in those days, even in those difficult circumstances, were less concerned with quality than we are now.

As we sampled the tiny stream of crystal-clear liquid that dripped from the still the second time around, tasting every few minutes as different volatiles evaporated and condensed, I understood what he meant. After the acetone of the heads had faded and before the flabby coarseness of the tails kicked in, right in the heart of the distillation was a moment of beautiful purity: the liquid tasted like essence of peach, bright, clean, sweet, long.

At the end of the day we had collected 400 millilitres of spirit at 64 per cent alcohol. From 20 kilos of peaches to just under half a litre of overproof peach eau de vie. Not all the funk of the cyder had stayed behind in the still – the spirit had a touch of coarseness and faint echoes of that mousy taint – but it was drowned out by the peachy aromatics, pleasant hints of almond-kernel bitterness and a soft, icing-sugar-like sweetness. This magical stuff was eminently drinkable. Even George Caley would have thought it worthy of commending to Joseph Banks.

And I understood, not just in an abstract sense but on a visceral level, the *value* of distillation. At the beginning of the day, I had been burdened with 10 litres of dodgy peach cyder that I couldn't bring myself to drink, let alone give away. Now, I had almost half a litre of spirit that was good enough to not only share *but also to sell*. In 1806, I thought, someone would have paid very good money for this.

––––––––––––

The line separating home brew from commercial grog production is a fine and fluid one, and crossing it changes the way you think about what you're making and why. It can change the relationship you have with the drink.

At Ras Dashen restaurant in Footscray, Wondimu Alameo has been serving his wife's homemade t'ej to customers as a gesture of hospitality, a symbol of cultural exchange. Now he is considering taking the next step and working with a manufacturer to scale up production and perhaps sell bottles of t'ej to other restaurants and retailers. A local brewer has shown interest in developing the product with him. And he's not the only member of the Ethiopian community exploring the option of commercialising their t'ej.

Naz Mahari and her chef partner, Dawit Kebede, are co-owners of Mesob restaurant on High Street in the inner-urban Melbourne suburb of Northcote. It's hipster central here: the woodfired pizza joints and artisan-woollens shops and craft-beer bars on this strip are full of bearded young men with topknots and tattooed young women in vintage dresses. Naz and Dawit's Ethiopian restaurant is one of the busiest venues in the street.

Naz's family came to Australia in the 1990s. Her mum makes t'ej at home using fresh gesho grown by the Eritrean community in Melbourne; she also uses the gesho to make an Eritrean beer-like drink called *suwa*, brewed from teff (the same grain used in the injera flatbread) and sorghum. But at Mesob, it's Dawit who not only makes the t'ej but is also the chef. According to Naz, this is unusual: 'Traditionally Ethiopian men don't even go into the kitchen.'

The t'ej here appears on the menu alongside the dessert wines: Dawit likes to serve flasks of the honey wine when it's only just started to ferment, so it doesn't contain much alcohol at all and is still quite sweet (although the flask I enjoy with my meal has clearly been fermenting a bit longer and has a lovely hint of sour tang). 'In Ethiopia,' says Naz, 'when it is first made and still sweet, t'ej is even given to children to drink.'

Naz says she has reservations about bottling t'ej. Yes, she can see the commercial opportunity. There is growing interest in Australia in drinks made from fermented honey, particularly in home-brew circles, but in bars and restaurants, too, always keen to find the Next Big Thing. Naz and Dawit run a small bar next door to the restaurant where bottled t'ej could be more popular than the flasks.

'I just wonder what it would taste like,' she says. 'Whether it would be the same as homemade t'ej.'

She's concerned that the essence of t'ej – its mutability, the fact that it is traditionally drunk at various stages as it ferments, from sweet and child-friendly to dry and very adult, from light and fresh to strong and savoury – could be lost by capturing it in a sealed container, adding preservatives, fixing it in a moment in time, and selling it to people who will then drink it without cultural context.

I have thought a lot about selling my own cider, too. About scaling-up production, turning my backyard hobby into a business. But I've never followed through on this plan, never crossed that line. If I did, I think I'd lose sight of why I make cider in the first place: to embrace that feeling of cultural connection.

The Salthouse champagne:
A taste of luxury

On Saturday 27 November 1841, a 260-ton ship called the *William Salthouse* sailed into the entrance of Port Phillip Bay. It was the final day of a voyage that had begun in June that year, when the trading vessel left Montreal in Canada and sailed via Cape Town to the six-year-old settlement of Melbourne. The ship was carrying a valuable cargo: £12,000 worth of building materials, salt pork, beef and fish, vinegar, flour, and plenty of alcohol – barrels of whisky and cider, bottles of sweet wine, baskets of champagne.

As any sailor knows who has navigated the narrow entrance of Port Phillip Heads in rough weather, if the wind is blowing up hard from the Southern Ocean and the tide is flowing out from the bay – as it was that November day in 1841 – it is treacherous to find safe passage through the hidden reefs. Not being familiar with this part of the world, the commander of the *Salthouse* tried his best to steer his way but the ship struck submerged rocks, snapping the rudder and gouging the keel.

Water rapidly filled the hull and the ship became unmanageable, eventually running aground on a sandbank called the Pope's Eye, near the small coastal squatter camp then called Shortland's Bluff and now known as Queenscliff. The crew were saved, but before salvage vessels were able to reach the ship and retrieve the cargo, the *Salthouse* sank off the sandbank into deeper water, taking its casks of herring and bottles of booze to the bottom of the bay.

There the wreck lay until 1982, when two scuba divers came across it sitting upright on the sea floor still full of cargo. Although the barrels of whisky and cider had long since broken apart and lost their contents, many of the bottles of champagne and sweet wine were intact, still packed in their wicker baskets and pine boxes. News of the discovery attracted amateur divers, treasure hunters keen to plunder the wreck, and although much of the contents were taken or destroyed, the Victoria Archaeological Survey (VAS) was able to conduct conservation and excavation work, including the retrieval and preservation of around 100 of the bottles.

In early 1994, to coincide with the launch of an exhibition about the history of wine at the Museum of Victoria, then housed at the State Library in Melbourne, VAS conservator Sera-Jane Peters arranged a tasting of some of these old bottles, keen to get the impressions of expert tasters to see if they could add any insight to the archaeological evidence and chemical analysis of the wines.

The VAS and Museum organisers thought it would be a good idea to hold the tasting in public, to promote the exhibition. On the day a curious crowd (including me: I had just started writing for *The Age* newspaper) gathered in an imposing 19th-century hall of the State Library to watch a panel of eminent experts, including Yarra Valley–based wine writer James Halliday and chief oenologist for

champagne house Moët et Chandon Richard Geoffroy, subject themselves to the rare experience of tasting 150-year-old shipwreck wines.

Peter Leske, a winemaker for the Australian Wine Research
Institute, carefully extracted the crumbling corks from a couple of the
old bottles and poured small samples of amber liquid. We all watched
and waited as each of the tasters picked up their glass, examined
the contents suspiciously, swirled the liquid and brought it up for a
sniff, then took a sip, spat it out and pronounced on the experience.
Surprisingly, perhaps, the experts didn't react to all the samples by
screwing up their noses and suppressing a desire to vomit. Yes, the
salt water had contaminated every bottle to varying degrees – as
you'd expect after they'd been under the sea for 150 years – but the
characteristic flavours of some of the wines, the tasters said, were still
clearly visible underneath the brine.

In his report on the tasting for the *Weekend Australian* newspaper,
Halliday described the champagnes as particularly notable. 'Overall,
the champagnes had been less affected by saltwater intrusion [than
the sweet wines],' he wrote, 'no doubt because the internal pressure
of the wine had long resisted the pressure of 17 metres of seawater …
The best examples still had a brilliant deep yellow colour, [and]
despite the pervasive saltwater contamination, the style of early 19th
century champagne was easy to see … One ached to taste an example
which did not have the half-chemical (gunpowder and flint) half-
fungal (mushroom) aroma and salty finish.'

I was standing close to the tasters that day. At one point Peter
handed me an almost-empty glass of brown, flat champagne to
taste. Carefully, nervously, I took a sip. And although sea water was
indeed the predominant unpleasant flavour (imagine mixing a little
old white wine with warm oyster juice), you could taste the grapes
behind it. You caught a glimpse of the long-ago golden sunshine of

northern France, preserved by alcohol, shrouded for a century and a half by the sands and seaweed at the bottom of a bay on the other side of the world.

––––––––––

The *William Salthouse* story is remarkable in many ways. It was the first ship to attempt direct trade between the well-established British colony in North America and the brand-new colony of the Port Phillip District. In doing so, it was blatantly flouting a British law prohibiting such intercolonial commerce. Melbourne was in the middle of its first population boom at the time; established in 1835, it had grown from a small settlement of just 5000 people in 1839 to a sizeable town of 20,000 around the time the *Salthouse* sank near the entrance to the bay. More than 300 ships arrived in Port Phillip in 1841, most from other ports in Australia but many from Britain and other colonial ports in South Africa, India and Indonesia.

There were significant profits to be made from selling essential supplies to the rapidly expanding colony. That's why the ship was laden with hundreds of casks of flour – which had been in short supply in Port Phillip the year before – as well as barrels of salt fish and meat, and large quantities of building materials: sawn timbers and nails for house construction. The Canadian whisky and cider, also shipped in cask, would hopefully have found a ready market, too, among the proprietors of the town's fifty new hotels and their thirsty clientele.

It's not so obvious at first, though, why fine sweet wine and fancy champagne were included in the cargo on the *William Salthouse*. These wines weren't staples: they were luxuries. As Sera-Jane Peters observed at the time of the tasting of the old bottles, much of the population of Port Phillip in 1841 were having a great deal of difficulty surviving: 'They weren't able to feed themselves and yet someone was importing large quantities of very expensive French wines and champagnes.'

Dessert wines, particularly fortified sweet wines such as vintage port and madeira and unfortified sweet wines from Sauternes in Bordeaux and other parts of Europe, were held in the highest regard by connoisseurs around the world in the late 18th and early 19th centuries, often commanding prices far in excess of dry wines. And these sweet wines had had a place at the dining table of well-to-do arrivals in the British colony of New South Wales since its foundation more than a half-century before, indicators of the refined tastes considered essential to being civilised.

In October 1787, en route to Botany Bay, the First Fleet stopped off in Cape Town to replenish provisions and buy animals and plants for the new settlement. While the convicts were left to languish for weeks on board, the British officers and marines went sightseeing on dry land – and indulged in a spot of South African wine tourism.

'The Cape is celebrated for producing in the highest perfection all the tropical and other fruits,' wrote soon-to-be lieutenant governor David Collins in his journal. 'Wines of their own growth formed a considerable article of traffic here; and the neatness, regularity, and extent of their wine-vaults, were extremely pleasing to the eye; but a stranger should not visit more than one of them in a day; for almost every cask has some peculiarity to recommend it, and its contents must be tasted.'

After assiduously sampling his way through the Cape's cellars, Collins singled out one particular wine for praise. 'Constantia', he wrote, 'has a very fine, rich, and pleasant flavour, and is an excellent cordial.'

Constantia was one of the most famous sweet wines in the world at the time. Notable devotees included Casanova, George Washington and Napoleon Bonaparte. Jane Austen, Charles Baudelaire and Charles Dickens – like David Collins – all wrote glowingly of it. And although he doesn't say so, it's easy to imagine a few bottles of the 'excellent cordial' making their way with Collins to the new colony, to be relished in his tent soon after arriving.

This, then, helps explain why ten wooden crates full of bottles of sweet muscat originally shipped from the port of Cette (today spelt Sète) in the south of France were found on the *William Salthouse*: wine merchants were selling Muscat de Lunel and Muscat de Frontignan – both produced near Cette – in Sydney and Hobart as early as the 1820s. But what's more interesting to me is the greater quantity of champagne on board: twenty wicker baskets, each holding a dozen bottles.

Despite many people in the colony initially battling hardship and shortages, some settlers also developed a taste for champagne in the booming Port Phillip District, and were prepared to pay the exorbitant prices charged for the luxury. In its round-up of retail prices in March 1840, the *Port Phillip Gazette* listed champagne as the most expensive wine available, selling for between £3 and £4 per dozen bottles, two to three times more than port or sauterne, and about the same price as 100 pounds (45 kilograms) of finest flour.

French sparkling wine soon emerged as a symbol of the booming optimism of the time. Conspicuous consumption of champagne became a key feature of colonial life, thanks in part to the vast sums being made by land speculators. The day before the *Salthouse* sank, for example, in the pages of the *Gazette* a property developer enticed buyers to an upcoming land sale of thirteen 1-acre allotments on the banks of the Yarra River – 'beautifully situated for Villa Residences and Gardens' – by promising 'a plentiful Repast, with Champagne, on the Ground'. These 'champagne breakfasts' became such common sights at land sales across the district that by 1843, Governor George Gipps reported that the suburbs were 'thickly strewed with champagne bottles'.

The Australian thirst for champagne turned into a frenzy with the gold rush in the 1850s, as recalled by Melbourne writer Garnet Walch, reminiscing about the era thirty years later. 'Not satisfied with ordering and opening half-a-dozen cases at a time for the benefit of all and sundry who chose to partake,' he wrote, 'the *nouveaux riches* of Diggerdom had a lordly taste for playing skittles, with bottles of champagne for pins, or for piling fifty bottles or so in a corner and demolishing them with a shovel.'

The connection between champagne consumption and celebration became entrenched in Australia during this period and continued long after the gold rush had faded – particularly, writes historian David Dunstan, at rich men's tables and at civic dinners: 'When the new Melbourne Town Hall was opened in 1870, Mayor Samuel Amess staged a huge banquet, ordering at his own expense one hundred cases of the best French champagne.' But it wasn't just the upper classes who indulged their passion for bubbly. As Dunstan puts it, after the gold rush the taste for champagne 'extended to low life as well as high'.

Alicia Bond arrived in Melbourne from Ireland in the mid-1850s, and by 1862, with three children and a consumptive husband to support, had opened a brothel on Lonsdale Street. Like many other madams at the time, she chose the notorious working-class area in the north-east corner of the city known as Little Lon to locate her business. We know that clients and sex workers regularly drank champagne in the Little Lon district because since the 1980s, as the old 19th-century buildings have been torn down and replaced by office blocks and apartment towers, archaeologists have retrieved thousands of artefacts, including hundreds of bottles that once contained alcohol. And in the rubbish in the backyard of Mrs Bond's brothel, researchers found seventy-seven champagne bottles – outnumbering spirits bottles seven to one – and more than 300 oyster shells.

We know, too, what brands of champagne these were. Dunstan relates an account of a party of prostitutes celebrating Melbourne Cup Eve in a hotel in Swanston Street in 1876, opening bottles of Moët et Chandon, Pommery and Krug by the dozen – all brands popular at the time and still exported to Australia.

Remarkably, we also know what brand of champagne was on board the *William Salthouse* when it sank in 1841. The bottles retrieved from the bottom of the bay are a very distinctive fat skittle shape, and half of the corks in the bottles are branded with the word *Aÿ*. Today, the village of Aÿ is home to many top champagne producers. But in the 1830s, when the wine inside those bottles was made, there were only a handful of wineries there. And one of those producers, Gosset, the oldest house in Champagne (established in 1584), claims to be the source of the *Salthouse* bottles: the company has 19th-century records of shipping wine to Montreal, where the ship had loaded its outbound cargo; and Gosset not only branded their corks with the name Aÿ, but the winery also still uses the same distinctive 'antique'-shaped bottle today.

We even have a good idea of the style of wine inside those old bottles. In his article on the *Salthouse* tasting in the *Weekend Australian* in 1994, Halliday described the Gosset bottles as being typical early-19th-century champagnes, 'much sweeter than those of today, with less careful juice handling leading to higher levels of phenolic flavours'. The tasters all noted a distinct soft sweetness in the champagnes they tried at the State Library of Victoria that day. And Moët et Chandon's Geoffroy observed that champagnes of the time were also made from a high proportion of red pinot noir grapes (as opposed to the blends of white chardonnay and red pinot typical in modern champagne) using less gentle techniques, resulting in coarser, heavier, more astringent flavours.

Geoffroy's description echoes journalist Richard Twopenny's rather snooty account of mid-19th-century champagne preferences in his 1883 book, *Town Life in Australia*. '"Body", or what captious folk would call "heaviness" is the first condition of good wine to the colonial taste,' he wrote. 'The lower middle and lower classes also like it sweet.'

By the late 1880s, however, tastes in champagne were becoming a little more sophisticated. The era of Marvellous Melbourne was in full swing and the city was groaning with extravagantly furnished places where one could eat and drink. In a glowing review in 1889 of the Palace Hotel, one of the largest and grandest of the new venues – complete with rooftop terrace – on the corner of Bourke and Swanston streets, a *Weekly Times* journalist praised the 'choicest of liquors' on offer in the establishment's many bars, especially the clarets and light wines. 'But the wine which calls for special notice', he wrote, 'is the *dry* Monopole champagne, of Heidsieck and Co., of Reims, established since 1785. This brand of champagne is rapidly taking a foremost place amongst the favourite wines in the Australian colonies.'

———

The 1880s also saw the emergence of locally produced 'champagne' on a serious, commercial level. There had been a few attempts at making fizzy wines in Australia before. In 1875, Marie Blampied and Jean Trouette, pioneering French vignerons in Great Western, near Ararat in western Victoria, produced a sparkling wine from the unremarkable ondenc grape. And the same year, at Yeringberg vineyard in the Yarra Valley east of Melbourne, Swiss émigré Baron de Pury recorded in his diary that he was putting aside some of his white wine made from 'tokay' (probably muscadelle grapes) to turn into 'champagne'. But the extra level of technical know-how, costly equipment and labour-intensive methods required to produce larger quantities of proper, bottle-fermented bubbly meant that very few vignerons persisted with the style.

One of the first to take the plunge into commercial production was Louis Lawrence Smith, a flamboyant Melbourne doctor, entrepreneur and politician and at times controversial self-promoter (*The Bulletin* slyly nicknamed him '££ Smith'). Smith had four 'model' farms outside Melbourne; he grew grapes, owned racehorses, was a patron of the Richmond Football Club, bred bloodhounds. And he had earned a somewhat fraught reputation as a promoter of the local food and wine industries.

In November 1867 – twenty-six years almost to the day since the *William Salthouse* sank in Port Phillip Bay – Smith organised the ill-fated Free Banquet, a huge feast on the banks of the Yarra River to celebrate the visit to the colony of Prince Alfred, the Duke of Edinburgh. Enormous quantities of food and drink were laid out that day, including a vast, 500-gallon oak wine barrel, painted gaudy red and raised 6 metres above the crowd on a dais, with pipes running to a series of taps that would dispense colonial claret to the assembled multitude. But the event turned out to be a complete fiasco.

Smith had expected 10,000 people to turn up – but eight times that many came for the free feed. The hot November northerly whipped up a mighty hunger and a grating thirst in the huge crowd, and when the prince failed to arrive, they rushed the tables of food and drink.

'Roughs and rowdies' ransacked the provisions tents and were seen skulking out from under the canvas with bottles of wine in their pockets. Others smashed open the heads of beer barrels, dipping bread into the ale and chucking the sopping loaves at one another. Still more pocketed what they couldn't eat, making off with cutlery and crockery. Four or five revellers even managed to clamber up on the huge red cask feeding the fountain and hand out goblets of wine to their mates – who proceeded to throw it in each other's faces.

Undeterred by this public relations disaster, by the end of the next decade Smith had established a cellar – which he grandly dubbed a 'champagne manufactory' – in the Eastern Market, on the corner of Bourke and Exhibition streets. There was a substantial amount of self-interest at play here: at the same time as he was producing sparkling wine himself, Smith was also advocating heavy import duties on champagne from France. Importantly, rather than rely on the patchy local knowledge of fizz production, Smith secured the services of a French winemaker, Auguste D'Argent, who had arrived in Melbourne in 1877 claiming four decades' experience in the industry, including a stint in the Champagne region.

One of the first sparkling wines D'Argent made for Smith, using grapes grown in his boss's vineyard at Nunawading, was called Crème de Bouzy, a knowing reference to the French town of Bouzy. When this wine took out second prize at the Melbourne International Exhibition in 1880–81, Smith immediately capitalised on the acclaim by floating his Victorian Champagne Company and selling shares to various members of Melbourne society – actors, lawyers and politicians. More show success followed, including medals in Bordeaux and Amsterdam, and success looked to be assured – but just a couple of years later D'Argent died and the company went into voluntary liquidation.

In 1888, another Frenchman – this time one who had actually been born in Champagne – caused a stir at the Melbourne Centennial International Exhibition by winning first prize with the sparkling wine he'd made in his cellar at Hindmarsh in Adelaide. Joseph Hippolyte Foureur was born in the village of Hautvillers, in the heart of the Champagne region. He worked at Moët et Chandon for a decade and gained experience in the production of aerated waters before arriving in South Australia with his family in 1874. After a short stint working for Thomas Hardy at his Bankside vineyard, Foureur took charge of Bickford's water factory, and in the early 1880s started making 'champagne' as a small side business.

The following decade, yet another Frenchman, Edmond Mazure, started making sparkling wine on a commercial scale at Auldana cellars, near Penfolds' Magill Estate on the outskirts of Adelaide. Mazure came from a winegrowing family west of Champagne and had worked in Burgundy and Spain before arriving in South Australia in 1884. He established a sparkling winemaking dynasty by hiring and training a young local lad, Hurtle Walker, at Auldana: Hurtle's son, Norm, went on to make champagne-method fizz at Seaview cellars in the 1970s and in turn mentored other sparkling winemakers. In 1890 Mazure also created St Henri 'claret', a wine that was subsequently revived by John Davoren at Penfolds in the 1950s.

But the Frenchman who had possibly the most lasting influence on Australian sparkling wine in the late 19th century was Charles Pierlot, who in 1890 took up the position as 'champagne' maker at

Hans Irvine's winery at Great Western, conveniently located on the railway line that runs between the two major markets of Melbourne and Adelaide.

—————

The cellars at Great Western are extraordinary. They were originally tunnelled out in the 1860s and 70s by Joseph Best, a prospector-turned-farmer-turned-vigneron, using miners from the nearby gold diggings. When Best died in 1887, Ballarat businessman Hans Irvine bought his vineyards, winery and cellars, and saw the potential for maturing bottles of sparkling wine. In his book *Journey to Wine in Victoria*, Sam Benwell described Irvine's vision to reproduce the great chalk caverns of Epernay in Champagne by utilising all Best had done, and employing the Ararat miners to carve even further into the workable subsoil.

'These men from the old diggings could use a pick like a precision tool,' wrote Benwell. 'Their six-inch stroke marks are there by the million on the doughy walls underground.'

'Doughy' is the perfect word. The tunnels are still all there and you can take a guided tour through them. As well as the earth itself being surprisingly soft, a century-and-a-half of sooty mould has accumulated on the surface of the walls and roofs of the narrow long cellars, soaking up all light and all sound. Known as 'drives', these eerily silent tunnels stretch through the dark for kilometres underground. Over the decades they have held millions of bottles of slowly maturing fizz.

Charles Pierlot was well qualified for the job at Great Western. Born in 1854 into an old family of vignerons near Reims in the heart of Champagne, he worked for four years at Pommery before travelling to Australia in the late 1880s. As soon as he arrived at Great Western he joined Irvine to expand the business at a rapid rate. As well as laying down thousands of bottles of wine to undergo the slow secondary fermentation in the cool cellars, and travelling to Reims to buy champagne-making equipment, Irvine and Pierlot planted more than 50 acres (20 hectares) of new vineyards, specifically including two of the grape varieties – pinot meunier, or 'Miller's burgundy' as it was known locally in Great Western, and 'black pineau', or pinot noir – that traditionally make up much of the plantings in Champagne. This was an innovation: prior to this, most sparkling-wine makers had to make do with whatever grape varieties they could get their hands on. D'Argent, for example, made his Crème de Bouzy in 1879 using 'pinow' (presumably but not necessarily pinot noir) blended with riesling, tokay (possibly muscadelle) and chasselas, a Swiss white variety.

The wines that Pierlot produced soon started to beat all the competition at wine shows, and Irvine's business acumen translated this critical acclaim into swift business success. By 1905 Irvine had opened an export office in London and had more than 40,000 bottles maturing in the cellar at Great Western. Pierlot retired in 1912 and in 1918 Irvine sold his business to the large South Australian winemaking family firm of Seppelt, who expanded production even further, sourcing grapes from further afield and making the Great Western name synonymous with sparkling wine. For decades, generations of Australians reached for Great Western champagne in the bottle-shop fridge when they were going out to celebrate at the local BYO. Many other brands of champagne-style sparkling wines came and went, from Penfolds' Minchinbury in New South Wales (developed in the 1900s by Leo Buring, who had worked briefly for Irvine) to Yalumba's Angas Brut, but Pierlot's legacy lived on.

In 1990, at the age of twenty-two, I took my first interstate train journey, from Adelaide to Melbourne, via Ararat. Halfway through the eight- or nine-hour trip and bored out of my brain, I went to the dining car for lunch. I can't remember what I ate: a meat pie, perhaps, or a salad sandwich. But I can remember what I drank: a half-bottle of Great Western champagne, sipped from a plastic cup. I didn't realise it at the time, but as I drank that sparkling wine, I was probably trundling past the cellars where, a century before, the brand had been born.

––––––––––

The French helped shape the development of Australian sparkling wine once again in the late 20th century. Driven by a global thirst for top-quality sparkling wine and faced with a finite amount of vineyard land available in the Champagne region itself, by the mid-1980s some producers were expanding operations into other countries. Two of the most prominent, Moët et Chandon and Louis Roederer, had already set up wineries in California and were looking for cooler spots in other parts of the world.

After exploring various sites in Victoria, Moët et Chandon settled on the Yarra Valley in 1985, and the following year started planting vineyards and building cellars across the highway from Yeringberg, where Baron de Pury had dabbled in sparkling wine production in the 1870s and where the baron's grandson Guill de Pury had been one of the first to replant grapevines in the Yarra in the late 1960s. This was an enormously influential moment in the region's history. Not only did it provide international validation for the Yarra as a fine wine area and introduce a new level of quality fizz to the local market, but Chandon also encouraged many growers to plant pinot

noir and chardonnay in cooler sites across southern Victoria, such as
in the higher-altitude red-soil hills of the Upper Yarra – vineyards
that then helped build the reputation of the region even further.
This is also why Moët's chief oenologist, Richard Geoffroy, attended
the tasting of the *William Salthouse* shipwreck wines in 1994: he
was travelling to Chandon in the Yarra every year to help blend the
winery's various cuvées.

In South Australia, the Bollinger champagne house bought
into Brian Croser's Petaluma wine company and helped develop
the Croser sparkling wine brand, and Deutz went into partnership
with Yalumba to develop a new product. But Roederer decided that
Tasmania would be the best place to make top-quality sparkling
wine, and in 1985 it formed a joint venture with Heemskerk vineyard
in Pipers River, which had been established a decade earlier by
Tasmanian wine pioneer Graham Wiltshire. This eventually became
the Jansz brand, and was bought by Yalumba's Hill-Smith family
in 1997.

The exceptional quality of the cool-climate sparkling chardonnay
and pinot noir that came out of the Roederer-Heemskerk venture
and other vineyards established in Tasmania in the mid-80s changed
the course of Australian wine history by encouraging other mainland
producers to explore Tasmania's viticultural potential. One sparkling-
wine maker, Hardys' Ed Carr, who had been mentored by Norm
Walker at Seaview cellars in the 1970s, was particularly impressed by
Tasmania and started sourcing grapes from the island in the mid-
1990s for his new Arras label.

Twenty years ago, I sat down with Ed to taste the first wines
he made from that fruit. The bottles he opened that day changed
the way I thought about Australian fizz: they had more character,
complexity and finesse than most top-shelf bubbly I had tried before.

Now, as the vineyards have matured, as Ed has learned how to extract the best from them, and as the wines have been allowed to develop to their full potential maturing for a long time on lees (the yeast that settles as sediment in the bottle after finishing fermentation), the Arras wines are widely regarded as the best in the country. And they are every bit as good as the finest French champagnes.

————————

But much as Australians have enthusiastically embraced locally grown sparkling wine over the last century or so, we have never lost our taste for champagne – the 'real thing', from France. One of the legacies of our prodigious 19th-century consumption is the fact that Australia is the seventh-biggest market for champagne in the world – larger than Italy or Spain, despite having a fraction of the population – and Australians boast by far the largest per capita consumption of champagne outside Europe. Each of us drinks twice as much as the average German, and four times as much as the average Spaniard. Australia is now the largest market outside France for well-known brands such as Mumm and Piper-Heidsieck, both of which have been shipped here since the 19th century. Not only that, but we're drinking more than ever: imports of champagne have tripled in the last ten years alone.

And as good as those top Tasmanian sparkling wines are, when it comes to choosing a bottle of fizz for really special moments, or to signal the same kind of status or prestige that our mid-19th-century forbears were striving for, fine French champagne still gets the nod.

One of the biggest supporters of the Australian wine industry is Qantas. The airline spends $15 million a year buying around 2 million bottles of locally produced wine. Whether you're drinking in Qantas economy, business, first or the lounges, all the wines on offer are exclusively Australian – except the bubbly up the pointy end of the plane. Passengers who take their seats in Qantas first or business are still offered top-shelf French champagne such as Krug Grande Cuvée – the same brand, you'll recall, enjoyed by partying prostitutes in Melbourne in the 1870s.

Not that I can be too judgemental here. The last time I sat down with family and friends to Christmas lunch – 30°C in the shade, platters of succulent prawns and freshly shucked oysters on the table – we had bottles of ten-year-old prestige cuvée champagne in the ice buckets, rather than Tasmania's finest. For Sophie's fortieth birthday party I bought some of her favourite blanc de blancs champagne, made by a small grower near Reims. And after our son Riley was born, on 27 November 1998, 157 years to the day since the *William Salthouse* hit the reef in the entrance to Port Phillip Bay, we celebrated with champagne. Fittingly, it was Gosset Grande Reserve, in the distinctive skittle-shaped bottle identical to those packed into the wicker baskets on the ill-fated ship.

It was, after all, a special occasion.

Sherry Cobbler

Sydney, 1857

If drinking fancy French champagne was an opportunity for the *'nouveaux riches* of Diggerdom' to flaunt their new-found wealth in the 1850s, the fact that they were able to drink it *cold* was also a symbol of conspicuous consumption.

Before the introduction of commercial refrigeration towards the end of that decade, one of the only ways to chill drinks down was to use ice. And in the hot summer months in Australia, the only way to ensure a steady supply of ice was to carve it out of frozen lakes in the Northern Hemisphere and ship it in enormous blocks in insulated containers halfway around the world.

The ice trade had been flourishing since the early 19th century. Much of the ice came from Massachusetts, with one source, Wenham Lake, becoming a brand name synonymous with all imported American ice. Around the same time, the American fashion for mixed drinks was taking off in Australia, with variations on alcohol-plus-sugar-plus-ice – the Mint Julep, the Brandy Smash, the Sherry Cobbler – becoming popular in the 1850s.

Cocktail historian Sebastian Reaburn has found an evocative account of a particularly harsh and hot day from the era that helps explain why the Sherry Cobbler in particular was embraced with such thirsty gusto in Australia.

Recently arrived English journalist Richard Rowe, writing under the pseudonym Peter Possum, wrote in *The Sydney Morning Herald* in February 1857:

> When the blue sky glares, like a maniac's eye, with hot unrest; when the glowing sunshine streams down sarcasmic as molten gold; when the shrivelled leaves rattle in the breeze – parched and parching as a furnace-breath – like the smoke-chapped tongues of witches ... when all mere mortal muscle is in danger of frizzling up like an overdone rasher, blushing vitreous-purple like an overbaked brick, and the most succulent humanity seems turning into toast; when, in short, the mercury stands at 120° [49°C] in the shade (wherever that may be) ... sherry-cobbler-drinking is certainly the only rational mode of spending an Australian summer.

Edward Abbott has a recipe for a Sherry Cobbler in his *English and Australian Cookery Book*, published in 1864, when the drink was still at its height: 'Take a lump of ice; fix it at the edge of a board; rasp it with the proper tool; collect the fine raspings in a capacious tumbler; pour thereon two glasses of cool sherry, and a spoonful of white sugar, with a few small pieces of lemon. Stir with a macerator, and drink through a tube of macaroni.'

One warm evening in early summer, my son Riley and I tried Abbott's recipe. Not having any Wenham Lake ice or a 'proper' rasper to hand, we made do with plain old ice cubes from the freezer, crushed in a hand-cranked ice crusher – which we felt was appropriately old-school technology. We used Spanish fino sherry, almost identical in style to the sherry available in Sydney in the 1850s. And we used paper straws, because using a tube of macaroni just sounded silly.

The result was a bit ho-hum. The drink is improved enormously, I think (sorry, Mr Abbott), if you muddle the lemon pieces with the sugar and crushed ice, and vigorously shake the drink rather than stir it, to turn it into a lemony alcoholic slushie. The next time I make a Sherry Cobbler I might also drink it through a pasta straw (although I reckon longer bucatini would be more useful than stubby macaroni), and I'll do it on a day as 'parched and parching as a furnace-breath' for maximum effect.

Seppelt Angaston Bitters:
When drinking was good for you

Bill Seppelt turns the lock in a big wooden door and it gives out a slow horror-movie creak as it swings open. We go through and our footsteps echo off the stone walls of the old cellars. We approach another heavy door, the key clanks, some more cinematic creaking. And another. Deeper and deeper, through layers of history at Seppeltsfield, the Barossa Valley's grandest 19th-century wine estate, originally founded by Bill's great-great-grandfather Joseph Seppelt in 1851.

As we descend a flight of wooden steps leading to the final door, I begin to smell a dull perfume of cloves and cinnamon and aniseed. Bill turns the key, we duck through the doorway into a small, low-ceilinged whitewashed room, and the source of the scent is revealed. The snug space is lined with shelf upon shelf of bottles dating back over a century and a half: small sample vials of fragrant flavourings, pharmacy flasks of essential oils, large flagons of aromatic tinctures. And dozens and dozens of bottles of the many different drinks produced here in the late 19th and early 20th centuries using those oils and essences: vermouths, tonic wines, bitters and cordials. It's El Dorado for flavour-geek history buffs. All I can manage is an awestruck 'Wow'.

'This is the inner sanctum,' says Bill, now in his early seventies, the Seppelt family archivist. 'Originally, this room was dug in the early 1850s as the cellar for my great-great-grandmother's dairy, before there was a winery here. This was where the cream and butter were kept cool. But then, when the first wine was made – in 1856, we believe – it became a cellar for wine barrels, presumably to the old bird's chagrin.'

Joseph's son Benno expanded the winery in the 1860s, adding the first of the larger stone cellars that we've just walked through. This small whitewashed room became the place where generations of Seppelt men stored these bottles of intensely flavoured concentrates and essences and mixed them together according to closely guarded recipes.

'This was the essence room until my father retired in 1976,' says Bill. 'He was the only one who knew the recipes for the liqueurs and spiced vinegars and that sort of thing, and he mixed them in here. Then I used to mix them for a while.'

We've come here to the essence room, the inner sanctum, for a special reason. Rather than just having me admire these precious old bottles and try to reconstruct, from the scents that have permeated the stone walls over a century and a half, a flavour image of what they must have tasted like, Bill's offered to open one and let me try it.

He picks up a bottle wrapped tightly in brown paper and printed with the words 'B. Seppelt & Sons, Angaston Bitters'. Angaston is the name of a nearby Barossa town. It's also cheekily similar to 'Angostura', the world's best-known brand of bitters. This drink was produced, thinks Bill, about 100 years ago.

He eases out the cork, pours a dark-brown dribble into a small fluted schnapps glass and hands it to me. I hold the glass to my nose and a cloud of dank herbs and brown spices and wet bark fills my nostrils. This old liquid is full of life! Wide-eyed and smiling, I take a sip and a bitter cavalcade of flavour digs a groove along my tongue. It tastes extraordinary, intense, as though Benno Seppelt made the drink yesterday, blending his collection of essences with spirit distilled here on site.

'It's the alcohol,' says Bill, smiling at my stunned reaction. 'That's why it's still so fresh. It's probably about 50 per cent alcohol. And the extreme bitterness acts like a preservative, too. It'll live forever.'

I feel strangely invigorated. This drink has done exactly what its maker intended: it has *stimulated the drinker*. I pick up the bottle and read the words printed on the brown-paper wrapping: 'These excellent Bitters are recommended as an unfailing, quick and effective remedy for weak digestion, loss of appetite, flatulence and kindred ailments. Furthermore, these Bitters can be used as a tonic and a stimulant to incite the appetite.'

Suddenly, I also feel terribly hungry.

I never imagined myself as a middle-aged man who collects antique bottles. But, well, there we are: that's exactly who I've become.

It started innocently enough when Sophie and I moved into an old house in Melbourne's south-eastern suburbs twenty years ago and uncovered a cache of bottles discarded long ago in the back shed. Most were broken, but a couple – an imperial quart Irish whiskey bottle from around 1900, a squat brown Leo Buring Rinegolde bottle from the 1940s – were intact and in good condition, so I kept them. Not on display or anything, just tucked away in a box in a cupboard. I liked having that connection with previous inhabitants; I imagined the house's original architect-owner in 1906, and the matriarch of the family who bought it after he died in the 1930s, both sitting in my front room, pouring themselves a drink from one of those bottles.

Then I started bringing empties home from particularly amazing wine tastings I'd been to and putting them up on a shelf in my office to remind myself of how incredible they'd tasted: bottles of Woodley 'Treasure Chest' Coonawarra reds from the 1950s with beautiful labels featuring 19th-century engravings; the 1961 Yalumba Galway Claret I brought home on the train in peak hour one day, me looking and smelling like the young pisspot I was.

People soon started giving me old bottles they'd inherited from aunts and uncles, some of which were still full. A 1987 Cab Mac. A 1990 Ben Ean Moselle. Countless old ports. And the more I learned about the history of drinking in Australia, the more I stumbled across gems in op shops – gems like the 1960s Mac's Cider bottle I picked up recently for ten bucks, or the 1940s sherry bottle from Crittendens' licensed grocers I found hiding behind some biscuit tins. When I caught myself online chatting with a collector in Gippsland about a particularly beautiful and rare 1930s vermouth bottle – gorgeous fine turquoise hue, lovely embossing – I knew I'd become … *one of them.*

This is how I ended up in the essence room at Seppeltsfield with Bill. A couple of months before, I'd been trawling through eBay and found a bottle of Angaston Bitters for sale. I knew Seppelt had made a lot of different wines 100 years ago, from fortifieds to sparkling, from claret to hock, but I wasn't aware at that point of its extensive range of now-long-defunct vermouths and bitters and tonics. So this bottle was a surprise. Even more surprising was the fact that it was full: the cork was still in it. And it was 'only' $100 – which to a normal person (i.e. not a middle-aged antique-booze-bottle collector) might seem a lot to spend on something that might taste terrible, but which seemed to me like a bargain.

As soon as I'd secured my purchase, I contacted Seppeltsfield and was put in touch with Bill. I was eager to know if he had any information about this old curio, whether he'd ever tasted it, whether he knew what it might have been made from, whether the contents might, by some miracle, still be drinkable.

'Ah yes,' he said, nonchalantly. 'I've got one of those bottles on my sideboard at home. I use the bitters in cocktails. It's a lovely drink. Next time you're in the Barossa we'll try it. I've got a few other old things you might want to taste, too.'

Bill inherited a stash of old bottles, including the already-opened Angaston Bitters, when his father, Hilton Seppelt, died. He also inherited his father's exercise book full of labels of the old drinks that Seppelt used to produce. And, most precious of all, recipe books dating back to the time in the late 19th century when Benno, his great-grandfather, was in charge of blending in the essence room.

Which is why, now, as we sit in that small room at Seppeltsfield and pore over the recipes and exercise book, Bill pours me a small taste of orange bitters also made by his forebears 100 years ago. So many of the bottles on the shelves here, and the labels pasted onto the pages of the book, have a medicinal feel, like the stimulating properties promised by the Angaston Bitters. Tonic wines, reviving cordials, and one of Bill's favourites, Red Hot Punch: 'An excellent antidote in cases of indigestion, dyspepsia [or] heartburn, etc. Taken in lemonade or soda water, it proves a capital thirst quencher. Try a dash in spirits, wine or beer.'

It was normal in the 19th and early 20th centuries for a large wine and spirits manufacturer like B. Seppelt & Sons not only to include many tonics, cordials and stimulants in its portfolio, but also to promote its regular wines, ports and brandies by emphasising their health-giving properties.

In the blazing heat of midsummer in 1908, a French visitor to the outback mining town of Broken Hill in far west New South Wales was treated to an afternoon in the cellars of Seppelt's regional warehouse by a journalist, who wrote an account of the visit in the local paper, *The Barrier Miner.* The three of them – the Frenchman, a Monsieur Le Croix, who had some knowledge of the wine trade and had spent time in Cognac; Seppelt's manager, Mr Paynter; and the unnamed journalist – spent several hours in the large, cool, airy store crowded with hogsheads and crates, tasting almost everything the company had to offer, from freshly opened bottles of clarets and hocks to cask samples of muscatel and sherry.

'Like bees in a clover field we moved from barrel to barrel, noting and tasting, tasting and noting,' wrote the journalist, describing how the trio eventually ended up in the manager's office, where they found a glass of whisky rather 'refreshing after our travels'.

It was a massive drinking session: towards the end of the day, after enjoying his tenth glass of wine in Mr Paynter's office (and that's *after* the refreshing whisky, mind), M. Le Croix 'grew voluble', proposed a garbled toast to his new best friends, picked up a bottle and kissed it. Along the way, the journalist also managed to give us a valuable insight into how these drinks were promoted at the time.

'Of Port we have four qualities,' Mr Paynter told his visitors. 'Simple Port at 4s. 6d. per gallon up to Medicinal Port at over three-times the cost.' He let them sample the good stuff and the journalist was impressed: 'It was nectar, a luscious, clinging grape juice.' But Mr Paynter reminded him it was expensive – and rare. 'It is chiefly for invalids,' he said. 'But I know some wine drinkers who will take nothing else.'

A little later, after some cherry brandy and vermouth, Mr Paynter offered his guests Quinine Champagne. 'A magnificent tonic. Come, your glasses.' The reaction? 'Lavishly palatable, surely a splendid invigorator or pick-me-up.' And then another tonic wine: Sedna, possessing properties that give it 'a high position as a stimulant and strengthener'.

In the essence room at Seppeltsfield a century later, Bill finds the old Quinine Champagne and Sedna labels pasted into his father's exercise book. Sedna was the king of tonic wines. A concoction of coca leaf, kola nut and beef extract infused in strong port, the label promised it was an effective cure for 'the pressure of business and overwork, weak stomach, sleeplessness and seasickness', among countless other ailments.

'We made Sedna under licence for the original Irish manufacturers,' says Bill. 'And because it was a tonic wine, that meant it could be sold in chemist shops; during the era of six o'clock closing [from World War I to the 1960s in most parts of Australia], it was the only alcoholic product you could legally buy after hours.'

Back in Broken Hill, the intrepid trio of tasters 'flitted from the wines to the Brandies, the purest flavoured the palate could conceive' and M. Le Croix began to quote French poetry. But Mr Paynter, ever the salesman, stayed valiantly on-message, explaining how Australian doctors had taken up Seppelt's Grape Brandy and how it was now used 'throughout the Commonwealth in hospitals and sick-rooms'.

He went on to spruik the purity of the other Seppelt spirits – such as the Old Tom gin that I tasted a few minutes ago, and the

Queensland rum that Bill has just poured into another schnapps glass for me to taste next.

'This is probably 100 years old, too,' he says casually. The small whitewashed room underneath the Seppeltsfield winery fills with the fiery memory of sunshine and molasses. 'Another one I got from my father. It's overproof rum they would have shipped down from the Beenleigh or Bundaberg distillery and aged in barrel here in the Barossa. I've got a full flagon of it at home. It's wonderful if you've got a cold.'

————————

I wish I had a flagon of that extraordinary overproof rum at home. I don't think I'd ever get sick if I did. Until I died of cirrhosis, that is. What I have instead is a half-bottle of brandy with a stick of cinnamon in it. We call it 'medicinal brandy' in our house, because we read something somewhere about someone (can't remember their name or where we read it) who'd lived to a ripe old age and swore by cinnamon-infused brandy, mixed with warm water, taken at the first sign of flu. I tried it once and it appeared to help, so we've kept a bottle on hand ever since. I still take it whenever I'm feeling a cold coming on. And should the medicinal brandy not do the trick, I combat the sickness with hot toddies – lemon, honey, hot water and whisky – until I feel better. And I remember my stepfather's mum, who lived to the age of 101 and put her longevity down to the glass of whisky and milk she drank every day.

The belief that alcohol can be beneficial to our health was once deeply ingrained in many societies. The idea of drinking as therapy was mainstream from the late 18th century – the First Fleet ships' surgeon, John White, like many naval doctors of the day, prescribed wine to those on board to combat scurvy and dysentery – through to the middle years of the 20th century.

This is one of the reasons why so many of Australia's best-known wine companies were founded by doctors. Henry Lindeman and Christopher Penfold, for example, both studied medicine at St Bartholomew's teaching hospital in London before migrating to Australia in the 1840s as young doctors and establishing vineyards in New South Wales and South Australia respectively. Although they and their descendants went on to plant substantial vineyards, build large cellars and establish commercial empires, Lindeman and Penfold were initially attracted to wine by its beneficial effects.

Wine historian Philip Norrie, himself a doctor-vigneron, writes that 'Dr Penfold believed in the medicinal use of wine, especially in using red wines to treat anaemia', and that soon after they arrived in their new home just outside Adelaide in 1844, 'he and his wife planted their vineyard and produced mainly fortified wines (ports and sherries) for patients'.

Lindeman laid out his views in a letter to the *New South Wales Medical Gazette* in 1871, calling wine a 'therapeutic agent' and advocating for it to become the 'national beverage' for Australia. There was, he said, a great need for his fellow colonists to plant vines and start making 'pure exhilarating wine to take the place of ardent spirits and of adulterated wines and beers'. These stronger, impure drinks, argued Lindeman, induce diseases 'arising from derangement of the liver; to suffer from which too often robs life of enjoyment by enveloping it in a perpetual fog of mental depression'. Instead, he argued people should be drinking 'pure, dry, and thoroughly fermented wine … light in alcohol, resembling as much as possible the pure growths of Bordeaux and the Rheingau'.

The same styles of wine – also known as claret and hock – were recommended by Sydney surgeon Thomas Fiaschi in a lecture to the Australasian Trained Nurses' Association in 1906, entitled 'The Various Wines Used in Sickness and Convalescence'.

Fiaschi was an important but now little-known figure in Australia's wine history. Described as 'tall and handsome with keen, searching eyes, fine physique and erect military bearing', the Italian-born doctor was an imposing figure in the military, medical and viticultural worlds. He was an outstanding surgeon: the striking statue outside Sydney Hospital in Macquarie Street of a wild boar – a replica of the famous 17th-century bronze *Il Porcellino*, in Florence – is a monument to him. He was a war hero: he fought with the Italians in Abyssinia in the 1890s and was decorated for his bravery in the Boer War, ending his military career as an honorary brigadier general. And he was a pioneering vigneron: he established vineyards in both the Hawkesbury and Mudgee regions, was president of the Wine Producers' Association of New South Wales for many years, and imported Italian grapevines such as the muscat-like aleatico into Australia.

He was also an unequivocal supporter of prescribing wine to his patients. 'Frankly,' he told the nurses in his 1906 lecture, 'I consider the temperate use of wine a valuable support to a healthy man in this thorny path of life, and ... the judicious use of it has proved itself to me of incalculable benefit in the treatment of the sick and convalescent.'

As well as recommending champagne as a stimulant in cases of weak heart action, and hock for convalescence, gout or rheumatism, Fiaschi told the nurses that claret 'acts as a tonic and reconstituent, and is a valuable aid to digestion ... In this climate, claret is especially useful on hot days, when the stomach becomes languid and unable to digest the amount of food required to keep up the nerve strain entailed in the struggle of civilized life. It tones both the stomach and the heart.'

With this kind of clinical endorsement, it's no surprise that so many wineries at the time sold their products by linking consumption to medical terminology. Hans Irvine's Sparkling Burgundy from Great Western in Victoria was just one of many wine brands 'recommended for invalids', and Penfolds' advertising for both its Hospital Brandy and a tonic wine called Irona – which, like Sedna, was a blend of beef extract, malt and wine – featured a nurse dressed in angelic white, cradling a bottle like it was holy water.

Sparkling burgundy, tonic wine, claret, hock: fermented products of the grape weren't the only drinks aimed explicitly at convalescents. A type of dark beer called invalid stout enjoyed a brief period of international popularity with frail drinkers towards the end of the 19th century. Irish brewery Guinness first produced a beer called Nourishing Export Stout – also labelled Invalid Stout – in 1874, helping to build the brand's 'healthy' reputation and leading to the 'Guinness is Good for You' advertising campaign that became famous during the 20th century. Unlike the company's regular dry stout, the invalid stout was a little lower in alcohol, contained more 'nutritious' sugar and tasted sweeter. According to Guinness historian David Hughes, the company sent bottles to hospitals, and doctors prescribed it for ailments such as influenza, insomnia and anxiety.

The style didn't take off in Australia to quite the same extent as the new refreshing lager-beer also being introduced around the same time, but invalid stout did become part of the portfolio of a few enterprising breweries. The Adelaide Malting and Brewing Company, producer of the Macclesfield brand of beer, was making an invalid stout – and tonic ale – as early as the 1880s. In Hobart, the Cascade Brewery introduced an invalid stout in 1903. And just before World War I, the Melbourne Co-operative Brewery started making Abbotsford Invalid Stout, a brand that still exists today.

Like Penfolds' Irona tonic wine, early advertising for Abbotsford Invalid Stout employed an angelic nurse dressed in white, smiling and tempting the viewer with a tray holding a freshly poured glass of the beer and a plate of biscuits.

Other alcoholic drinks made extravagant claims about their therapeutic properties, too. In 1917, Melbourne cider manufacturer Kitz started promoting its products by stressing the health value of fermented apple juice. 'Cider gives good complexions and prevents rheumatism,' promised one advertising leaflet, while another quoted a London doctor who claimed 'cider is the most hygienic of all beverages in the world', and 'cancer is almost a thing unknown among regular cider drinkers'.

———————

Today, of course, modern food-labelling laws forbid the use of such extravagant health claims – or any health claims at all – on the packaging of alcoholic drinks. The Alcoholic Beverages Advertising Code also prohibits any suggestion in marketing material that a product might 'offer therapeutic benefit or (be) a necessary aid to relaxation'. But that doesn't stop producers and consumers thinking about and talking about how drinking can be good for us – and how certain types of drinks can be better for us than others. As the 'wellness' trend grows at a staggering rate in the world of food, winemakers, brewers and distillers are beginning to dabble once again in semi-medical language, even making new, allegedly therapeutic products. And they often sound uncannily similar to their 19th-century predecessors.

When I visited cider maker Clive Crossley at his orchard south of Hobart, we talked about the old English and French apple varieties

he had planted, and how their bittersweet characters, often derived
from the astringent polyphenols in the juice, are so important for the
deep golden colour and tangy flavours in traditional cider.

But Clive also talked about the potential medical benefits of
drinking cider. He told me he was developing a research project
looking at the chemistry of the polyphenols of cider apples and their
effect on the gut microbiome.

'I'm interested in going beyond the antioxidant capacities of
apples,' he said, pouring me another glass and echoing the words
of the Kitz cider company a century ago. 'I want to look in much
more detail at cider as a functional food. I want to encourage people
to drink it because it's good for them.'

Modern producers of 'natural' wine – made from grapes farmed
without synthetic chemicals, fermented and bottled with few or
no additives – also talk a lot about how their wines are better for
you than conventionally made wines. Indeed, the emergence of the
natural wine movement over the last decade has been boosted by
the wellness trend: as consumers become increasingly concerned
with all the 'toxins' they've been putting into their bodies, they are
embracing organic, biodynamic and preservative-free wines.

A few years ago I interviewed Alex Podolinsky, who founded
the Demeter Bio-Dynamic Method in Australia in the 1950s and
influenced a number of top Australian wine producers to convert to
his system of organic farming. 'Wine is the aristocrat of the meal,'
he told me. 'You don't have to have too much. You just have to have
what is established as very important for your digestive system in
good red wine. I might only have a quarter of a glass in the evening –
but I still want the stimulation and digestive power and aristocracy.'

'Digestibility' is a word you hear a lot in natural wine circles.
One maker told me that because he lets the wild yeasts and bacteria

do their thing in the ferment and doesn't filter his wines, they have greater 'digestibility' and 'tonicity'. Another claimed that 'digestibility' is improved in his wines because he picks his grapes earlier, resulting in fresher acidity and lower alcohol. And a prominent merchant who specialises in natural claims that wines made this way are particularly 'more-ish, sapid, refreshing [and] digestible'.

The Cannabis Co. is a new start-up business selling hemp-based products: flour, protein powder, essential oils – and gin. The company is based in an industrial park in Ringwood, in Melbourne's outer-eastern suburbs, and when I visit, biochemist and co-owner Dr David Stapleton takes me on a quick tour of the premises. He opens a door into a concrete-slab warehouse where boxes of hemp doggy biscuits and hempseed oil for pets ('a drop on the tongue does wonders for dogs with anxiety') await dispatch, and shelves lining the walls are stacked with bubble wrap and orange high-vis vests.

Another door takes us through into a corporate boardroom, with a whiteboard in one corner and sheets of A3 paper Blu-Tacked to the walls, covered in texta-scribbled strategy planning. On the table is a bottle of the company's gin. It was distilled using fourteen aromatic botanicals, including juniper berries (the quintessential ingredient in gin), coriander, orris root, hemp (of course) and a terpene called myrcene. David explains that terpenes are aromatic, sometimes oily compounds found in many plants; myrcene, for example, is a component of the complex flavour profile of hops, mangoes, bay leaves – and cannabis. The gin is certainly punchy: lots of fruity, citrusy perfume, and interesting woody, herbal hints from the hemp.

According to David, myrcene – along with other terpenes also found in cannabis, such as linalool and beta-caryophyllene – is also thought to have therapeutic qualities. He's a little cagey about those benefits ('a lot of scientists don't want to go near this because of the associations with marijuana'), and admits that research still needs to be done into how the process of distillation might affect the potency of terpenes.

But on the company's website, the benefits of the botanicals in the gin are spelled out in unequivocal detail. 'Myrcene', says the blurb, 'is known as an antibacterial, anti-diabetic, anti-inflammatory, anti-insomniatic, anti-proliferative, antipsychotic, and anti-spasmodic.' But wait, there's more. Juniper berries, apparently, are also valued for their 'anti-inflammatory properties, ideal for relieving pain due to rheumatism and arthritis'.

It sounds a lot like an 'unfailing, quick and effective remedy for weak digestion, loss of appetite, flatulence and kindred ailments'. So I try the gin again. And another sip. And while I can't testify to any noticeable beneficial health effects, my mood does change slightly. But that's mostly because the gin is 40 per cent alcohol.

1930 Dalwood cabernet:
Two centuries of wine

In the late summer of 1930 in the Hunter Valley north of Sydney, a man named John Davoren made a red wine that changed the course of Australian history.

Davoren made the wine using grapes harvested from old vines that had been planted at Dalwood, on the banks of a slow bend in the Hunter River, during the very earliest years of colonial winegrowing. Three decades after it was made, in 1960, a rare bottle of that Dalwood wine inspired another winemaker, Max Lake, to plant his own boutique vineyard – which in turn helped encourage dozens, hundreds, thousands more winemakers to follow.

That single bottle, then, can be seen as a pivot point on which our whole national wine story balances. As historian Julie McIntyre has observed, the story of where it was grown, Dalwood – from its beginnings in 1828 to its phoenix-like rebirth almost 200 years later – is like 'a journey through the rise and rise of the Australian wine industry'.

February 1835, Dalwood vineyard, Branxton, New South Wales

George Wyndham's first forays into winemaking at Dalwood were a bit of a disaster. The 29-year-old well-to-do English settler from Wiltshire planted his first vines here in 1830. Those vines died. So he planted more, and then some more, and in the summer of 1835 he and his convict labourers picked enough grapes to start filling barrels. It started well enough, but soon the heat and Wyndham's inexperience begin to take their toll.

'Began my vintage,' wrote Wyndham proudly in his diary one hot February Monday, describing how he'd filled a barrel with 'black cluster', a common name at the time for the grape we now know as pinot noir.

Despite his wife, Margaret, having given birth to a new baby son less than a week before (one of fourteen children she would bear over a twenty-year period) in their newly built sandstone house up the hill, Wyndham spent more time checking on his casks than with his young family. After a day's nervous wait in the cellar with nothing happening in his barrel, by Wednesday morning he saw 'a froth rising', then by the afternoon 'a head foaming thick, and a vinous smell'.

But as the days grew hotter – nudging 100°F (38°C), so typical in the Hunter in February – the ferment became violent and the sweet taste of the grapes was quickly replaced by what Wyndham called a 'harshness'. Despite trying to cool things down by draping 'blankets' over the barrel, and to stop the ferment by racking into smaller casks and by adding sulphur, it was too late to save the wine. 'It is sharp and promises to make good vinegar,' he wrote bitterly in his diary the following Monday.

Not to be discouraged, the next day Wyndham filled the barrel with fresh black cluster grapes, and a few days later he harvested some white grapes and filled an old beer hogshead with the juice. By the end of the month, as the weather began to cool, things were looking up: one vat, he wrote, has 'a splendid bouquet ... I like its promise.'

George Wyndham was one of a number of well-educated, well-off and well-travelled early-19th-century settlers keen to see a wine industry established in the colony. His contemporaries included James Busby (who supplied Wyndham with his first batch of vines), William Macarthur (from whom Wyndham sourced better vine cuttings in subsequent years) and other prominent Hunter pioneer vignerons such as Dr Henry Lindeman.

As well as farming vines at Dalwood, Wyndham ran sheep and cattle – he brought the Hereford breed to Australia – and established pastoral runs at Inverell in New England, in northern New South Wales. Much of this agricultural activity was 'experimental', in the sense that few people at the time knew for certain what varieties of plant or stock would work in the colony's hot, often harsh environment.

This is one of the reasons Wyndham had planted a 'fruit salad' of grapes at Dalwood. He established his vineyards over many years – just a few hundred vines to start, then a couple of acres here, a few more acres there – and every new planting brought with it a new selection of varieties, to see which would be best suited to the climate and soil. It was the same in his garden and orchard: detailed plans sketched and catalogued by Wyndham in the 1840s list dozens of different fruit trees. This is why Dalwood became home to grape varieties that were traditionally planted hundreds of kilometres away from each other in Europe in vastly different climates but here were all planted on the same land: the cabernet and petit verdot of Bordeaux alongside the shiraz of the Rhône Valley, Iberian grapes called 'Black Spanish' and 'Oporto' (possibly tempranillo and touriga) next to the Burgundian 'pineau blanc' (the grape we know today as chardonnay).

For Wyndham and many other 19th-century vignerons, growing grapes and making wine was explicitly intended as a *civilising* act on the frontier. A way of bringing order to the chaos of colonisation. Poet and author Judith Wright, a descendant of Wyndham's, wrote that George saw Dalwood as a bulwark against the hostile country and that he continued to yearn for the meek and orderly traditions of rural Wiltshire. The exchange of vine planting material between the new landowners, the deliberate attempt to establish a wine industry, was, as historians Julie McIntyre and John Germov point out in their book on the region, *Hunter Wine*, a way of creating 'strong bonds of social kinship that consoled settlers distant from their close ties with family and society back in Britain'.

The 19th-century history of Dalwood set a pattern for the boom-and-bust nature of the Australian wine industry. Just ten years after his first vintage at Dalwood, an extended economic downturn – and the end of convict transportation to New South Wales in 1840 – forced Wyndham to leave the property in the hands of a manager and explore new pastoral opportunities further north. When German naturalist and explorer Ludwig Leichhardt visited Dalwood in 1842, Wyndham told him he wasn't able to harvest his vineyards due to the shortage of labour, and had let his cattle in to eat the grapes instead. And he lamented that the kinds of wine he made weren't to everyone's taste. 'As Wyndham remarked to Leichhardt,' write McIntyre and Germov, 'most elite colonists preferred drinking tea to consuming colonial wine.'

George's eldest son, John, took over in 1857 (George died in 1870) and began to build Dalwood and his family's other vineyards at Inverell into a prosperous business as markets expanded and tastes changed following the discovery of gold in the 1850s. John built new wine cellars at Dalwood, introduced more innovative winemaking equipment, and started exporting wine to the UK, as did many of the other wine estates in the Hunter and across the country. Then, as now, a good review was helpful in marketing wine, and Australian winegrowers became enthusiastic participants at the great exhibitions that were all the rage in Europe's capital cities in the late 19th century.

In 1882, Australian winegrowers bombarded the Exposition Universelle des Vins in Bordeaux with samples, hoping to please the judges. Remarkably, John Wyndham's handwritten entry form for this exhibition has survived, and it gives us a detailed picture, in a dense forest of tiny script, of Dalwood at the time.

Eleven different grape varieties – including the cabernet and petit verdot and the pineau blanc (chardonnay) that are crucial to this story – covered 70 acres (28 hectares) under vine, and had been planted from 1854 onwards using cuttings taken from his father's original 1830s vineyards. John boasted that Dalwood wines had won 'over 100 prizes ... too numerous to particularize in this space' at various exhibitions over the years. And he itemised the more than two dozen wines he was sending to be judged in Bordeaux. Three reds made from the verdot grape garnered gold medals, and John proudly boasted that his name was 'placed first among all the wine exhibitors from the Australian colonies'.

By the end of the century, Dalwood had become one of the largest and most successful vineyards in New South Wales. Which is why, following the removal of intercolonial trade barriers following Federation, it was bought in 1904 by the large South Australian wine company Penfolds, as the first stage of what would become a major expansion into new markets.

Penfolds was, and would remain for many years, the country's largest wine business, and although it relied heavily on its South Australian vineyards, it also developed a very important presence in New South Wales. The company bought the Minchinbury winery close to Sydney in 1912, and in the 1920s established another vineyard in the Hunter near Dalwood called Sparkling Vale, as well as setting up a new winery in the emerging irrigation district of Griffith in central New South Wales. Then, in the 1930s, Penfolds started leasing a vineyard that had been planted by the Hunter Valley Distillery in 1908, eventually purchasing it a decade later. This vineyard, known as HVD, also plays a very important part in this story.

Throughout this period, Penfolds was lucky to have two of the Hunter's great winemakers at the helm at Dalwood. The first of them was born in Branxton in the 1860s and worked at Dalwood all his life.

———————

February 1930, Dalwood vineyard, Branxton,
New South Wales

John Davoren took off his hat and wiped his brow. It must have been 100 degrees in the shade but the veteran winemaker was dressed formally, white shirtsleeves rolled up above the elbow, dark waistcoat, heavy woollen trousers, dusty boots. He looked at the grapevines in front of him, wilting in the muggy heat, their gnarly trunks bent low towards the sandy ground, carrying a dense canopy of dry-edged leaves. Somewhere among the foliage lurked jewel-like clusters of black grapes, almost ripe, almost ready to be picked. Davoren reached into the canopy, picked a couple of grapes, popped them in his mouth, chewed on the skins, spat out the seeds and made some quick calculations in his head. Not long now to harvest, he thought. And it could be another good one.

These were petit verdot vines, some of the oldest at Dalwood. In 1886, a photographer had come through and snapped a picture of them and they were thick and gnarly even then, having been planted at least twenty years before. Early accounts of Dalwood frequently made special mention of the verdot variety and the excellent, award-winning wine it produced. Originally from Bordeaux in France, where it's traditionally blended with better-known varieties such as cabernet sauvignon and merlot to make the region's red wines – famous clarets from big-name chateaux – the verdot grape is clearly at home in the Hunter, too.

That vintage, in 1930, Davoren harvested those verdot grapes, enough to fill a couple of barrels with wine, and blended this with another couple of barrels of wine made from cabernet sauvignon. It wasn't much. But in the early 1930s in Australia there was very little demand for reds like this. Fortified wines – ports, sherries, muscats, sweet and strong, mostly – were what people drank. Not fine, dry, 'claret-style' table wines. And as the Great Depression began to bite, what little demand there was for wines like this dropped off so sharply that Davoren's Dalwood cabernet/verdot was classified as 'surplus to requirements' by Penfolds and sold to a wine merchant who shipped it to England and sold it bottled under his own label.

Penfolds kept Dalwood going, though, by adapting to the changing market – and by hiring another talented winemaker.

———————

Winter 1945, Penfolds head office, Sydney

Perc McGuigan nervously looked around the tasting room at Penfolds' Sydney headquarters, waiting for his boss, Frank Penfold Hyland, to pronounce on the six glasses of young white wine in front of him. Perc had only been working for the company for a couple of years, and this vintage he'd tried a new blend of chardonnay and semillon. He wasn't sure how the wine would go down with the older man, who was studiously sniffing and sipping each glass.

Perc was a Hunter Valley boy, born and bred. His parents had a few rows of vines at Rothbury when he was growing up. In 1921, when he was eight, he got his first job in the HVD vineyard shooting birds, to stop the little bastards eating all the grapes in the lead-up to vintage. As an older kid he graduated to harvesting, and one of the places he worked was Dalwood, under the watchful eye of old John Davoren. 'While I was still going to school I worked in the holidays in the picking of grapes and the tally keeping,' Perc told an interviewer in 2000. 'And I used to work in the winery when I was about fifteen, sixteen years old.' He probably helped Davoren pick and crush and ferment the petit verdot grapes during the 1930 vintage.

Then, in 1941, 29-year-old Perc was offered Davoren's job of manager at Dalwood. Penfolds had built a new winery there after taking over in 1904, locating it closer to the river, down the slope from John Wyndham's old cellars. A visitor in the early 1930s described the operation as 'easily the best and most up-to-date in the Hunter [with] hydraulic presses and steam-driven machinery [that] reduce much of the drudgery of winemaking experienced by some of the smaller vignerons'.

Despite the 'modern' (steam-driven!) machinery, Perc recalled that, when he started, there was still quite a bit of drudgery involved.

'I made wine for eight years without electricity,' he said. 'The electricity hadn't been reticulated to the Dalwood area until 1949 ... You might wonder how we made wine at all when we weren't able to control the rate of fermentation. Well, we used to get eight and ten tons of ice.' Perc remembered having to drop the ice in the ferments during heatwaves, when they'd get at least eight or ten consecutive days over 100°F. 'And there's no way in the world that you can make a good wine – a top wine – if the temperature gets up above 90.'

One of the first vineyards that Perc harvested during his first vintage in 1942 was HVD. He picked enough chardonnay to fill a 500-gallon (2200-litre) cask. He did the same the following year, and the next. But after a very dry summer, the 1945 vintage yielded enough grapes to make only 300 gallons of wine. So Perc made up the shortfall by adding semillon grapes to the cask.

Old Mr Davoren had always referred to the chardonnay on the HVD vineyard by its 19th-century name, 'pineau blanc'. Wine writer John Lewis believes this is because HVD was possibly planted using cuttings that had come from Dalwood. And if 'pineau blanc' was good enough for John Wyndham and John Davoren, it was good enough for Perc McGuigan. Similarly, for 19th-century historical reasons the semillon grape was often called 'riesling' in the Hunter. Which is why Perc labelled his unusual new blend of chardonnay and semillon 'pineau riesling' when he took it down with some other wine samples to show his boss a couple of months after they'd finished fermenting.

Perc was even more nervous now. Frank Penfold Hyland had finished tasting the line-up of wines, but he kept going back to the glass that contained the new blend. Finally, he delivered his verdict.

'He said, "Pineau riesling. Why have you done that, McGuigan?" And I told him the reason. That I had no alternative but to fill [the cask] so I called it pineau riesling. And I remember well. He picked the glass up, and he held it up to me, and he said, "You keep doing that, McGuigan. That's the best wine that's ever come out of the Hunter Valley." And until 1976, Penfolds still made a pinot riesling.'

It seems silly to us today that a blend of chardonnay and semillon could be so misnamed. We accept truth in labelling without thinking about it. If we pick up a bottle labelled 'riesling' we don't consider for a second that the grapes used to make the wine wouldn't be riesling. But Australian wines were still being labelled inaccurately as late as the end of the millennium: I remember selling Tyrrell's Vat 47 Pinot Chardonnay from the Hunter when I worked at bottle shops in the early 1990s. Even though the wine was 100 per cent chardonnay, the 'pinot' name was still hanging around, a tangible legacy of the colonial era.

That wine, the Tyrrell's Vat 47, is another good example of how so much of the history of Australian wine over the last two centuries radiates out from Dalwood. In the late 1960s, winemaker Murray Tyrrell was keen to make chardonnay, but there was hardly any planted in Australia at that time and cuttings weren't commercially available from nurseries. Having tasted the quality of the white wines that Perc McGuigan had made at Dalwood from chardonnay grown on the then sixty-year-old vines at the HVD property, Tyrrell famously jumped the fence in winter 1968 after the pruners had been through and pilfered cuttings to plant his own vineyard. In 1971, he released the inaugural vintage of Vat 47 and promoted it as the first commercial varietal chardonnay in Australia. This always made Perc chuckle: as he told me when I interviewed him very late in his life, he'd been making straight varietal chardonnay for decades before Murray Tyrrell came along; the only difference was that it wasn't *labelled* as chardonnay.

In 1982, Murray bought the HVD vineyard, and Tyrrell's now make a single-block wine from those original 'pineau' vines. Tasting the finesse and concentration of flavour in the Tyrrell's Old Vines HVD Chardonnay – made from that 1908 planting – you can see what impressed Perc about the vineyard in the 1940s.

Dalwood was also the birthplace of John Davoren Jnr, younger son of John Davoren Snr. About the same age as Perc McGuigan, John – like his older brother Harold, who had moved to Penfolds' Griffith winery – was recruited to work in other outposts of the company empire, eventually making his way in the late 1940s to Auldana, an old winery established in 1853 across the road from Penfolds' Magill Estate on the outskirts of Adelaide, and acquired by the larger company in 1943. Here John worked with company scientist Ray Beckwith, and Max Schubert, installed as winemaker at Magill around the same time. The two winemakers developed what wine writer Huon Hooke, Schubert's biographer, called 'an intense but, Max insisted, friendly rivalry'.

Schubert made his first vintage of Grange Hermitage – Australia's most famous red wine – at Magill in 1951. It was intentionally radical: fermentation and maturation in smaller new oak barrels, lots of power and concentration. Many dismissed it. John Davoren Jnr famously called it 'a very good dry port, which no-one in their right mind will buy – let alone drink'. Which only encouraged Schubert to make it a success.

In 1953, Davoren made a small batch of a trial red wine in response to Grange – like a poet composing a reply to another poet – that was quite different but no less ambitious. Named St Henri after a highly regarded red wine first produced in the 1890s across the road from Magill at Auldana cellars, Davoren's creation was, according to author and master of wine Andrew Caillard, a 'homage' to classic

Australian claret. It was also very much informed by his upbringing at Dalwood.

Davoren's first trial vintages of St Henri were blends of cabernet from the Barossa, mataro from Auldana and shiraz from Paracombe, in the Adelaide Hills. Like his father bringing cabernet and petit verdot together a quarter of a century before at Dalwood to create a wine greater than the sum of its parts, Davoren Jnr was working out how to combine these disparate flavours into a harmonious whole.

As George Wyndham had done in the early years of Dalwood, Davoren fermented his first vintages of St Henri in old barrels turned on their end with one head taken out, to create impromptu small vats. Like Wyndham, he also included some of the grape stalks in the ferment, to help extract colour and bring a brightness and lightness to the wine.

At the same time as Davoren Jnr and Schubert were creating exciting new wines in Adelaide in the 1950s, back at Dalwood Perc McGuigan was facing declining yields in the old vineyard and a series of at times almost insurmountable obstacles. During vintage in 1955, after three days of nonstop rain, the Hunter River burst its banks in the worst flood in recorded history, inundating the winery. The floodwaters came to within a few centimetres of the tops of the vats full of juice that had just started to ferment. Then, in 1959, Penfolds decided to pull out the vines at Dalwood and establish large, new, modern vineyards on cheaper land at Wybong in the Upper Hunter. Winemaking operations carried on for a few years at the old winery, but it was the end of an era for Dalwood.

It would take another decade and a radical change in Australia's wine culture for the next era to begin. And that change would be inspired, in large part, by the wine John Davoren Snr had made at Dalwood in 1930.

Sometime in 1960, Doug and Judy Crittenden's house, Melbourne

Wine merchant Doug Crittenden clutched the thirty-year-old bottle firmly in one hand and gently eased the cork out with the other. His Sydney visitor, renowned surgeon and wine lover Dr Max Lake, held out his glass in expectation.

'It's from the cellar of a deceased estate I've been asked to value,' said Crittenden, carefully pouring the wine. 'Don't know much about it, other than the box it came in said Hunter River Cabernet, 1930.'

Crittenden poured and Lake brought the glass to his nose, sucked in all the wine's perfume, closed his eyes, took a large sip and rolled it around his mouth before swallowing. After what seemed like minutes of rapture, the surgeon opened his eyes and beamed with joy.

'Ambrosial! Incredible! Extraordinarily complex, subtle, elegant. I've never tried anything like it!'

Lake wrote about this epiphany many times in subsequent years, describing how tasting that thirty-year-old cabernet blend led him to search for the perfect site to plant his own vineyard and make a wine like it. In 1960, most Australians were still drinking much more fortified wine – sherry, port, muscat – than fine red table wines like Davoren's Hunter 'claret'. If they did drink table wine, it was likely to be one of the new styles of fruity, cold-fermented rieslings that Crittenden had been successfully promoting through his family's licensed grocery in Malvern since the early 1950s. Or one of the growing number of sweet sparkling wines then gaining popularity, inspired by the success of Orlando's Barossa Pearl, launched to coincide with the Melbourne Olympics in 1956. Only a handful of new wineries had opened in Australia since the war, and almost none of those were the kind of small, high-quality operation that Lake had in mind. Crucially, too, he was the first of what would become a flood of professionals from outside the wine industry – doctors, lawyers, television producers – to establish their own boutique vineyards over the ensuing decades.

Lake was already familiar with the Hunter Valley. A passionate wine lover, he had first visited the region in 1954 under the guidance of Johnny Walker, Sydney restaurateur and wine merchant. At that time, a low point in the Hunter's history, only five wineries remained. Walker introduced Lake to legendary Mount Pleasant winemaker Maurice O'Shea, and published Lake's first article on wine – an essay on the 'claret style in Australia' – in his newsletter in 1959. This article attracted the attention of Max Schubert at Penfolds, and he and Lake soon became friends.

After the life-changing tasting at the Crittendens' house in Melbourne, Lake drove around the Hunter for three years, talking to old-timers about which bits of the valley used to produce the best wine, digging holes to examine the vine-growing potential of the soil, visiting dilapidated sheds that once held barrels and vats. Eventually, in 1963, he bought 25 hectares of deep-red volcanic soil in the heart of the valley, across the road from O'Shea's Rosehill vineyard, and started planting his own. As it turned out, the property, which he called Lake's Folly, had once been the site of an old vineyard that may even have contributed to his epiphany wine.

In *Hunter Winemakers*, one of many books that Lake wrote throughout his life, he describes a conversation with a local farmer who remembered pulling vines out of the future Lake's Folly site in 1933, when it was owned by the Kime family. Lake also wrote about a visit to Harold Davoren at Penfolds' winery in Griffith:

'Old Mr Davoren ... told me that as a boy his father (John Davoren Snr) had taken him across to the Kimes' from Dalwood. Both he and his father thought some of the best wine in the valley came off that hill.'

Mary Ryan is an archivist at the State Library of South Australia. She is also the daughter of John Davoren Jnr, the maker of St Henri, and granddaughter of John Davoren Snr, who made the 1930 Dalwood cabernet. She has read through her grandfather's copybooks and letters to Penfolds' head office and although – frustratingly – the records from the 1930 vintage are missing, she has found references from 1929 to him visiting other makers in the region, such as Wilkinson and Tyrrell, to buy casks of wine from them. And she found a mention of her grandfather buying 'good, clean' wine from 'Kime'.

Which means it's possible that the cabernet wine Davoren Snr blended with Dalwood petit verdot to make the 1930 Hunter River red that inspired Lake to plant his own vineyard may have come from the very spot where Lake ended up establishing the Folly thirty-three years later.

Like Max Lake, many of the new wave of 'gentleman vignerons' who emerged in the 1960s were inspired by old bottles from bygone eras of Australian wine history – as well as being inspired by Lake's pursuit of his Folly. Stuart Anderson, who founded Balgownie Estate, one of Victoria's most influential modern boutique vineyards, in 1968 was encouraged by both.

Stuart had fallen in love with wine as a student in Melbourne in the early 1950s: at the Oxford Hotel, one of the few wine-friendly dining rooms in the city at the time, he'd drunk all the great Hunter wines made by Maurice O'Shea. After graduating, he worked – like his father and grandfather before him – as a pharmacist in Bendigo and continued to buy wine and travel, visiting vineyards in Europe, kindling the flame.

'Then one day,' Stuart told me when I interviewed him a few years ago, 'an old woman brought an old leather shopping bag into the pharmacy and said, "I think you might be interested in these." There were six – full – bottles of Bendigo wine going back to the 1880s. When I saw these wines, I thought: if it was done last century it can be done again.'

After planting a small trial plot of vines, Stuart decided to expand to a proper vineyard, called Balgownie, encouraged by his friend and mentor Max Lake. Wine circles were small back then; everyone knew everyone else.

'Max was a great supporter in the early days,' said Stuart. 'Because it was a pretty lonely existence when I started. There was no other winemaker just down the road I could talk to. At the time, there were only seven new vineyards in Victoria and we all got to know each other. There was a certain feeling for all of us of being out on a limb. But in those early days there was a great camaraderie, too.'

As well as inspiring people further afield, Lake's Folly also acted like a magnet in the Hunter in the late 1960s and early 70s, pulling in dozens of professionals from Sydney and further afield, attracted by what looked like the glamorous lifestyle of the vigneron. People like Don Francois, New South Wales Director of Fisheries, who established Chateau Francois vineyard near Tyrrell's. People like Peter Dobinson, who planted a vineyard called Millstone that would come to play an important role in my life twenty years later. And people like wine merchant, judge, consultant and writer Len Evans, who was busily reshaping the culture of Australian wine.

———————

Early spring 1967, somewhere on Sydney Harbour

Evans was in his element. A stolen Sydney afternoon, perfect for a spot of yachting. White flecks on the water, sun on full sails, the rigging taut and singing in the wind. While the crew put the blue-hulled 50-foot sloop through its paces, Evans, garrulous, ruddy-faced, beaming, put a few bottles of Hunter wine through theirs. Drinking out of plastic cups, chomping on large turkey rolls.

'One of the huge UK liners steamed in full of migrants and apprehension,' wrote Evans a few days later in his 'Cellarmaster' column in *The Bulletin*. 'We went over to welcome them to Australia. Keeping to windward, we went very close and the liner listed as almost all the settlers waved to us. And as we waved back we could imagine them saying, at the first sight of their new country, "Well, it can't be *that* bad, eh?"'

One of the wines on board the yacht that day was a 1962 Penfolds Pinot Riesling, the blend Perc McGuigan had developed twenty years before and was still making at Dalwood, from chardonnay ('pineau/pinot') and semillon ('riesling') grown on the HVD vineyard.

Evans raved about this wine in his column and described the changes taking place with the brand. That year, 1967, Prime Minister Harold Holt had opened Penfolds' new, efficient, more commercially viable winery at Wybong in the Upper Hunter. The company had closed the old winery on the slow bend in the river at Branxton after the 1966 vintage, uncoupled the Dalwood brand name from the property, and taken it – and the winemaking equipment and old oak casks – with them to Wybong.

The late 1960s was a dynamic time for Australian wine, thanks in no small part to Len Evans. He was everywhere during this decade, relentlessly enthusiastic, witty, tireless. He was a wine columnist,

TV celebrity, restaurateur, even for a time official industry spokesperson: when he joined the Australian Wine Board as promotions executive in 1965, Australian per capita consumption of table wine was one bottle. When he quit two years later it was six bottles.

Evans encouraged the new wave of boutique winemakers like Max Lake and Stuart Anderson. He even started his own winery in the Hunter Valley, Rothbury Estate, as part of a consortium that also included Murray Tyrrell. More than fifty new wine companies both big and small opened in Australia in the 1960s. Over 200 appeared during the following decade. And one of these new brands was Wyndham Estate, located in the old Dalwood winery at Branxton, which Penfolds sold in 1968 for just $24,000.

The purchaser was Perc McGuigan, who chose the new name as a tribute to Dalwood's founder – and also because Penfolds owned the Dalwood brand name. Perc began replanting vines and getting the 65-year-old winery back into shape to start producing again. Just two years later, though, ill-health forced him to sell Wyndham Estate to three new owners: mining magnate Digby Matheson, Sydney stockbroker Tim Allen – both looking for an investment to write off against tax – and Perc's second son, winemaker Brian.

Brian McGuigan had learned his craft working alongside his father at Dalwood and under other Penfolds winemakers such as Max Schubert and John Davoren. In his 1967 *Bulletin* column, Len Evans described him as 'one of the bright, dedicated young wine men one meets more and more these days ... he will be part of the expansion that is in store for the wine industry. A significant part, I predict.'

It didn't take long for Evans's prediction to come true. As good a winemaker and blender as he was, Brian's true talents lay in marketing and promotion, increasingly important skills to have as a wine boom kicked off in Australia the 1970s. He had an uncanny ability to read the minds of wine drinkers and develop products and experiences that were perfectly tailored to their changing tastes.

Wyndham Estate was soon inundated with a flood of wine tourists. Matheson claimed that he and his business partners were the first to offer food in large quantity to the busloads of visitors who started turning up every weekend: 1500 steaks were marinated in port on Friday night to be barbecued for the hordes the following day.

'Once we realised that we were getting large numbers of people up to the winery, we decided to have entertainment,' Matheson told an interviewer in 2003. 'We hired Marcia Hines to put on a big concert … Well, from the road there at Branxton – it's about five or six or seven kilometres – the traffic was just banked up. Thousands of people. We counted money for days afterwards. We had suitcases full of money. It was unbelievable.'

The owners of Wyndham Estate realised that wine was capturing the imagination of a new generation of Australians. And Brian intuited that a good way to expand that potential market even further was to make a wine with plenty of perfume and some residual sweetness. So, following in his father's footsteps and inspired by similar styles he'd seen made at Penfolds in the 1960s, he blended fruity, spicy gewurztraminer with lean, citrusy semillon and called it 'traminer riesling'. He also made full use of then cutting-edge technology such as machine-harvesting and temperature-controlled fermentation to ensure the wine could be made cheaply and consistently.

The wine, first released in 1972, was a huge hit, spawning dozens of copycat brands. It became one of the era-defining brands of the decade, along with Lindeman's Ben Ean Moselle, another sweet white. And when Wyndham Estate rebranded the wine as TR2 in the early 1980s, sales climbed even higher.

'We were selling hundreds and hundreds and hundreds of thousands of cases,' said Brian. 'I suppose I was fortunate to recognise pretty early that what we had to do was to deliver what the consumer wanted, not necessarily what the professional winemaker thought the consumer should have. So, I learned that lesson and I staked the whole future of the company on one particular product, which was Traminer Riesling.'

That's not to say Wyndham Estate only produced semi-sweet white wine. The company also became well known for other styles that sound anachronistic to 21st-century ears but were the height of sophistication in the 1970s and early 80s – wines such as Chablis Superior and Graves Exceptional. And vintage 'port', a wine style that was still popular especially if it came in collectable sets with labels featuring famous racehorses or sporting legends of the day or – in Wyndham Estate's case – politicians: Matheson remembered selling over 20,000 sets of Prime Ministers Port, with Bob Hawke even visiting the winery for a photo opportunity when it was his turn to feature on a bottle.

A decade later, one hot Hunter Valley evening in summer, I came face to face with a dozen bottles of port made at Wyndham Estate during this era. Not, unfortunately, a set of Prime Ministers: this cache of bottles was unlabelled, unusually strong, and had almost been forgotten.

February 1993, Wandin Valley Estate, Lovedale, New South Wales

My father-in-law, Jim Davern, invited 100 of his closest friends to help him celebrate his sixtieth birthday. A big marquee was set up on the lawn at the vineyard he and Philippa had recently bought in the Hunter Valley. The place used to be known as Millstone, but Jim renamed it Wandin Valley Estate after the fictional location of *A Country Practice*, the TV series he produced and the profits from which he was now ploughing into the new business. Jim had a tenuous connection with the wine industry and with the Hunter: although not directly related, his Davern ancestors originally came from the same part of Ireland as the Davorens of Dalwood: both names are derived from O'Davoren.

As I was the newest member of the family, and because I was fresh from working in the wine trade in the UK, Jim gave me the job of opening and decanting a dozen bottles of port for the guests to drink later in the evening. The bottles were covered in dust, and had no labels. And Jim referred mysteriously to the wine inside as 'the Silver Shed port'.

'It's bloody mother's milk,' he said, smiling. 'But watch out: it's strong.'

As I carefully prised the stubborn cork out of each bottle and poured the contents into a decanter, Jim told me the story of how the port got its name and how he ended up with hundreds of bottles of the stuff.

In 1993, Jim's winemaker at Wandin Valley was a bloke called Geoff Broadfield. Back in 1979, Broadfield was working for Brian McGuigan at Wyndham Estate. One particularly hot sunny day, it was Broadfield's job to make some port by pumping high-strength spirit into a vat of fermenting shiraz to fortify it: the sudden addition of extra alcohol stops the yeasts working, leaving unfermented sugar in the resulting rich purple wine. The next thing Broadfield knows, he's being yelled at by Brian to 'wake up and turn the bloody pump off!' Thanks to the fumes and the sun, Broadfield had nodded off and over-fortified the port. Instead of raising the alcohol content to the desired 18 per cent, it was sitting at 22 or 25.

Broadfield and McGuigan decided to bottle the port anyway and lay the bottles down, unlabelled, stacked up in a big wire cage shoved in a corner of an old warehouse at Wyndham Estate known by the workers there as the 'silver shed'. And that's where it stayed until 1990, when McGuigan sold Wyndham Estate to South Australian wine firm Orlando, owners of – among other brands – Jacob's Creek. The merger of the two companies created one of the country's largest wine businesses, Orlando Wyndham, a major player in an era of corporate takeovers and rationalisation.

By this time, Broadfield was working at Wandin Valley. When he heard that the new corporate owners were auctioning off some old equipment and stock, he went along with my father-in-law to the sale. And they returned with the big wire cage full of hundreds of bottles of Silver Shed port, purchased for the giveaway price of ten bucks a dozen. Which is why I was able to open bottle after bottle at Jim's sixtieth-birthday party. The over-strength wine went down a storm with the old-timers from the local wine community, too: the irrepressible Don Francois, resplendent in a safari suit on the dance floor, became more and more voluble with every sip.

Orlando Wyndham was happy to let the Silver Shed port go at such a ridiculously low price because by the early 1990s this style of wine was no longer fashionable. Neither was the sweet TR2 that Brian had made at Wyndham Estate. Throughout the 90s, Orlando Wyndham replanted the vineyard at Branxton mostly to chardonnay, which was then a far trendier grape variety. It was a time of massive expansion in the wine industry, fuelled mostly by an unstoppable export boom but also by a local market thirsty from the recession we had to have. In 1993 there were around 700 wineries in Australia: by the end of the decade that number had more than doubled. During the same period the value of wine exports increased almost tenfold, much of it driven by the extraordinary growth of Jacob's Creek in the UK. And the wines that new consumers wanted to drink both here and overseas were not semi-sweet 'moselles' and heavy ports: they were sunshine-kissed golden chardonnays and ripe, oaky shiraz.

A few months after Jim's sixtieth, I had my first wine article published in a newspaper. *The Age*'s 'Epicure' section ran a story I'd written on Yeringberg, a 19th-century wine estate in the Yarra Valley that had been revived in the late 1960s by the grandson of the original owner after encouragement by various wine figures – including Max Lake. I wrote the story on a typewriter – which seems almost inconceivable now – and delivered it to the desk of the 'Epicure' editor after a photographer friend who worked at *The Age* literally got me in the back door.

I'd written that story because I'd become fascinated by the rich heritage of Yeringberg and the other great 19th-century estates in the Yarra Valley and across Australia since moving to Melbourne in 1992. But heritage wasn't a priority for many in the Australian wine industry at the time. It was all about the new, the shiny, the modern; growth, expansion, takeovers, investments. When I travelled to Adelaide a couple of years later for a press conference about the booming export figures, I took a bus out to the 150-year-old Penfolds Magill Estate, the home of Grange and St Henri, now world-famous wines. I expected it to be a showpiece cellar door, a fittingly upmarket tribute to the status of the brand and its wines. A pilgrimage for any wine lover.

In the mid-1990s it wasn't even open to the public.

Orlando didn't buy the Wyndham Estate business in 1990 for its heritage value. It was a successful commercial brand that just happened to come with a bit of history and a bunch of old buildings. And while Orlando Wyndham – itself bought a few years later by giant French drinks multinational Pernod Ricard – continued to make some wine at the old property at Branxton, it felt increasingly like a remote outpost of a corporate empire, not the spiritual home of the entire Australian industry. Eventually, all winemaking for the Wyndham Estate brand was moved to other Pernod Ricard sites around the country, and in 2012, the cellar door and other facilities were closed down. The once-thriving property was abandoned. Again.

––––––––––––

November 2018, Dalwood homestead, Branxton,
New South Wales

I'm sitting on the verandah of the house that George Wyndham's convict workers built two centuries ago. The broad flagstones are rounded and weathered underfoot; rough convict tool marks are gouged into the sandstone wall blocks. The place is crumbling. Wooden support beams hold up one side of the building. A sheet of corrugated galvanised iron covers a gap in the shingle verandah roof. Exposed dirt emerges from below dissolved floorboards. Behind the house, a few echoes of the Wyndham family orchard remain: a giant bunya pine planted in the 1870s, a straggly peppercorn, a wizened old orange tree bearing exhausted, sour fruit. The place feels forgotten and remote and spent. In the words of poet Judith Wright, it has 'an indefinable air of loss … woebegone and old'.

But there is good news here at Dalwood. In December 2016, local property developer and pub owner Sam Arnaout purchased the place from Pernod Ricard and hired talented winemaker Bryan Currie. A year later, Arnaout bought the Dalwood trademark back from Treasury Wine Estates, the parent company of Penfolds. And in early 2018, he opened the old winery building again as a cellar door selling wines from the other Hunter vineyards Arnaout owns, Hungerford Hill and Sweetwater, as well as new wines from Dalwood's own 25 hectares of vines. After almost three decades of corporate ownership, Dalwood was once again in private hands. And after half a century apart, the estate and its original name were reunited.

'That was a champagne-popping moment,' says Bryan, 'when we put the brand and the property back together.'

We walk back to the old winery buildings and Bryan tells me his plans for Dalwood. The vineyard is currently mostly planted to chardonnay – a legacy of Pernod Ricard's priorities in the 1990s – plus some semillon and shiraz. But he is grafting some of those vines over to varieties that have historical resonance here, such as the Spanish red grape tempranillo and the Portuguese red grape touriga: echoes of George Wyndham planting 'Black Spanish' and 'Oporto' back in the 1830s.

Bryan doesn't, unfortunately, have any plans to grow petit verdot again at Dalwood. Which is a shame. That would have been a neat full circle to this story. But he has embraced the concept of the classic Hunter 'claret' blend: the best red wine he pours me at the tasting room is a shiraz cabernet, elegant, grippy, firmly structured, destined for a long life in the cellar. It's a wine that would have tasted familiar to the Wyndhams, to John Davoren, to Perc McGuigan. Bryan also plans to start using the old basket press and big, round open fermenting vats in the 1904 winery.

Dalwood is not the only Australian heritage wine estate to return to private ownership recently. In fact, it's a trend. Over the last few years, other prominent Australian wine entrepreneurs have been busily acquiring historic sites from corporate businesses. In the Barossa Valley in South Australia, Warren Randall has returned the 170-year-old Seppeltsfield estate to much of its former glory since taking over from former owners Treasury Wine Estates, and is set to repeat the exercise at the Ryecroft winery (established in the 1880s) in McLaren Vale and Quelltaler (1860s) in the Clare Valley. Griffith-based Casella Family Brands, owner of the huge Yellow Tail wine label, have bought the Baileys of Glenrowan winery (1880) and 144 hectares of vineyard in north-east Victoria from Treasury, following the acquisition of Rutherglen fortified specialist Morris Wines (1859) from Pernod Ricard. And in the Hunter Valley, Brian McGuigan and another local wine identity, Colin Peterson, have purchased the 147-year-old Ben Ean vineyard and winery from Treasury. All these veterans of the wine business clearly believe there is a future in the past.

So, too, do some of the larger corporate wine companies. Penfolds' Magill Estate, closed to the public when I first visited in 1995, is now one of the world's great wine tourism destinations, after its owners spent millions of dollars on restoring the old winery buildings and vineyard and installing restaurants and tasting rooms. And Pernod Ricard has modified its Wyndham Estate brand, replacing it with two new brands that focus more on the name of the founder, George Wyndham himself.

Half a century ago, in the late 1960s, author Ivan Roberts and photographer Douglas Baglin visited Dalwood while researching their book *Australian Wine Pilgrimage*. The place was at a low ebb: John Wyndham's old vines had been pulled out a decade before, and all the old casks and winemaking equipment had been transferred to Penfolds' new winery at Wybong. The land and the buildings were abandoned. They spoke to Perc McGuigan, who, unknown to them at the time, was just about to buy the place from Penfolds and start replanting the vineyard.

'Who knows?' said Perc, hamming it up for his visitors (imagine the twinkle in his eye). 'With interest in growing and making wines these days so great, I wouldn't be surprised to see "old" Dalwood live again.'

White Lady

Angaston, 1936

This old-bottle-collecting obsession is getting out of hand.

My latest purchase is a bottle of Niblik, a premixed cocktail first produced in Angaston, South Australia, by Barossa Valley wine company Yalumba in 1936. I found it in an antique shop that specialises in Art Deco items. You can see why it appealed to the owners of the shop, and to me. The bottle is shaped like an octagonal cocktail shaker, angular, tapered, very Deco. It has a dark-green Yalumba-branded Bakelite lid. Remarkably, the label is intact: 'Niblik Cocktail, White Lady Type' and an image, in silver silhouette on a crimson background, of a golfer (the niblick is an old type of golf club, apparently).

Unlike my Seppeltsfield Angaston Bitters, though, the Niblik bottle is empty. So I went looking for White Lady recipes from the era, to try to imagine what it would have been like to – as the Niblik label implores – 'Shake well and serve icy cold'.

As with so many now-classic cocktails, the origins of the White Lady are disputed. Legendary bartender Harry MacElhone claimed he first made a drink called White Lady in 1919, perfecting the blend of gin, triple sec and lemon juice at his Harry's New York Bar in Paris ten years later. The Savoy in London asserts that *its* legendary bartender, Harry Craddock, invented it at the hotel's bar and included it in the influential *Savoy Cocktail Book*, published in 1930.

Whoever originally invented the drink, Sydney's *Sun* news-paper first printed a recipe for it, syndicated from England, in 1929: 'If a cocktail is wanted on a grizzling hot day,' suggested Scottish cookery writer Elizabeth Craig, 'mix equal quantities of gin, Cointreau, and lemon juice, and you have a refreshing and stimulating White Lady.'

This differs from Craddock's recipe in the *Savoy Cocktail Book*, which mixes two parts gin to one part each of Cointreau and lemon juice. So I tried a taste comparison of the two recipes (any excuse to get the cocktail shaker out) and can report that, if you're looking for something refreshing on a 'grizzling hot day', Craig's lighter, more citrusy version is the better option. But if you're looking for a cocktail that tastes like a *cocktail*, punchy and full of the flavour of gin, Craddock's White Lady is the one to try. And if you want to emulate the Niblik, try a half-and-half blend of lemon and orange juice instead of just lemon: Yalumba advertising from the period emphasises the inclusion of 'just the right tangy dash of lemon and sun-sweetened oranges' in the drink.

I also love my Niblik bottle because it's a tangible reminder that premixed cocktails, a dynamic trend in the second decade of the 21st century, have a very long history in Australia.

In the 1850s, enterprising Melbourne hotelier Michael Moran started selling 'blended and bottled' gin, brandy and sherry cocktails from his Central City Hotel in Collins Street to people heading off to the races. A decade before the introduction of Niblik, in 1927, at the height of the cocktail boom, Yalumba released a blend of vermouth and gin cheekily labelled Ver-Gin: 'A Cocktail of outstanding quality, made from an old Italian recipe, from the finest imported herbs'. Other big wine companies in the 1930s such as Penfolds and Orlando sold pre-bottled Manhattans and other cocktails.

During World War II, American soldiers stationed in northern Australia brought their preference for drinking rum mixed with Coca-Cola. Queensland's Bundaberg distillery had been awarded the government contract to provide rum to the armed services and, responding to the drinking habits of the visiting GIs, started bottling rum blended with cola; I was delighted to find a couple of these bottles, still full, on display at the distillery's museum when I visited. Bundaberg tried to sell this ready-to-drink blend to Australians after the Americans had gone home, but it didn't catch on until the mid-1980s, when Bundaberg launched rum-and-cola in ready-to-drink cans. Today, more than 40 per cent of all the rum the distillery makes is sold in RTDs.

Premixed drinks in cans also have a longer history in Australia than most people realise. Technology that enabled the canning of fizzy drinks without the carbonated liquid corroding the container was perfected in the late 1950s, and a few American producers started putting cocktails into cans at that time. The innovation arrived in Australia in 1965, when Sydney wine and spirit merchant Douglas Lamb teamed up with Schweppes to market a range of canned drinks – brandy and dry ginger, gin and bitter lemon, vodka and orange – under the Alfresco label. While that brand didn't last, another brand launched at the same time by United Distillers Limited, UDL, originally incorporating spirits made at the Corio distillery in Geelong, lives on to this day: Australian bottle-shop fridges are still full of UDL cans.

Victoria Bitter:
A big cold beer

You can get it ridin'
You can get it slidin'
You can feel it comin' on about four …

I wasn't expecting this. There's a strange, sudden warm swelling in my chest. Could it be … pride? I can't remember feeling this way about a beer before. Certainly not a beer I don't even drink very often.

I have driven past the huge CUB Abbotsford brewery on the banks of the Yarra River countless times over the last twenty-five years. I've waited at the traffic lights on Victoria Street for B-doubles full of clinking bottles to negotiate the tight corner into Bond Street. I've wondered what goes on behind those massive red-brick walls; pictured the giant mash tuns and steaming kettles and miles of gleaming pipes needed to produce the millions of litres of beer that emerge from this brewery every year. I've thought about this place whenever I've drunk CUB beers across the country, whether it's a pot of Melbourne Bitter in a sticky-carpet pub in Richmond around the corner, or a schooner of Carlton on the muggy verandah of the Darwin Hotel.

Now, after years of wondering, I've spent a day inside discovering why the company's iconic beer brand, VB – Victoria Bitter – tastes the way it does. I managed to convince the giant multinational company to let me in through its gates, to peek behind those massive walls, to see the giant mash tuns and kettles up close (they're even bigger than I imagined), to learn the secrets of this quintessential Australian beer. Eight hours in a high-vis vest and safety specs, smelling the yeast, tasting the hops, sipping the sugary wort. No wonder I'm overwhelmed by the sheer unique bloody Australian-ness of it all.

You can get it in a hole
Or up a pole
You can get it doin' nothin' at all

Victoria Bitter is the perfect single brand to tell the broader story of Australian beer because, unlike other equally historic Australian brands, it has nationwide appeal: where XXXX is fiercely Queensland, and Swan Lager belongs to Western Australia, where Cascade is traditionally Tasmanian and Reschs is drunk in New South Wales, Victoria Bitter has a long-established market and loyal fans across the country. All these beer brands share a similar story arc, though: all were first produced by small-scale local breweries, all were swallowed by corporate takeovers during the 20th century, all are mass-produced to a consistent standard by industrial brewing techniques, and all are seeing their sales eroded by a new generation of small-scale local breweries.

The VB story starts in 1842 with the arrival of an entrepreneurial young Scot named Thomas Aitken in the young settlement of Port Phillip. Aitken founded his first brewery in Geelong in 1851 before moving to Melbourne the following year to set up the Union Brewery in Little Lonsdale Street, then shifting to a new, larger operation, the Victoria Brewery on Victoria Parade in East Melbourne, in 1854.

The second half of the 19th century was a boom time for new Australian brewers, fuelled initially by demand from thirsty miners on the goldfields, and subsequently by dramatic population growth. There were just seventy breweries across the country in 1850; ten years later that number had risen to 178; by 1890, there were almost 300.

Aitken's Victoria Brewery soon became one of the largest of these new operations, but it was far from the only substantial producer of beer in Melbourne. Three in particular are important in the VB story. The Carlton Brewery, whose bluestone facade still stands in Bouverie Street on the fringe of Melbourne's CBD grid, was founded in 1865 and soon became one of the major players in the colony. Two brothers from New York, keen to make and sell the lager style of beer, established the Foster Brewing Company in 1888 just a few streets away from Aitken's Victoria Brewery. And in 1904, in response to the market power of the big breweries such as Victoria and Carlton, a group of hotelkeepers opened the Melbourne Co-operative Brewery in a former distillery at Abbotsford on the banks of the Yarra.

By the turn of the century, competition had become so fierce and breweries had overcapitalised to such an extent that some rationalisation needed to take place, and in 1907 the six major players, including the Victoria, Carlton and Foster operations, amalgamated to become Carlton and United Breweries. This was the beginning of a series of mergers and acquisitions around the country (including, in 1925, the Melbourne Co-operative Brewery in Abbotsford, makers of Invalid Stout) throughout the 20th century that would see CUB become Australia's largest company, while the total number of breweries shrank to just a couple of dozen in 1980.

The first Victoria Brewery Bitter Ale with the distinctive VB initials on the label appeared around the time of the merger in 1907. The brand was widely advertised and marketed in all states and territories. Following the enormous success of the 'hard-earned thirst' TV ad campaign that started in 1968 (and which I'll come back to later), sales grew steadily until, by the 1980s, one in three beers sold in Australia was VB.

But there's another reason why I wanted to get closer to the heart of the brand. I have a sentimental attachment to VB. It was an integral part of my early Australian drinking life.

———————

You can get it rollin'
You can get it bowlin'
You can get it ridin' a line

———————

It's Christmas 1977. I'm nine years old, out in Australia visiting my stepfather's family in the western suburbs of Sydney. This isn't like Christmas back home in England, where beer is something my grandad sips from a pint glass in a dark, wood-panelled pub. Here, while the sun blares down and cicadas rip the air and everything feels raw and overexposed, I watch as squinting uncles and sunburnt cousins in singlets and stubbies and thongs rip the ring-pulls from can after can of cold lager: gold cans of Tooth's KB and green cans of Victoria Bitter. This is my first glimpse of Australian beer and Australian beer drinking.

Now it's late December 1993 and I've been living in Australia for a year and a half. I've just flown back into Sydney from London, returning from a visit to see my English relatives over Christmas. Yesterday Sophie and I were tramping through London's slush and grime and biting cold. Now we're smothered by Sydney's humming humidity.

We arrive at my in-laws' house late in the evening, struggling with jet lag, wading through sweet clouds of frangipani. I feel like I'm flickering in and out of two worlds: I haven't been away from England long enough to shake the pangs of homesickness, and haven't lived in Australia long enough for it to feel comfortable and familiar. As the kitchen fan whirls overhead, I open the fridge and look for a midnight snack. A couple of minutes later, I'm tucking into a leftover roast lamb sandwich and washing it down with a cold can of VB. I feel I've come home.

More memories. Lugging cases of VB longnecks from the delivery truck into the coolroom at a drive-through bottle shop in Fitzroy, selling slabs of cans to blokes in utes, sixpacks of stubbies to students in black jeans and flannos, the first proper job I got after moving to Melbourne, the year that Essendon won the flag. Drinking jugs of VB in the front bar at the Esplanade Hotel at sunset, listening to mates' rock bands and playing pool, surprised when we didn't blow .05 on the drive home and thanking god the bastards at the hotel had watered the beer down. Visiting my stepfather, a veteran actor, backstage after a show, him nursing a can of VB in one hand, a cigarette in the other. Ditto at backyard barbecues. And theatre openings. And family birthdays.

That was all a while ago now, though. Over the last twenty-five years, like millions of other Australians, I've become far more interested in craft beer from independent brewers. Which means, yes, you could call me a bit of a beer snob. I would much rather drink a wild-fermented sour ale brewed with foraged ingredients by some bearded hipster than reach into the fridge for a can of industrial beer brewed by a corporation.

In fact, before my adventure at Abbotsford, the only time I'd drunk VB in the last decade was a few years ago, when I ordered a pot in the pub across the road from my house at 10 a.m. on Melbourne Cup Day, a rolled-up form guide in my back pocket, a couple of sure-fire bets safely placed at the TAB. Sophie and I had survived a near-fatal car crash a couple of weeks before, me with a few bruises, her with multiple broken ribs and sternum. After the crash, for some reason – shock? survivor's luck? – I started gambling, just a small punt here and there. By Melbourne Cup Day I'd got into the swing of things. Drinking a pot of VB before midday didn't seem all that unusual. Neither did betting a little more every time. They both felt like the kind of normal Aussie things that Aussie blokes do. Luckily, I came to my senses when a little old lady spotted my form guide and asked me for tips. I put down my pot and walked out. Which was lucky, as those sure-fire bets turned out to be fizzers.

So when I sat down with the CUB communications manager to see if I could arrange a tour of the Abbotsford compound and watch the brewing process up close and he asked me whether I drank VB myself, it stopped me in my tracks. What did the brand mean to me, he asked. Did I feel the same way about VB as the millions of Australians who were fiercely loyal and protective? Did I love it? *Did I drink it?*

'Um, yes?' I said. 'Well, not for a while. I mean, no. But I used to.'

I could understand his suspicion. I flaunt my beer snobbery in my newspaper and magazine writing. I have been openly critical of various CUB products at times, and downright hostile at others.

And here I was asking CUB to be generous and transparent with the intellectual property of one of their most important and valuable brands. No wonder it had taken me six months of email to-and-fro with head office to finally get to this meeting. If I were CUB, I'd be wary of me, too.

So I was surprised when, six weeks later, the comms manager got back to me with a suggestion. 'I've been speaking to a senior brewer at Abbotsford who's had an idea,' he said. 'Instead of doing just a tour, do you want to brew some VB from scratch?'

You can get it squeezin'
You can get it pleasin'
You can get it breakin' your back

Claude Nyaguy has been working for CUB for forty years. When he started with the company, first in quality control, then as development brewer, they were still making beer in the original bluestone Carlton Brewery in Bouverie Street, before all operations moved to Abbotsford. He looks a bit like a tall, enthusiastic Hungarian-Australian Harrison Ford. He surfs, he's fit and he's full of energy and enthusiasm for his job, for VB.

'But I reckon they only hired me because they wanted me in the CUB footy team,' he says, smiling.

Claude runs the Research Pilot Brewery, a small operation in the heart of the Abbotsford compound. This is where the company develops new products, brewing small, 1500-litre batches for appraisal by the sensory analysis team and the marketers and the head brewers before production is moved to the real, gigantic brewery that surrounds us. Today, Claude is going to brew a scaled-down batch of VB following the company's recipe. He says he will take me through every stage of the process, from the moment the first grains of malted barley are milled, to the moment the yeast is added. I can make notes, he says, ask questions, help with the various stages, press buttons, turn taps, add ingredients to the tanks, take photos. The only thing I can't do, he says, is take photos of the sheet of paper with the recipe on it. Oh, and drink. I can't drink. The whole Abbotsford worksite has a zero-tolerance alcohol policy. No sampling of the beer during the day. No enjoying a pot of the product at the pub around the corner at lunchtime. All employees and visitors must be completely sober at all times.

Claude hands me a knife to cut open the first sack of malted barley, which we tip into a noisy mill to be ground into a fine powdery meal that is then placed in a tank called a mash tun and mixed with hot water. This is the basis of beer. The malting process, where barley is germinated then dried, turns the starch in the grain into fermentable sugars that the yeast, added later, can turn into alcohol.

The malt used for VB is a pale malt, made from Australian-grown barley processed to CUB's specifications by the big malting company Barrett Burston, based a few blocks away in Richmond, behind the grain silos on the banks of the Yarra and the old Victoria Bitter sign that generations of commuters have driven past on their way up and down Punt Road. The way the malt is processed is key to the final style, flavour and character of a beer. The more the grains are roasted during the malting, the darker and fuller-flavoured the end product. For VB, it's crucial that pale malt is used, to deliver the recognisable pale-gold colour – that enticing sunlight-yellow sparkle that countless designers and photographers and ad directors have worked so hard to capture – and the famously straightforward character of the drink.

Claude scoops out a handful of grains from the sack and I pick a few to chew on. Crunching through the husk, the barley tastes faintly of sweet biscuit, like one of your nana's Milk Arrowroots. It's not a strong flavour. Clean, simple.

This is exactly the base flavour CUB is looking for in VB. The expectation, the ideal drinking moment, the end point of the whole process, is when someone pours a glass, ice-cold from a tap in a bar, or pulls a can from an esky, or a stubbie from the fridge. At that instant, when the very cold beer enters the mouth of the drinker, it needs to taste exactly as everyone involved expects it to taste – the brewer, the marketer and especially the consumer.

This, remember, is a big cold beer designed to satisfy a hard-earned thirst. Which means it needs to be easy to drink, not too taxing, not too heavy. Claude says VB is 'perfectly suited to our climate', so it should be 'refreshing, not complex'. Beer marketers call this quality 'sessionable'. What it really means is that VB needs to be the kind of beer that people can drink a *lot* of, long after their hard-earned thirst has been quenched. It needs to be a beer that matches the culture of the 'shout'.

I first heard this word used in 1977. I was straight off the plane from London and my Australian grandma offered to shout me an icy pole. I had no idea what she was talking about: it had to be explained to me that she was offering to buy me an ice-cream.

The first time I came across the alcoholic version of shouting was not long after I moved here in 1992, when Sophie and I visited friends of hers in Tamworth, north New South Wales, the country music capital of Australia, and I went to a local pub with a couple of farmers, both big country lads, to see a band. When we arrived, one of the farmers bought a round of beers and we sat down to watch the show. After a couple of minutes, I was still halfway through my cold middy of Tooheys when the larger of the two farmers, without taking his eyes off the band, thrust his empty glass in my chest. Not quite sure what to do, I looked at the other bloke for etiquette assistance.

'Your shout, mate,' he said, draining his glass and handing it to me.

Beer writer David Downie neatly defines 'shouting' as '[purchasing] a round of drinks ... with the expectation of reciprocation ... The consequence of the shouting ethic is, of course, a fairly rapid and consistent pace of drinking.' He says the culture was established during the gold rush and quotes an 1855 article in the *Australian Brewers' Journal* explaining that 'a lucky miner, intent on "knocking down his pile" [spending all his money] was accustomed to go into the road and shout for all hands to come and drink with him, so that in time "shouting" came to mean "standing drinks for the crowd"'.

In the late 1990s, Melbourne drinks writer Mark Shield codified the complex and strict rules of the shout that had developed over the previous 150 years:

> Thou shalt not miss your turn. Thou shalt drink at the same rate as the others in the drinking school – no slower. Thou shalt not leave the school until the first round is complete or you have had your turn in the chair. People who go to the dunny when they should be in the chair should be treated with suspicion. People with death adders in their pockets shall be expelled from the school and sent to Coventry ...

The introduction of lager-style beers like VB helped entrench this culture of 'rapid and consistent drinking'. Take, for example, one of the most infamous events in Australian beer history, when cricketer David Boon drank fifty-two cans of VB on a Qantas flight to London in 1989. It's really hard to imagine Boonie being able to achieve such a feat with the kind of beer made in this country before lager came along.

You can get it strivin'
You can get it divin'
You can get it mixin' cement

For the first hundred years of its existence, Australian beer was dark, heavy, and drunk warm – like it had been back in 'the old country'. There's an account of drinking in the journal of Philip Gidley King, lieutenant on the First Fleet and future governor of the New South Wales colony, that brings this old style of beer vividly to life.

On 19 January 1788, King and an exploratory party in three boats skirted around the shoreline of Botany Bay, looking for inlets and rivulets of fresh water. Finally, in the south-west corner of the bay, the party went onshore and ate salt beef and 'in a glass of Porter drank ye healths of our friends in England'.

When I read King's words I wondered: what did that porter taste like? What did it feel like to drink that beer on that beach in January 1788? Or that style of beer in countless other hot summers across the country in the early years of the colony? I became a bit obsessed with finding out. So 230 years later, almost to the day, I travelled by train and bus across Sydney to Sandringham in the south-west corner of Botany Bay and went for a walk on the beach.

I took with me some slices of corned beef and a flask of beer I'd blended up in an attempt to re-create the style of strong, cask-matured porter King and crew had with them: English porter for authentic flavour, barrel-aged Scandinavian porter for the cask character, and an old, past-it bottle-aged Australian stout I'd forgotten I had in the cellar, to hint at the months at sea King's beer would have endured before he drank it.

By blending these disparate components the day before in the flask and keeping it at ambient temperature rather than in the fridge, letting the beer go flat and start to oxidise, and by choosing to drink it on the shore of Botany Bay in the middle of a Sydney summer, I wanted to emulate what I assumed would have been a not terribly enjoyable experience back in 1788.

That's not what happened, of course. When I arrived at the beach, a strong chilly breeze was churning up the surf. I found a sheltered spot away from the paragliders and dog walkers, and as QF19 rumbled up into the clouds from Sydney Airport across the bay on its way to Hong Kong, I poured myself a cup of porter.

It was delicious. Warm, yes; flat, yes. But hearty and welcoming, too, somehow. After my long journey (not, admittedly, quite as harrowing as eight months on the *Sirius*), the flavour of this strong dark beer filled my senses and served as a touchstone, like my homemade cider, a reminder of home that I had brought with me.

It was only after I'd drained my cup and was walking back to the bus that I saw the council sign prohibiting alcohol consumption on the beach.

Dark beers like that porter, sweet from the roasted malt, heavy from warm fermentation, dominated tastes to such an extent that early attempts to introduce the lighter style of lager, fashionable in Europe and the US in the mid 19th century, initially failed to attract much interest from the Australian drinking public.

Theodore Rosenberg was probably the first person to brew lager commercially in Melbourne and Australia, in 1858, when he began producing what he called 'genuine Bavarian lagerbeer' at his Union Brewery in Bouverie Street, which became the Carlton Brewery seven years later. It didn't catch on: the business was offered to let the following year.

By the early 1880s, a few brave breweries had managed to establish a small market for the new style of beer, with the Cohn brothers' Victoria Brewery in Bendigo and the Anglo-Australian Brewery in Sydney both making and selling lager. But Melbourne's drinkers resisted the inevitable: when a trio of ambitious brewers established the Gambrinus Lager Beer Brewery in Collingwood in 1885, it took less than a year for the locals' indifference to see the company fold.

Everything changed in 1888 when two New York brothers, William and Ralph Foster, set up operations a few streets away from Thomas Aitken's Victoria Brewery, installing specialised equipment, an ice-making plant and a German-trained brewer from the USA, with the express intention of making lager. The company struggled for the first few years, but by the mid-1890s Foster's Lager had become hugely popular in Melbourne, thanks partly to cutting-edge quality control put in place by chemist Auguste de Bavay, and partly because every delivery to retail outlets, whether in bottles or kegs, came with a free supply of ice to keep the lager cold. This was the turning point. For the next 100 years, the lager style of beer would grow in popularity across Australia until it had almost completely replaced the old dark ales of the past. And the brand that would come to exemplify the Australian lager style in the second half of the 20th century was Victoria Bitter.

Which is weird, really. To many outsiders – British beer drinkers who have just arrived in Australia, for example – the name is contradictory. To them, 'bitter' is a brown ale, top-fermented, warm, with a strong malty character and pronounced bitterness. And yet, as soon as you pour a glass of Victoria Bitter you can see it's obviously a lager: pale in colour with a lacy, persistent white foam, bottom-fermented cool, and best drunk cold. In the very early days, the beer that started life as Victoria Brewery Bitter Ale was probably exactly what it said on the label: a bitter ale. Sometime in the middle of the 20th century, the beer's style changed, bringing it more in line with the lager style then proving to be more fashionable. By that time, though, the Victoria Bitter name was rusted on.

Most Australians who've grown up with VB couldn't give a stuff, of course, about this disconnect between nomenclature and stylistic integrity. To them, VB is just beer.

You're buildin' a shed
Or movin' a bed
You're blowin' so hard you could burst

'Are you sure you want to do that?' says Claude. 'It's incredibly bitter. You'll still be tasting it on your tongue next week.'

He's just handed me a glass measuring cylinder half-full of dark-golden, slightly viscous liquid. It's hop extract, an intensely concentrated form of the compounds found in hop flowers that give beer its astringency and bitterness. He wants me to add this liquid to the brew kettle, to boil up with the sweet wort before being pumped into the fermenting tank. But before I do, I ask him if I can taste it. This, I think, is the beating heart of VB, extract of Pride of Ringwood, a variety of hop bred especially for CUB in the 1950s. What better way to understand the beer than to taste the hop in its essential form – even if the extract is several thousand times more bitter than it'll be once it's diluted in the brew.

Despite Claude's warning, I dip the end of my little finger into the golden fluid and dab a droplet, perhaps half a match-head, onto the side of my tongue. For a fleeting millisecond, my mouth fills with the intensely aromatic resinous flavour of hop flowers. And then the drying, rasping roughness of the hop oils kicks in. While not quite hanging around for a week, the taste is still with me when I go to sleep that night.

Hops have been used in brewing for centuries to add aromatic flavour and bitterness to beer: hop flowers contain essential oils and bitter resins that leach into the liquid when they are added to sweet wort. Historically, hops were also prized for their preservative qualities: the bitterness in the flowers helped subdue microbial activity and spoilage in beer before refrigeration and sterilisation gave brewers more control.

In the early years of the colony, Australian brewers were dependent on shipments of hops from England. It wasn't until the 1820s that hop cultivation began in New South Wales, and not until the 1850s that growers realised the plant was far better suited to the cooler climate of Tasmania. When Thomas Aitken established the Victoria Brewery in 1854, Tasmania had become the main source of hops for brewers across the mainland, but in 1866 hop farms also began to appear and flourish in cooler parts of Victoria.

In the 19th century, Australian growers planted English varieties of hop such as Fuggles and Canterbury Golding, which had the right kind of mild perfume and bitterness suitable for the ales, stouts and porters popular at the time. The more aromatic Californian Golden Cluster hop took over as the most widely grown variety in the first half of the 20th century as the lager style of beer began to dominate the market. But few of the imported hop varieties were ideally matched to the harsher Australian landscape; growers often struggled with yields and disease was a perennial problem. Many brewers also found the flavours in Cluster to be harsh. So in 1950, keen to explore the possibilities of new varieties of hop for its ever-expanding business, CUB instigated a breeding program, hiring top New Zealand hop researcher Albert Nash and installing him and his young family at a research station at Ringwood, then on the rural fringes of Melbourne.

Nash's daughter Margot, who went on to become a performer at Melbourne's Pram Factory theatre in the 1970s and then a film-maker, wrote a vivid memoir of her time growing up in Ringwood, 'running through the hop fields into the forbidden territory down the back where the creek marked the border of our land from the bush; where the bellbirds sang and tiny green tree snakes curled through the branches'.

She remembers her father working seven days a week to breed thousands of different hops, looking for 'that one magic hop that might solve all the problems'. Traumatised – as many of his generation were – by combat experience in World War II, she writes, Nash drank heavily and suffered acute paranoia and regular nervous breakdowns. And yet he kept working, eventually breeding a hop that exceeded expectations by crossing an English variety called Pride of Kent with a wild Tasmanian hop. He named the new variety Pride of Ringwood.

'When "Pride" was released [in 1959] it was the highest alpha-acid-yielding hop in the world,' remembers Margot. 'Alpha acids are found in the resin glands of the female flowers, and produce the unique bitter taste of beer, but "Pride" also had a distinct citrus aroma. It would become the main hop grown in Australia, flavouring Victoria Bitter and Foster's Lager, and accounting for about 90 per cent of Australia's hop production.'

Pride of Ringwood also gave higher yields and had better disease resistance, and it was enthusiastically embraced by the Victorian industry, with the area under hops across the state almost tripling in the decade after its introduction.

Despite all these advantages, Pride of Ringwood was still being used in brewing the old-fashioned way, with sacks full of dried hop flowers – called cones – manually tipped into the boiling kettle. As well as being labour intensive, it was inefficient: only about a third of the alpha acids are utilised in the beer. So in 1960 CUB established a team of scientists to find a more efficient way of extracting the flavouring and bittering compounds in the hops.

Hop extracts and concentrates had been used in Australian brewing in a minor way since the 1880s, but the CUB scientists applied recent advances in the understanding of hop chemistry and made the extraction process better, constructing a custom-designed extraction plant in 1965. The company's chief chemist, Frank Harold, described how his team had discovered a way to remove the alpha acids from the extract, leaving all the other flavouring materials behind to be put in the boiling kettle, then adding the alpha acids at the end of fermentation to achieve a 95 per cent utilisation rate.

'We had a world first,' he said. 'We won the plant of the year award. We have exported the extract around the world. We still do.'

———

You're climbin' a pole
Or diggin' a hole
Or comin' so close you seem cursed

———

Another crucial ingredient in the VB recipe is the yeast. As Claude pumps the sweet, malty, hoppy liquid – the 'wort' – from the boiling kettle to the fermenting tank via a heat exchanger to cool the liquid down, he brings a small stainless-steel keg out of the coolroom and hooks it up to the pipes leading to the tank. Inside the keg is a slurry of yeast captured from a previous ferment.

The CUB brewers have been using the same yeast culture to make lager since 1923. That yeast originally came from the Carlsberg brewery in Denmark, where it had been isolated and used for the commercial production of lager in 1881. The same yeast culture has been kept alive and used and reused in countless brews by CUB ever since. While the fermenting tank slowly fills with wort, Claude takes us to see the vast, spaceship-hangar-sized yeast room, where enormous stainless-steel tanks, each bigger than the entire capacity of most craft breweries, store the yeast, ready to be used to make more and more beer. Not all of the yeast from each brew is reclaimed, though. Since 1933, a lot of CUB's spent yeast has been sent to Kraft Foods in South Melbourne to make that other iconic Australian product, Vegemite.

As well as converting the sugar in the wort into alcohol, the yeast contributes to the distinctive flavour of the beer, along with the malt and the hops. Because it's the same yeast used, year-in, year-out, there's consistency of flavour. And because the same yeast is also used in other CUB lagers, from Melbourne Bitter to Carlton Draught, there's a certain family resemblance in how they all taste.

What differences there are between the beers derive from the kinds of malt and hops used, and how the beer is finished. In VB's case, after a week or so it finishes fermenting with an alcohol volume of around 6.5 per cent. It's then chilled before being diluted back to 4.9 per cent alcohol – importantly, a little stronger than Melbourne or Carlton. Some extra hop extract is added to meet the required flavour parameters, and the beer is filtered, carbonated and packaged, either in keg, to be sold to pubs and restaurants around the country, or in bottles or cans.

For most of the 20th century, VB was bottled in long-neck 750 ml brown bottles. The brand's popularity soared across Australia in the late 1960s when it was sold on draught and then put into cans – a move that coincided with the launch in 1968 of a now-legendary television advertising campaign.

You can get it walkin'
You can get it talkin'
You can get it workin' a plough
Matter o' fact I got it now

You can probably hear the tune in your head as you read those words. The VB ad is one of the most instantly recognisable TV commercials in Australian history. But, as online beer magazine *BrewsNews* discovered, it started life as an ad for another beer altogether.

In 1965, CUB was having problems selling one of its Queensland beers, Bulimba Gold Top. It approached advertising agency George Patterson, who came up with a campaign emphasising what creative director Bruce Jarrett called the 'masculine' quality of the 'B' in the brand name: 'A big, big thirst needs a big, big beer'. Jarrett briefed a composer to come up with a *big* backing track – something 'rough and gutsy', like the theme tune of the hit film *The Magnificent Seven* – and hired John Meillon, an Australian actor with an equally gutsy baritone voice, to do the voice-over.

The ad was a huge success. Gold Top was soon outselling XXXX, the quintessential Queensland lager, in Brisbane. People were playing the soundtrack on jukeboxes. So, when George Patterson were hired to come up with a campaign for Victoria Bitter a couple of years later, they decided to simply use the same format, swapping one two-syllable brand for another. It was a sensation.

Prior to the TV ad, in the mid 20th century VB was advertised in newspapers and on billboards much like every other beer brand in the country: on its quality – 'The best that's brewed' – or how good it was for you – 'The most nourishing and refreshing beverage'. What George Patterson successfully tapped into, first with Bulimba Gold Top and then VB, were notions of true-blue Aussie masculinity that were coalescing in the 1960s. It was the right ad at the right time.

Depending on when you first saw the ad, you'll remember it slightly differently. The first ad in 1968 featured a succession of blokes, jackaroos, steelworkers, footy players, farmers, doing blokey things, working, sunbaking, sweating a lot, and a couple of sheilas dutifully pouring their thirsty, weary men a big cold beer. This formula continued into the 1970s and 80s in what became a long-running series of ads. Lots of construction workers, blacksmiths, woodchoppers, miners. All of them blokes. All very Anglo-Aussie. Women seldom made an appearance – sometimes not at all – and when they did appear, the gender roles were usually well defined: the husband downs a Vic while his wife does the dishes; an older man drains his pot while a young woman looks up at him admiringly.

The tone began to shift slightly in the early 1990s – one ad featured a bloke working up a sweat as *he* did the dishes, while his long-suffering wife looked on – and by the late 90s, the brand started trying to reach new consumers: one or two hardworkin' non-Anglo characters began to appear, and occasionally women were given screen time drinking cans of VB. But during the 2000s and 2010s, as the formula moved away from the original rhyming-couplet format, the campaign mostly descended into a series of ads riddled with cringeworthy misogyny, overt ockerism, crass sport tie-ins or hyper-masculinity: deeper and deeper voice-overs, lots more sweat.

The more money CUB spent on these ads, though, and the further they drifted from the original, simple concept, the less effective they seemed to be. The shift in tone coincided with other corporate changes. Sales of mainstream beers were steadily declining. Craft beer was on the rise. The company was going through a series of major takeovers. Huge amounts of loyalty had been invested in the VB brand by generations of drinkers, and people didn't like having that loyalty challenged – as the company discovered dramatically in 2009 when it dropped the alcohol content in VB to 4.6 per cent.

There was uproar. Consumers boycotted the brand. Claude Nyaguy was part of the team that worked on the modified beer, and he recalls the backlash: 'The beer tasted the same as the 4.9 version. The most highly trained sensory evaluation people in the company couldn't tell the difference. But customers were angry. "You've changed my beer," they said. "It's not like it was when I was young. Change it back!"' So they did.

In 2018, the CUB marketing team decided it was time to refresh the brand. They changed the packaging, made it look more like it did in its heyday in the 1970s and 80s. And, half a century after the first VB ad went to air, they brought back the classic formula for a new series of commercials: the old theme tune, images of people hard at work, a baritone voice-over by actor William McInnes.

But this time, a few strands of diversity and inclusion were woven into the fabric of the brand. One ad featured a rock band with a female, Asian lead singer. Another ad showed hospitality workers – male chefs, a female waiter – enjoying a few beers together after knock-off. The voice-over talked about the modern flexibility of knock-off, 'a time-honoured tradition that no longer has a time'. The message was clear: even though we're not living in a white-bread, nine-to-five world anymore, you can still rely on good old VB.

A hard-earned thirst needs a big cold beer
And the best cold beer is Vic
Victoria Bitter

The brew day is over. I hand my high-vis vest and safety goggles and earmuffs back in at the front office and walk out of the gates. It's a beautiful crisp Melbourne spring afternoon and I'm thirsty. So I walk around the corner to Moon Dog, a craft brewery and bar that opened in 2014.

When I started writing about booze in 1992, you could count the number of small, independently owned Australian craft breweries on two hands. The market was almost entirely dominated by a few very large beer companies, such as CUB. That has changed beyond recognition since people like Cam Hines and Dave Bonighton opened their pioneering Mountain Goat brewery a few blocks away from here in Richmond in the late 1990s. Since then, hundreds of craft breweries have popped up across the country, echoing and exceeding Australia's first beer boom in the 19th century. There's something lovely about the fact that one of those small breweries, Moon Dog, is literally in the shadows of CUB's Abbotsford behemoth.

My new-found respect for VB and for large-scale Australian beer production will stay with me after leaving CUB. Later that evening, on the tram, I'll look differently at the bloke carrying a sixpack of big-brand beers he picked up at a bottle shop on his way home. But this afternoon, here at Moon Dog, I walk past the bearded boys and tattooed girls and order a pint of dark, old-fashioned, deeply satisfying porter.

A flagon of McWilliam's Port:
Breaking the rules

The radio was always on at the Fitzroy drive-through bottle shop where I worked in the early 1990s. Triple J would crackle through tinny speakers on Friday afternoons as people rolled up in their cars and utes to pick up a slab or a cask on their way home from work. And one of the songs on high rotation was Archie Roach's 'Charcoal Lane'.

The title track of Roach's first album, 'Charcoal Lane' referred to a place off Gertrude Street in Collingwood, a few blocks away from the bottle shop, where Roach spent much of his heavy-drinking days in the 1970s. In the song, Roach sang about stopping at the Builders Arms Hotel in Gertrude Street to catch up with friends and family, recalling the time when this area of Melbourne was home to a big Aboriginal community and that pub was a favourite haunt. After closing up at the bottle shop, I'd often drink at the Builders.

In 'Charcoal Lane', Roach name-checks the brand of booze he used to drink: a flagon of McWilliam's Port. Almost two decades later, working on this book, I wanted to talk to Roach about the flagons, about the joy and pain that came with drinking. I wanted to talk to him, too, about how he gave up the grog in his mid-twenties, went into rehab, started writing songs. I contacted his manager, Jill Shelton, who understood my request but eventually turned it down. Archie, she told me, was in the process of writing his autobiography and it was bringing up a lot of raw, difficult memories. Instead, she suggested I go to a gig Archie was playing the following week and listen to the songs and the stories he told. That, she said, might give me some insight.

The band room at the Corner Hotel in Richmond was full of Archie Roach fans, including lots of his family and friends, some in wheelchairs or on crutches, many wearing the red, yellow and black colours of the Aboriginal flag. The atmosphere was charged. The air conditioning struggled to keep up. It was hot and muggy in the sticky-carpet room as Roach and his musicians worked through their set.

Between each song, Roach told the audience stories, giving context for the lyrics, describing moments from his life. As he led into 'F-Troop', he recalled his heavy-drinking years in Collingwood in the 1970s, hanging around with a group of Aboriginal people who'd named their drinking school after one of their favourite TV shows, meeting his brothers and sisters for the first time since they were taken from their mother years before, separated as scattered members of the stolen generations.

When Roach sang, his broken vibrato rippled out into the room. It was bittersweet, a nostalgic recollection of the happiness of dancing, singing and drinking with family, sharpened with a sense of loss, an acknowledgement of the dark side of drinking too much, the fighting, the neglect, the slow slide to sickness and death. When the song was over, there were tears.

As the applause died down and the crowd started to chatter, the musicians attended to their instruments in readiness and quietly, half off-mic, Roach said, of F-Troop, 'There's only two or three of us left now.'

He paused, then collected himself.

'Anyway, here's the next song.'

————————

In his book, *Tell Me Why*, Roach writes with particular clarity about his first drink. In his mid-teens he left his foster home in Melbourne and travelled to Sydney to track down his long-lost brothers and sisters. Soon after arriving, feeling lost and wondering where to go, he was befriended by an older Aboriginal man sitting on a park bench near Central Station. To make up for the disappointment of not finding his family, the man offered Roach a 'charge': a drink from a bottle of sweet, strong, fortified brown muscat he was keeping in his coat pocket.

'As I slugged from the bottle,' remembers Roach, 'my throat burned like bushfire.'

He managed to keep that first mouthful down and soon found the muscat was making him feel warm, and made talking easier. 'The booze seemed to be flattening everything,' he writes. 'Loss and fear, sound and light, time and space. I liked it.'

Roach quickly fell in to the pattern of drinking every day with other Aboriginal people in the pubs and in the park, often living hand-to-mouth, hustling, sleeping on the streets. It's a pattern that was repeated when he moved back to Melbourne, and then when he travelled to Adelaide, where he met Ruby Hunter, his soulmate. A lot of his drinking stories describe times during this period of being 'carefree and happy', but he writes that, with hindsight, he can also now see 'the darkness that would have touched every moment unless we numbed it with beer and port and sherry'.

We sold a lot of port and sherry at the drive-through, as well as beer: cheap flagons of potent fortified wine, bought by old men and women who smelled of yesterday's stale booze and who, like Roach's drinking school, had scraped together enough change today to buy another flagon and do it all again.

Later, I learned that Roach's lyrics in 'Charcoal Lane' echoed the songs of another Aboriginal singer from a different time and a different part of Australia, a man who also sang about flagons of fortified wine.

───────────

Dougie Young was born in south-west Queensland in the mid-1930s. He left school in his teens and worked as a stockman, moving to Wilcannia on the Darling River in north-west New South Wales in the early 1950s. This is where Young met a local woman, had kids and, after a riding accident that prevented him getting any more work as a stockman, started writing songs, inspired by the country artists he'd heard on the radio as a kid.

The songs chronicled his life and, because Young was a self-confessed 'drunk', included lots of references to drinking. In 'They Say It's a Crime', he sang about being addicted to the booze from birth. In 'Pass Him the Flagon', he sang about running out of grog and needing to hustle on the streets to buy more – lines that Archie Roach echoed thirty years later in 'Charcoal Lane'.

When Dougie Young started writing his songs about drinking, and performing them to his friends and family in Wilcannia, Aboriginal people were legally banned from buying and consuming alcohol in hotels – which is where most Australians traditionally drank – unless they had an exemption certificate, known colloquially as a 'dog-licence'. Race-based laws prohibiting the purchase and consumption of alcohol by Aboriginal people were first introduced in 1838 in New South Wales, and were brought in across all other states and territories over the ensuing century. Not that that stopped Indigenous people drinking, of course: although they weren't allowed in pubs alongside white people, they could usually buy grog on the sly, out the back. This became a lucrative market for unscrupulous publicans.

Young's songs are also full of the trouble he got into as a result of his illicit drinking – and how he had no intention of letting the law stop him and his friends doing it. In 'They Say It's a Crime', he sings about being released from the lock-up and vowing to give up for good – and then meeting a friend with a flagon of wine and going off on another bender, because it's up to him to decide to drink or not.

These early songs of Dougie Young were recorded in Wilcannia in 1964 by anthropologist Jeremy Beckett and released on an EP by a small folk label the following year. They were field recordings: you can hear his friends chuckling along in the background when their names and exploits are mentioned in the songs. You can hear dogs barking and bottles being knocked over as Young strums his guitar.

Beckett wrote that Young's songs were songs of defiance. An attempt to '[take] back the image of the anonymous, stereotypic "drunken Aborigine", making him ... once again a human being with a name, friends, and the gifts of music and laughter'. The songs were, Beckett pointed out, composed for and about the Aboriginal community on the fringes of Wilcannia, not for the white people in town. He wrote that the patterns of drinking prevalent in Young's songs showed how 'Aborigines had adopted the hard drinking of the frontier to reconstitute their shattered society, and that in defying official prohibition they were conducting a pre-political resistance'.

———————

Australia's state and territory laws banning the sale of alcohol to Aboriginal people were repealed throughout the 1960s, but the impact on Indigenous communities of a century or more of prohibition was profound.

Social anthropologist Maggie Brady argues that prohibition encouraged Aboriginal people to develop a social drinking scene of their own, segregated 'away from white man's eyes' in large groups, making it easier for drinkers to pressure family members for drink or money, leading to arguments and fights. Prohibition 'marked out Aboriginal and Islander people as different, inferior' and stigmatised their drinking, focusing the attention on getting drunk quickly. And not allowing Indigenous people to drink in hotels also excluded them from the evolution of Australia's drinking culture over time.

'Indigenous people missed the opportunity for a long-term familiarisation process,' Brady writes. 'They were denied the opportunity to experience the waves of change in patterns of consumption and attitudes to alcohol that affected the general population over the decades.'

Unfortunately, as she points out, the lifting of prohibition in the 1960s also coincided with a dramatic growth in the availability, accessibility and promotion of alcohol in broader Australian society. Six o'clock closing of pubs was finally abolished in all parts of the country in 1967, extending the hours in which people could drink. Liberalisation of liquor laws allowed single-bottle sales for home consumption and encouraged the proliferation of drive-through bottle shops. And the drinks industry developed a number of ways to make drinking easier, such as the introduction of beer and ready-to-drink cocktails in cans.

'Per capita consumption [of alcohol] increased by 20 per cent between 1969 and 1975,' writes Brady. 'Sales of sweet wine – the drink favoured by Aboriginal drinkers – grew by 40 per cent between 1970 and 1981.'

By the time Archie Roach tasted his first mouthful of sweet brown muscat in the early 1970s, Australians were drinking more than they had done since the gold-rush days of the 1850s. And two of the most important catalysts for this dramatic increase in consumption were the growing popularity of wine in flagons, followed by the introduction of the wine cask.

———————

Wine has been sold in half-gallon (2.2-litre) glass jars called flagons in Australia since the early 19th century. But in the 1950s, Melbourne-based wine company Wynns gave the large-format bottles a boost by releasing a new range of claret and chablis, port and sherry under the Wynvale label, all packaged in specially made barrel-shaped flagons. The development of the Wynvale flagon is often cited as being crucial to the popularisation of wine-drinking in this country. And for a lot of Australians, this was a positive development.

In the 1950s, for example, in Murrumbeena, then on the fringes of Melbourne suburbia, the Boyd family of artists would often embrace 'the raw essence of Australian Bohemia' at parties that 'included roasting whole sheep, Wynvale flagons and gaggles of kids [and where] Charles Blackman, Barry Humphries and other budding stars were carousing'. My mum remembers glimpsing some of this lifestyle when she lived in an apartment building in South Yarra in the mid-1960s with a bunch of other television people and actors, gathering for lunch every Sunday in someone's flat with bowls of salad and flagons of claret. Very civilised.

The democratisation of wine drinking developed further after South Australian winemaker Tom Angove patented the first design for packing a gallon of wine inside a bag inside a cardboard box in 1965. Angove's product didn't last long: the consumer had to open the box, take the bag out, snip off a corner to pour the wine, and seal the bag with a paperclip. A couple of years later, Penfolds came up with a design of its own: a bag of wine packed inside what looked like a paint tin. Again, not surprisingly, it didn't take off. In 1971, Wynns was the first wine company to perfect the cask concept by introducing a reliable tap mechanism that didn't leak, and soon other large companies such as Orlando had jumped on the bandwagon and were selling vast quantities of wine in cask.

Orlando had started selling wine in flagons in the 1960s under the Coolabah brand. The word *coolabah*, originally *gulabaa*, comes from the Gamilaraay language of northern New South Wales, and is the name for a species of eucalypt that grows in many parts of the country. The word features most famously in Banjo Paterson's 'Waltzing Matilda', and this folksy association is one of the reasons Orlando chose it as a brand name.

When Orlando started packaging its Coolabah wines in cask in 1973 the brand really took off, thanks in part to a series of television commercials with the tagline 'Where do you hide your Coolabah?', showing all the inventive ways in which happy white Australians would stash their cask to stop anyone else chugging on it: in the sand at the beach, behind a pot plant at a party. It was a campaign that actively encouraged furtive drinking.

Orlando's operations manager at the time, Perry Gunner, once explained to an interviewer why the campaign resonated so strongly with audiences:

> It was often said that with a cask of wine in the fridge, no-one actually quite knew how much you were drinking. You could go back and have a few more glasses, and instead of having to open a flagon that might oxidise before you got to drink it, here was a wine that was being preserved all the time during consumption. They even suggested that when Mum and Dad were away the children would go and help themselves to the cask of Coolabah in the fridge. So, it became omnipresent, as we used to say, in households around Australia.

The cask also became omnipresent in Aboriginal communities where, writes Brady, it became 'a stock item of the takeaway trade for home or outdoor consumption'. Fittingly, where Orlando had appropriated an Aboriginal name for their successful cask brand, it's likely that Aboriginal people gave the cask its now ubiquitous nickname, the 'goon bag'. According to the National Dictionary Centre, goon is possibly a variation of *goom*, or 'methylated spirits', derived from a south-east Queensland Aboriginal word meaning 'water' or 'alcohol'. It's a word that features in both the songs of Dougie Young (goom-and-lemonade was one of Dougie's regular tipples) and the memoirs of Archie Roach, who writes tragically about being 'pickled in goom' when his second son was born. You have to be desperately, hopelessly addicted to alcohol to resort to drinking meths: not only does it taste disgusting, it's also highly toxic.

Academic Marcia Langton says there is another reason why the wine cask replaced the flagon in Aboriginal communities: it's less harmful. Not the liquid inside but the container itself.

'The flagon is a large glass object,' she says. 'And in Alice Springs people were using them as weapons. Doctors and the Central Australian Aboriginal Congress lobbied back in the early 80s to stop the sale of port and such in flagons and the marketing of liquor in glass containers because of the terrible figures of injury and harm.'

———————

Langton has been writing for decades about the impact of alcohol on the Aboriginal population. When I meet her at the Indigenous Studies office at the University of Melbourne, she tells me she has little time for all the drinking songs.

'Yes, they're sentimental, and sure, we all love them, but they have had a harmful impact,' she says. 'This attachment among heavy Aboriginal drinkers to the mythology of alcohol, the flagons, sitting around in a drinking camp, it's actually not part of Aboriginal culture.'

Instead, she says, the songs have helped reinforce and legitimise the culture of excessive drinking, and strengthened the argument from some in the Aboriginal community that it is somehow their human right to continue to drink freely.

'There is a serious alcohol problem in Australia,' she says, 'and it has even more harmful impacts on the Aboriginal population because of the way that alcohol is marketed to areas with high Aboriginal populations by the alcohol industry. And the alcohol industry – I've got to say this very clearly to you – has opposed sensible policy reform despite [knowing about the] health consequences, in order to sell more alcohol.'

Langton and two colleagues, medical anthropologist Kristen Smith and research fellow in the Indigenous Studies Unit Shane Bawden, travelled to Kununurra in Western Australia's Kimberley region in 2016 to look at how alcohol was impacting the community. Takeaway alcohol sales are permitted in Kununurra, but there are restrictions on trading hours and the amount of alcohol a person can buy: sales of cask wines, for example, are not permitted. Those restrictions were tightened in 2017 following a report that found the rate of alcohol-related domestic assaults in the region was almost thirty times higher than in metropolitan areas elsewhere in Australia.

At the time, one of the biggest-selling brands of booze in Kununurra was Poker Face, a range of cheap wines that sold for around $6 a bottle. According to Smith, the most popular Poker Face wine was the sweet white moscato: despite the fact it was relatively low in alcohol, she said, 'it has developed an almost mythical reputation among drinkers as being an extra strong mixture of spirits and wine'.

In 2016, Elaine Johnson, who works at the Kununurra Waringarri Aboriginal Corporation's sober-up shelter, told a reporter that people who drank Poker Face acted erratically and out of character. 'Some people who drink it don't normally drink when they are out at communities, and when they come into town it makes them act like they are on some sort of heavy drugs,' she said. 'Sometimes people who drink it do things that they don't remember and it makes them violent.'

That year, Poker Face wines were singled out by Kununurra police officer Senior Sergeant Steve Principe as being a significant factor in alcohol-related harm in the community. The Shire of Wyndham-East Kimberley Council named Poker Face as a harmful product that should be banned. Community advocates in Kununurra wrote to the makers of the brand telling them about the harms of that particular drink. Poker Face was subsequently removed from shelves. But another brand quickly took its place as the wine of choice.

The companies that produce Australia's lowest-priced, highest-volume wines often also make the kind of smaller-volume, higher-priced wines that I write about in newspapers, magazines and books. I admire some of these companies for their innovation in both viticulture and winemaking and have awarded their wines medals and trophies at wine shows where I've been a judge. But I find it hard to reconcile my personal positive view of those companies with the fact that their wines are also sold in remote communities with large Aboriginal populations – despite the winemakers repeatedly being told by people in those communities how damaging their products are.

It's a critical question that can be asked of everyone involved in the manufacture, promotion and sale of booze: how do they – we – justify profiting from a product that can cause such profound harm?

I contacted one of the big wine companies to see if I could speak to them about this difficult dichotomy. The company's sales and marketing manager responded by email.

He told me that the company 'does not support the abuse of alcohol', but he did say that they had seen a 'surge in commercial wine sales [bottled wines that cost $10 or under] when cask wines were banned'. The company continued to sell wine into many remote rural areas, he said, through Metcash, a huge food and liquor distribution business.

I sent back more questions. I asked him whether the more recent alcohol restrictions in Alice Springs and Kununurra had affected the company's sales. I asked him about the plastic bottles of wine sold in these remote communities – hundreds of which have been photographed strewn across the bed of the Todd River. Does his company have a policy on working with communities around the supply of alcohol? Do they adjust how they market and distribute their wine depending on location?

'Our Australian sales are tracking well considering the recent natural disasters,' he emailed back (this was just after the 2019 Christmas bushfires). 'We bottle a few different products under PET [plastic] bottles ... We also bottle water in PET bottles which we donate to drought affected towns. Our products are offered in many different countries, we try to [do] uniform marketing but it is difficult.'

I asked if I could talk further with him about it on the phone. He didn't reply.

––––––––

Much of Australia's cheap commercial wine is made in the hot, irrigated inland Riverina region in central New South Wales. It was here, perhaps ironically, that a group of Aboriginal men established Australia's first Indigenous-owned wine business twenty years ago.

Murrin Bridge is near Lake Cargelligo on Wiradjuri land north of Griffith, about an hour and a half's drive from the Riverina region's large vineyards and wineries. It was initially set up as an Aboriginal reserve in 1949, and in the late 1990s was home to about 150 people. At this time, a group of Murrin Bridge men were studying market gardening at the local TAFE as part of the 'work for the dole' scheme when their lecturer, local vineyard owner Pat Calabria, asked if they wanted to do viticulture.

'We almost choked on our tea,' said Craig Cromelin, one of the men on the course, when he spoke to a journalist about the course in 2002. 'None of us had set foot inside a vineyard before, let alone a winery. We had no idea and we couldn't visualise it. We said, "blackfellas don't do that sort of thing.'" Other students were equally sceptical: 'Blackfellas makin' wine and growin' grapes – we drink it, but we don't make it!'

Despite the initial scepticism, the men decided to give grapes a go, and in 1998, with Pat's help and, eventually, some government assistance, planted 10 hectares of chardonnay and shiraz. By the early 2000s, when the first wines – made by another local Italian-Australian, Dom Piromalli – were about to hit the market, Craig had become a passionate advocate for the project.

I interviewed him when the wines were released, and was inspired by his vision that the wine business could provide real prospects for his community and could become a symbol of reconciliation. I remember how he dismissed criticism of the project: those who thought that because Aboriginal people had 'a problem' with alcohol, they shouldn't be encouraged to make wine – or, worse, those who said the Murrin Bridge people wouldn't be able to control themselves and would just drink everything they made.

The project attracted media interest both in Australia and internationally, but it didn't last – not because the Aboriginal participants were too interested in the product, but because they weren't interested enough. According to anthropologist Daniela Heil, who studied Murrin Bridge, by 2004 the community didn't view the vineyard as being any more important than other projects that had been initiated to encourage opportunities. And part of the reason for the lack of interest was that the market for the wine was not the people who grew the grapes, but mostly non-Indigenous tourists and consumers in the city. The community had proved that blackfellas *can* do 'that sort of thing' – grow grapes and make wine – but without any sense of cultural connection to the practice and the product, the exercise lacked meaning.

While Murrin Bridge was the first Indigenous-owned and -run wine business, historian Julie McIntyre and others have shown that it wasn't the first example of Aboriginal people being employed in Australian vineyards or wineries, rather than, as was often the case, being exploited.

In a 2016 oral history recording, Gavi Duncan, a descendant of the Darkinjung people in the Hunter Valley, said that his ancestors helped George Wyndham build his winery at Dalwood in the Hunter Valley; that the English winegrower considered the land still belonged to Aboriginal people and treated them fairly with wages; and that, as a tribute to this legacy, Duncan's middle name and his father's middle name are Wyndham.

Photographs and written accounts of Thomas Fiaschi's Tizzana vineyard on the Hawkesbury River from the late 19th and early 20th centuries show Aboriginal people from the nearby Sackville Reach reserve working alongside newly arrived young Italian migrants and descendants of the Hawkesbury's first English settlers. Fiaschi recorded in his diaries that the Aboriginal employees were more conscientious in their vineyard work than the Europeans.

Around the same time, in Victoria's Yarra Valley, Swiss-Australian winegrower George de Pury employed people from the neighbouring Coranderrk Aboriginal station to work in his Yeringberg vineyards and winery. According to his farm diary, in 1901 he paid a group from Coranderrk to pick 'red hermitage' (shiraz) grapes, and the following year he took on a 'black boy' to do post-vintage work in both the vineyard and cellar. This could be the same young Aboriginal man who appears in two group photographs taken around the time, one at Coranderrk and one at Yeringberg.

Long before they were employed to work on the vineyard, the community at Coranderrk had a reputation for growing some of the finest hops in the country. The station had been established on land near present-day Healesville in 1863, and hops were first planted in 1872. With the encouragement of their sympathetic and collaborative manager, Scotsman John Green, the forty or so Aboriginal workers at Coranderrk soon expanded the plantings to 8 hectares, with the hops from the farm fetching record high prices and winning awards at agricultural exhibitions. Indeed, the success of the hop-growing is thought to be one of the reasons why disgruntled local farmers and powerful allies a couple of years later forced Green's resignation and pushed to close down the station: they weren't prepared to have such a blatant example of Aboriginal self-determination flourishing in their midst.

At the same time as they were growing hops for beer and harvesting grapes for wine, of course, the people of Coranderrk were legally prohibited from drinking alcohol. Many had signed the temperance pledge to 'abstain from intoxicating liquors'. But that didn't stop William Barak, Wurundjeri Elder and *ngurungaeta* or 'head man' of the community, forming a friendly and respectful relationship with the de Pury family of winegrowers at Yeringberg.

Swiss émigrés Baron Frédéric Guillaume de Pury and his brother Samuel had arrived in the Yarra Valley in the 1850s, and soon established vineyards – Samuel at Cooring Yering in 1860, the baron at Yeringberg in 1863. The young settlers met Barak around this time: the baron is mentioned as one of 'a large number of white friends' who attended Barak's wedding at Coranderrk in 1865.

Barak became a frequent visitor to Yeringberg: there are many photographs of him there, both in traditional dress of possum-skin cloak, holding a boomerang, and in a formal European white suit, holding a fob watch. In the 1880s, he took the baron's teenage sons, George and Victor, out into the bush, teaching them his culture. Victor, a budding artist, drew pictures of what he saw on these trips, of kangaroo hunting and corroboree. And in 1899 he painted a haunting, melancholy, intimate portrait of Barak that still hangs in the de Pury house today.

In a sense, that portrait was Victor's response, in oils, to a picture that Barak had drawn in charcoal and ochre the year before.

Barak was one of the most important Aboriginal artists of the 19th century. All of his extant works depict scenes from traditional life: ceremony, corroboree, hunting – all except this one. This picture was different. It was of Samuel de Pury's vineyard: among the manna gums and sweeping hills is a house, a fence and neat straight rows of grapevines. And along the bottom, dictated by the artist, an inscription to Barak's old friend Samuel:

> *Native Name Gooring Nuring*
> *The English name is Bald Hill*
> *this is all your Vineyard and trees there*
> *all belong to you there*
> *your House alongside the vineyard where you stop*
> *this is the picture of it, what you see*
> *now I send you this paper*
> *I still remember you all the time*
> *not forgetting yous at all*
> *and your Uncle*
> *I am getting very old now*
> *I can't walk about now much*
> *William Barrak*

In 2015, Allan Wandin, Barak's great-great-nephew, read out these words in front of a large audience in the lecture theatre at the State Library of Victoria. Barak's painting of Cooring Yering vineyard was projected onto the screen behind him. I had invited Allan and other members of both the Wandin and de Pury families who still live in the Yarra Valley to participate in a talk I organised as part of my creative fellowship at the library, researching the story of the friendship between their ancestors. Sixteen-year-old Sam de Pury also read an extract from an essay his great-great-uncle George had written in the 1880s, at around the same age Sam was now, describing a trip to Coranderrk: 'We soon arrived at the house of an Elder called Bérak ... one of our good friends. I often went hunting with him for two or three days in a row.'

Before the talk, I sat down at Coranderrk with Allan and showed him the Barak painting of Samuel's vineyard. He immediately understood what Barak was trying to say: it was and is Wurundjeri culture to welcome visitors to their country – why not these Swiss people, too? There was probably a strategic element to the relationship: Barak clearly had a strong connection to the country where the de Purys planted their vineyards, and making friends with the family ensured his continued access to that country. But Allan felt strongly that the intimacy encoded in the inscription on the Samuel de Pury vineyard picture, and the way that Victor de Pury painted Barak's portrait, both suggested a deeper, far more affectionate relationship than one of mere convenience or strategy.

'It's a story about their friendship, really,' said Allan. 'They must have been good friends. They must have been really close. The record's there. That is the record. That transcribes what took place: we ate together, we drank together, that's our friendship. That tells it right there. Starting point to finishing point.'

After the talk at the State Library, we all walked up to Gertrude Street and had dinner at a restaurant that specialises in cooking with Indigenous ingredients and runs a social enterprise program training young Aboriginal people. The restaurant is called Charcoal Lane, and it's located in the same building that housed the Aboriginal Health Service back in the 1970s, when F-Troop drank in the park across the road.

Before we sat down for dinner, we gathered in the courtyard and tapped a keg of beer produced specially for the evening. A couple of days before, I'd met Wurundjeri Elder Aunty Joy Murphy Wandin, Allan's older sister, at a brewery in Healesville and she'd helped the brewers infuse the keg with freshly picked hops, harvested from a nearby backyard that was once part of Coranderrk. It was the first time she'd handled hops, smelled the flowers' pungent aroma, felt the stickiness of the bitter oils on her fingers from the plant her ancestors grew so successfully.

Aunty Joy doesn't drink. She says she's seen a lot of the harm that alcohol has done to her community, but that's not the only reason. She just can't 'get' the taste: perhaps, she says, all she needs is to try the right wine. But she's proud of the hop-growing at Coranderrk.

'It was something that made history,' she says. 'The land, the terroir provided for this plant that had come from another country, and nurtured it. So it was obviously the right place. And of course if you know the Yarra Valley today, there are any number of wineries that are doing well. So there is something in the soil that says: this land is here for everyone, and equally provides for all who live on it, so long as that land is cared for and nurtured, and treated with respect.'

At Charcoal Lane, Allan Wandin did the honours, hammering a tap into the end of the 40-litre keg and pouring himself a pot of the Healesville hop-infused beer. He poured more for everyone and then we sat down to a dinner featuring lamb and wine from Yeringberg, the tables festooned with garlands of intertwined hops and grapes. And as we ate and drank, Allan's daughter Brooke Wandin talked about plans to rejuvenate Coranderrk, now under Aboriginal ownership, to bring back farming on the property, to perhaps plant hops again to sell to the local brewers.

———————

Some of the best advice I've ever received about drinking came from an Aboriginal man.

Uncle Lewis Yerloburka O'Brien is an Elder of the Kaurna people in Adelaide. Born in 1930 at Point Pearce mission on the Yorke Peninsula, he has worked since the 1960s teaching Aboriginal languages and culture. Before the dinner at Charcoal Lane restaurant I visited him in his office at the University of South Australia to ask his thoughts on wine education in an Aboriginal context. A few weeks before, I had hosted a wine-tasting session for the trainees at Charcoal Lane; they were being taught to become hospitality professionals, and the service of alcohol is an integral part of Australia's restaurant industry so it was valid to integrate wine into the teaching program.

I was caught off-guard pretty much as soon as I started.

I opened a bottle of moscato and poured some into glasses for each of the trainees to try. I thought I'd start with a really fragrant grape, the same variety that got me into wine all those years ago, full of easy-to-appreciate aromas. And as soon as they took a sniff, it looked as though some of the trainees were indeed excited by the smell.

'It reminds me of my nana,' said one girl.

'Oh, that's good,' I said. 'You mean it smells like flowers? Like your nana's garden?'

'Nah,' she said. 'It smells like the goon my nana drinks.'

Uncle Lewis chuckled when I told him this story.

'I drink alcohol,' he said. 'But I know the rules. I taught myself the rules. By watching. I grew up with Italians. My mother married an Italian. They used to make wine in the backyard, used to make tomato sauces, used to collect olives. I got a head start living with them. I'd see them eating food, and they're drinking, and you're thinking, that makes sense. You must always eat when you drink. That's the basic rule.'

The second rule, said Uncle Lewis, is understanding that bodies like habits, and habits aren't good for you, so you must have a day off. Or two days, three days, it doesn't matter, but you've got to break it up somewhere. And the third rule: drink water – even if it means putting water in the wine, so you're only having half a drink.

'You'd work it by observation,' he said, describing how he learned the rules. 'You'd see the drunks on the street, you'd watch them and you'd suddenly think, they're getting crook and you'd think, they don't eat, and you've got the equation, and you'd work it out, it's there in front of you: the drunks on the street, why are they in strife? They're drinking as much as the Italians, but they're not doing it *by the rules.*'

I've thought about this a lot. Thought about what my own rules for drinking are. Who I learned them from. Who I'm teaching them to. And how often I break them. They're simple rules that reflect my own hardly usual circumstances, writing about booze. First: don't drink all the free tasting samples that come flooding through the front door every day (in other words, you don't have to drink it just because it's there). Second: don't drink on your own. Third: always have food around when you're drinking. Fourth: have time off the booze every so often.

As I say, I break these rules all the time because, to be frank, I like drinking too much. But when I stick to them, I'm happier, my mind is clearer, and I know I'm doing my body less damage. I know Uncle Lewis is right.

'You should write a rule book, mate,' he told me. 'People need to know these things. It's like what Shakespeare says: wine mucks up your performance if you have too much. It's about training and knowledge and sharing stories. That's how our people taught for centuries. You tell people stories and you tell them the rules, that's how people make sense of it. You don't tell people what to do. You say, here are some good rules to look at.'

Japanese Slipper

Melbourne, 1984

'Nobody has asked me about this before,' says Jean Paul Bourguignon. 'You are the first one. Well, no, my son has asked me. He always wants to know about it. But you are the first one outside the family.'

Jean Paul is now in his mid-sixties. Despite first arriving in Australia from Paris over four decades ago, he still has a rich French accent. These days he lives in the Blue Mountains near Sydney and runs a babywear company with his partner. But in the mid-1980s, when he was a young, enthusiastic bartender in Melbourne, he invented a drink that would go on to become the only cocktail from Australia to be included in the International Bartenders Association handbook. It was a gaudy green mash-up of cultural influences called the Japanese Slipper.

The place where Jean Paul created the cocktail, Mietta's Restaurant and Bar, was appropriately cosmopolitan. Constructed in Alfred Place in the heart of the city in 1886, the ornate building functioned as a hub for Melbourne's German community before becoming the Naval and Military Club and then housing a series of businesses until Mietta O'Donnell, from a well-known family of Italian-Australian restaurateurs, and her partner, Tony Knox, took it over in the early 1980s.

Jean Paul had worked at Mietta's first restaurant in Fitzroy briefly in the mid-1970s, when he was on holiday in Australia and learning English. Returning to Paris, he started training to become a bartender. He was inspired by the traditions of Harry's New York Bar, where the White Lady cocktail had been devised fifty years before.

'Because I knew Mietta and Tony, when they were opening up a new place in Alfred Place they proposed to me to come to Australia to set up the lunch place and bar downstairs,' says Jean Paul. 'In the 1980s Australia was a very different place. It was very, very strange. All the pubs were enclosed, you didn't have any people drinking outside, on a terrace. It was just beer consumption. When I went to an international hotel like the Hilton, the barman wouldn't even know what Campari was. I never saw that before, my god.'

Mietta was attempting to introduce a new kind of sophisticated hospitality to Melbourne with her Alfred Place establishment, says Jean Paul. She obtained a licence allowing drinks to be served until 1 am. The bar became a magnet for actors, artists, musicians. A salon. And then, one day in the bar, the young Frenchman dreamed up a drink that would capture the spirit of the decade.

'I had to write the cocktail list,' says Jean Paul. 'I invented a lot of cocktails while I was there, but only one survived. I was buying the liquor for the bar, and one day I received a sample bottle of Midori from Suntory. It was on the desk and I said, what can I do with that? I also had a bottle of Cointreau on the desk and I thought: I am French, I'm going to mix both of them. Then I put some lemon juice in, to cut the sweetness. My English was not too good when I arrived. I was reading books to learn. I had just learned a new word, "slipper", and Midori was

Japanese, so I thought: let's call it Japanese Slipper. I put it on the list and it went well. It went well because it was sweet. Remember that all the drinks were sweet at that time. Even the most popular wines were sweet.'

Something about the taste of the cocktail, the dynamic setting of its creation, the melding of cultures, the bright-green colour – made even more lurid by the optional garnish of a maraschino cherry – resonated with a generation of Australian drinkers. The drink adorns the cover of both the 1994 and 1999 editions of *The Australian Bartender's Guide to Cocktails*, the 'Official Manual of the Australian Bartenders Guild', with the authors describing Jean Paul's creation as 'one of the most popular cocktails in Australia'.

Twenty years later, hardly anyone drinks Japanese Slippers. If they do, it's with a kind of nostalgic irony. In fact, the Japanese Slipper is considered so passé that it's no longer on the International Bartenders Association list of official cocktails. Which is a shame, because it's a good drink.

I asked Jean Paul for his recipe for the Japanese Slipper. As per *The Australian Bartender's Guide*, he recommended equal parts, 30 millilitres each, of Midori, Cointreau and lemon juice – although, he said, 'you can go more in lemon if you want' – shaken and strained into a chilled martini glass. I followed his instructions and made one for Sophie, who remembers drinking Japanese Slippers in the late 1980s at Mietta's because it was one of the only European-style bars open in the city at the time. As soon as she took a sip, she smiled.

'Oh yes,' she said. 'That's it. That takes me straight back.'

Kanga Rouge:
Vineyard of the Empire

Oz Clarke places a forty-year-old bottle of Coonawarra shiraz gently on the table. He's been waiting a long time to open this. As he picks up his corkscrew, he sees my smartphone.

'Do you want to video this?' he says.

Of course I do. I've travelled all the way to Putney in South London, to the house of one of the world's most famous wine writers, for this moment, to share his last remaining bottle of 1978 Kanga Rouge, a serious wine with a silly name made at a time when Australia's reputation in the rest of the world was at an all-time low. It's probably the last remaining bottle in the world. I absolutely want to document it for posterity – or at the very least post it as an Instagram story. I pick up my phone, open the camera app, tap record and Oz slips immediately into performance mode.

'This', he says, grabbing the corkscrew and looking straight into the phone's tiny lens, 'is a moment that has got triumph and disaster writ large upon it in pretty much equal measure ...'

And with that, the decades disappear.

It's the late 1980s. I'm living in a share house in Brighton in the UK with a bunch of art students and dreadlocked anarchists. Being twenty-year-olds living in a share house, we spend a lot of time watching TV. And because I'm beginning to nurture an interest in wine – the taste of that formative Brown Brothers late-picked muscat still lingering on my lips – one of the programs that appeals to me more than to my housemates is *Food and Drink* on BBC2.

Food and Drink was a television phenomenon in the 1980s and early 1990s. Millions of viewers tuned in each week. The show had two wine presenters, both bursting with enthusiasm for the bottles they tasted and recommended: a posh-sounding curly-haired woman called Jilly Goolden, and a mischievous balding bloke called Oz Clarke. The pair were becoming household names thanks to the often colourful, sometimes ridiculous way they described wine. Many people dismissed the flowery language as an entertaining load of old twaddle. But I was fascinated by it. I was inspired by the way wine could evoke such outbursts of emotion.

As well as appearing on TV, Oz wrote about wine for newspapers and published an annual wine guide. I bought the 1989 edition when I got my first job at a high street wine shop, and it became a bible for me. (I still have it, dog-eared, well-thumbed.) I loved the way Oz wrote: conversational but comprehensive, entertaining but educational. I consulted his guide to help me buy wines, and when I started keeping a notebook, writing descriptions of the wines I was tasting and drinking, consciously or not I emulated Oz's style. In many ways, I still do.

A couple of years later, in 1992, I worked on the International Wine Challenge, a huge competition, in London – opening boxes, cleaning glasses, emptying spit buckets – and I met many of the UK wine writers, including Oz, all of whom appeared to be having a great time doing what they did. It was an experience that encouraged me to start writing about wine when I moved to Australia.

And now, almost three decades later, here I am watching a seventy-year-old Oz Clarke on my phone screen as he slowly, gently eases the cork from his dear, darling, much-loved last bottle of Kanga Rouge.

'Oh, I can't believe it's coming out,' he says, building up the tension for the camera. 'I'm sort of wondering, how much further can I dare go? I think it might be time to give it a pull.'

The cork comes out in one piece and Oz smiles proudly.

'Okay, what colour is it going to be?' he says as he reaches for a couple of glasses and begins to pour.

The wrong colour, unfortunately. The wine is a tragic muddy brown, a clear sign of oxidation. Oz groans and laughs through gritted teeth.

'Ah, it's a *sort* of colour,' he says, searching for the right lines as he pours. 'It's a colour *after a fashion*. The first glass is about as clear as … a bowl of shaving cream. The second glass is about as clear as … the Sargasso Sea at breeding time.'

He brings one of the wineglasses up to his nose and inhales deeply. The clenched smile becomes a grimace as the dreadful oxidised aromas claw at his nostrils. The wine's fucked.

'Ah, ah, see,' he says, smiling painfully into the lens. 'They don't make sherry like this anymore.'

Aaand – cut!

In the UK in the 1970s, when this bottle of Kanga Rouge was made, Australian wine was a joke. Literally. Only a few thousand litres of wine dribbled into England each year from down under – a fraction of the millions of litres flooding in from across the Channel from France, Italy, Portugal and Spain. A few fine Australian bottles made their way onto dusty, ignored shelves in Harrods and stuffy wine shops, but most arrived in the form of gimmicky brands like Oz's old bottle of Kanga Rouge, and Wallaby White and Bondi Bleach, or cheap, sweet fortified wines sold on tap in glum pubs up north. Monty Python's famous 'Australian Table Wines' sketch from 1972 was less satire and more reportage: when Eric Idle intoned, in his most laconic Aussie accent, 'Chateau Chunder ... is ... specially grown for those keen on regurgitation: a fine wine which really opens up the sluices at both ends', it probably reminded many in his audience of a real brand called Chateau Downunda, sold in UK off-licences in the 1960s.

It hadn't always been like this. In the second half of the 19th century, Australia was on its way to becoming the pre-eminent wine supplier to the British Empire.

In 1886, Yarra Valley vigneron Hubert de Castella wrote a book called *John Bull's Vineyard*, designed as an extended promotional pamphlet accompanying the Australian wine entries at that year's Colonial and Indian Exhibition. 'England', wrote de Castella, 'must become a large consumer [of Australian wine]. The federation of the British possessions, to-day in the hearts of so many Englishmen ... gives a special interest to Australian viticulture. Is it not in view of the closer bonds that may unite the English race that the products of the whole Empire are summoned to-day to London?'

De Castella's dream was for Australia to supply fine table wines to the Mother Country – wines like the elegant cabernet he produced at St Hubert's. That's not what happened, though. The style of wine the English preferred was 'Australian burgundy': full-bodied, strong red wine made from shiraz and grenache in warm regions such as McLaren Vale and Rutherglen. According to historian David Dunstan, these wines were often described as 'ferruginous', a term that had been coined by McLaren Vale vigneron Thomas Hardy in reference to the red, ironstone-rich soils of the region. 'As a consequence,' writes Dunstan, 'naturally rich Australian wines came to be recommended as suitable for people of anaemic disposition, invalids and elderly folk.'

One of the most important exporters was the Australian Wine Company, established in 1862 by Patrick Auld of Auldana winery on the outskirts of Adelaide, in partnership with a former customs officer in Britain. The company was modelled very much on the traditional wine shippers of the period, run by ruddy-faced gentlemen in between drinks at their club: a letter to a London newspaper of the period reports that 'Mr Auld has established himself at the back of the Mansion House, in a nice little cellar'. An entrepreneurial Australian ensconced in the heart of the Empire.

Like many of its competitors, the Australian Wine Company employed native animals in its marketing, registering the Emu brand for its wines in 1883; Hans Irvine of Great Western Vineyard in Victoria advertised his wines alongside a painting of a kangaroo.

As the 19th century flowed into the 20th, shipments of Australian wine – mostly ferruginous 'tonic' burgundy with a marsupial or two on the label – grew steadily, only dipping with the onset of World War I. And then everything changed. The Australian Government introduced the soldier settlement scheme, encouraging returned servicemen to take up blocks of land in the inland irrigation districts, where they planted vineyards. Much of this new crop of grapes found its way into the fortified wines – ports and sherries – that were increasingly popular in Australia at the time. Then, in 1924, to stimulate the export of these styles, the government introduced an export bounty on shipments of fortified wine. And the following year, the British Government brought in a policy of Imperial Preference – lower duty on wines from countries in the Empire. As a result, exports to England grew at a staggering rate: Australia shipped an extraordinary 19 million litres of now mostly fortified wine to the UK in 1927, up from less than 2 million litres before the war. By the mid-1930s, Britain was importing more wine from Australia than from any other country except Portugal, historically England's primary supplier – a remarkable cultural upset.

The tsunami of wine that crashed onto Britain's shores was sold less on what it tasted like and more on how 'good' it was for you. A promotional film from the 1930s, aptly named *The Vineyard of the Empire*, depicted vintage scenes at the Seppeltsfield winery in South Australia's Barossa Valley: 'To stand on the fringe of a vineyard such as this', says the narrator in that heartfelt, clipped Australian/British tone of the era, 'is to appreciate two vital characteristics that contribute towards the efficacy of Australian wines: warm sunshine and dazzling light. That subtle alchemist, the vine, performs a miracle of storing these health-giving properties in liquid form so that the less fortunate residents of colder climes may enjoy the benefits of bottled sunshine.'

Crucially, too, this solid trade to the UK kept many vineyards in South Australia viable throughout the Depression years of the 1930s, meaning that winemakers today are able to harvest grapes from vines that are now, in some cases, well over a century old. Imperial Preference in the 1920s is partly responsible for our modern preference for old-vine shiraz and grenache.

It all came crashing down during and after World War II. Exports dwindled to a quarter of pre-war levels, picked up a little into the 1950s, but then fell to less than a million litres a year in the late 1960s and half that again in the 70s. Some of the only drinkers keeping the Australian wine flame alive in the UK at this time were found in dark, wood-panelled pubs in the north of the country, such as the Yates's chain of so-called 'wine lodges' found in places like Blackpool and Leeds and Oldham.

A newspaper report from 1977 paints a grim picture of these lodges. '[They] have acquired a distinctly dismal reputation,' says the reporter, 'as if drinking [at] Yates's was only a hiccup away from drinking meths.'

Yates's had been selling Australian fortified wine for decades, most of it flagons of cream sherry and a 'sweet white' that the company sold on tap, mixed with brandy, as a proprietary drink known as 'The Blob': 'Just round the corner from the Liverpool lodge,' writes the reporter, 'there's a police station known as the billiard hall because you're *in off the white* – Yates's Australian white wine, which is said to be regarded as a panacea by some and by others as "lunatic soup".'

Lunatic soup. Chateau Chunder. Bondi Bleach. That's what most Poms thought of Australian wine – if they thought about it at all – when Oz Clarke made his first trip down under, in 1975. Oz was then a young up-and-coming English actor who had discovered wine as a student at Oxford; he'd led the university's competitive wine-tasting team; he'd even conducted a live blind tasting on television. But he had no idea what was awaiting him when he arrived in Melbourne as a minor cast member of the Royal Shakespeare Company's Australian tour of *Hedda Gabler*.

In the mid-1970s Australia was in the grip of a domestic wine boom, certainly as far as quality was concerned. As David Dunstan

has observed, the collapse of Australian wine exports to the UK
after World War II had had an unexpectedly positive effect on wine
consumption back home. 'Britain's loss was Australia's gain,' he
writes. 'Good red table wine ... that might have gone to the UK in
the 1950s and 1960s became plentiful and inexpensive in Australia
and helped lay the foundations for the great Australian enthusiasm
for wine that was already building.'

This was the enthusiastic environment that Oz discovered in
Melbourne in the mid-1970s.

'I was just a young squit in the theatre,' he says. 'I was there
with big stars, Patrick Stewart, Tim West, Glenda Jackson. Because
they knew I was interested in wine, I'd be sent off after rehearsals
in St Kilda to buy a few bottles. I'd come back with a bag full of
riesling and hermitage and chablis, you know, a dollar a bottle.
And we'd sit there, drinking these wonderful wines that tasted like
bottled sunshine.'

Then came an unforgettable tasting on a nudist beach. A couple
of years before his Australian trip, Oz had met a young Australian
winemaker, Andrew Pirie, working in the vineyards during vintage
in Bordeaux. So when the RSC tour got to Sydney, Oz rang him.
'I said, these two girls I've met want to go on a picnic, would you like
to come? And Andrew said, yeah, I'll bring the wine.'

When they arrived at the beach, says Oz, the two girls
immediately stripped off and ran into the sea, leaving the actor and
the winemaker no choice but to follow suit, with Pirie first burying
the half-dozen bottles he'd brought with him in the sand to keep
them out of the sun.

'After we'd been frolicking in the briny for about an hour,' says
Oz, 'we came out and of course all these bottles were lovely and
cool in the sand. So Andrew started bringing them out: there was a

1955 Grange, a Maurice O'Shea Hunter red [classic wines now worth thousands of dollars a bottle]. A couple of others like that. And we just pulled the corks out. Bollock naked, rolling around, plastic cups, just waving the flies out of them, with salt all over our lips, we poured and drank our way through Grange and Maurice O'Shea, all naked and happy and drunk.'

Oz was hooked. His crash-immersion in Australian wine and lifestyle was a revelation: fun, fruity flavours at the cheaper end of the spectrum and extraordinary, age-worthy reds at the other.

'And then I went back to England and I said, "There's a whole new world of wine out there!" But nobody was listening. Nobody cared. You struggled to find a single bottle of Australian wine in this country back then. At that time, there was virtually nothing. There was the Australian Wine Centre, next to a sex shop in Soho, and that was about it. But I kept remembering those flavours.'

He soon started appearing in West End musicals. *Sweeney Todd*, *Evita*. Got a reputation as 'the actor who knew about wine'. Began writing about wine for the *Sunday Express*. And in 1983 he went on a wine-drenched press trip to Australia, meeting legends of the industry such as Max Lake and Len Evans, opening more classic old bottles. When he got back to the UK, Oz was more enthusiastic and determined than ever to spread the word.

'I just said, "Australia – Australia! This! This!" Australia under-stands something about life that we've completely forgotten about in this country – if we ever knew.'

This time, he wasn't alone. A handful of Australian producers had started chipping away at the export market in the late 70s and early 80s: Brown Brothers with wines like the golden late-harvest muscat that introduced me to wine as a teenager; Rosemount with its groundbreaking 'diamond label' chardonnay; Orlando with a new label called Jacob's Creek that would quickly become the number-one brand in the UK. And a visionary Manchester-born Australian Trade Commission employee named Hazel Murphy had written a very positive, very influential report in 1982 about the potential for wine in the UK.

'[I'd been] given a range of products that I had to look after to help the exporters,' Murphy told a documentary filmmaker in 2012. 'I'd worked with steaming coal, coking coal, cardboard mousetraps, ugg boots, and they asked me if I'd look after wine as well. I had no background in wine, no knowledge about wine – I didn't know anybody who drank wine at all. They used to say "Chateau Chunder from Down Under", so we were climbing a pretty big mountain.'

Murphy set about changing the way Australia promoted its wines. First, she organised tastings where rough-diamond Australian winemakers would pour their latest vintages for members of the general public: 'The first year we did it,' she said, 'we probably did about 20,000 consumers at various events.' This seems like common sense to us now, surrounded as we are by a constant barrage of weekend wine festivals and pop-up tastings. But in 1980s Britain it was revolutionary: the entrenched traditional wine countries, the French and Spanish and Italians, simply didn't feel they needed to pour their wines for the public.

In 1985, Murphy organised a two-week visit to Australia by a group of British masters of wine. At the time, only 117 people around the world had passed the rigorous exams required to join the Institute of Masters of Wine, and thirty-five of those travelled down under that year, most for the first time. The response was overwhelmingly positive. Melbourne wine merchant Roy Moorfield told *The Age* that the MWs he met on their tour were 'staggered – flabbergasted – at the quality and diversity of the wines we are producing here'.

And because most of the MWs were buyers for UK wine shops and off-licence chains, that goodwill translated directly to export orders.

The increasing availability of Australian wines in UK super-markets was a blessing for Oz Clarke and Jilly Goolden and their weekly segment on BBC's *Food and Drink*. 'We were determined to democratise wine,' says Oz. 'It sounds so self-important now, but we were being watched by 9 million people a week. We had to find cheap wine that was delicious. Ripe, fresh, juicy. And I just said, I know where we're going to get it because I've been there twice. We've got to get it from Australia.'

Not just Australia, but also southern France and Eastern Europe and other parts of the globe where a new generation of young Australian wine-school graduates were being employed by UK wine merchants and supermarkets to bring a little of their up-to-date Aussie know-how to the local, old-fashioned, technologically 'backward' wineries. On one hand, these 'Flying Winemakers', as they were dubbed, imposed a kind of reverse oenological colonialism on the Old World, producing chardonnay in Romania in the image of chardonnay from the Riverland, but they also certainly helped 'democratise wine', and took some Old World philosophy back with them that would help change the nature of Australia's wine in years to come.

The value of the Australian dollar plunged in 1986, making the prices of Australian wine even more attractive to UK wine buyers. And throughout the decade, British television screens filled up with images of Australia's easygoing, sun-drenched culture, from the soap operas *Neighbours* and *Home and Away* to the ocker comedy of Paul Hogan to the pomp of the bicentennial celebrations in 1988, all reinforcing deep colonial links to the Mother Country. Exports of Australian wine to Britain doubled between 1985 and

1986 to more than a million litres. By the end of the decade this annual figure had leapt to 10 million litres worth $40 million, and the figures were doubling each year. For a generation of British drinkers, developing a taste for Australian wine – and wines made elsewhere around the world by Australians – became a new form of imperial preference.

'You know, we were going through a pretty dull time in Britain in the 80s,' says Oz. 'Mrs Thatcher's revolution was hard at work. Australia was this fantastic sunbeam of delight that just shone every time you opened a bottle of wine. It made a lot of dull, unhappy people happy.'

———————

Like Oz, I first tasted Penfolds Grange on a bright-blue Sydney day. Not on a nudist beach, though: my first sip was at a posh restaurant overlooking Circular Quay, in 1990. I'd been in Australia for a couple of weeks on a family holiday, and my senses were buzzing. The sun glittered on the water, the tablecloths were starchy stiff, the food served on big white plates. And the deep-purple wine flooded my mouth with pleasure.

Our first stop in Australia had been Adelaide, where a family friend took us on a tour of some of South Australia's best cellar doors. I was staggered – flabbergasted – by the experience. I can still taste the extraordinary essence of blackcurrant I found in the first cabernet I tried at the first winery we visited, almost obscene in its voluptuous concentration. I can still feel the thirst build at the back of my throat to try more new wines – a thirst I've been trying to quench ever since. For this 22-year-old wine newbie, used to knocking back cheap European plonk, it felt like someone had opened a door to another, far more delicious and rewarding world and invited me in. When I got to Sydney and was taken out to lunch by a wealthy relative who'd taken pity on the poor art student, and the waiter poured me a glass of Grange, I felt as though I'd reached the inner sanctum of that fabulous new world.

Unlike Oz, though, when I returned to the UK from this holiday in 1990, I didn't need to convince anyone that Australia was capable of making good wine. By that point, supermarket shelves were groaning with bottles of well-priced chardonnay and shiraz and cabernet. Nobody remembered Chateau Chunder anymore.

I found a job in a wine shop that specialised in Australian wine: when I told the manager at my interview that I'd just come back from a trip to the Barossa and Clare valleys, he asked me when I could start. I began drinking as many different wines as I could afford. Encouraged by the shop manager, David, who became a lifelong friend and has never stopped opening amazing bottles to inspire me, I became obsessed. I turned into a wine junkie. But a wine junkie on a shop assistant's budget.

One day, longingly browsing the expensive shelves at a rival wine shop, I happened to glance down and catch sight of a distinctive red capsule poking out from the shadows. There, lying dusty and unloved, was a bottle of 1980 Grange – with a price tag of twenty quid, half what we were charging for the latest vintage.

I went through the routine familiar to all shoppers who come across a bargain that looks too good to be true. First the eye-rubbing double take: perhaps I had misread the price tag. Then the furtive look: is someone having me on? Is this a prank? Then the nonchalant walk to the counter with your find, plonking the bottle down as though you buy Grange on a daily basis. And finally, the barely suppressed little yelp of victory when you leave the shop having just forked out a mere £20 for *a whole bottle of your very own ten-year-old Grange*!

My interest in Australian wine deepened when I worked at the 1992 International Wine Challenge in London, where Coonawarra cabernet triumphed over claret, and Hunter shiraz scored higher than Rhône Valley syrah. I blagged a ticket to a tasting of Penfolds Grange at Vintners' Hall in the city, in all its brown-panelled glory, where winemaker John Duval opened vintages going back to the 1960s. And I attended the huge Wine Trade Fair at Olympia exhibition centre and met members of the UK trade who'd just returned from another of Hazel Murphy's two-week fact-finding tours to Australia – dubbed the Wine Flight of a Lifetime – all of them still buzzing with energy and enthusiasm for what they'd seen.

'What Hazel did was fantastic,' says Oz. 'The restaurateurs and wine buyers that she took out would come back to the UK with their eyes just out on stalks at how wonderful the place was, and therefore every single time anyone came into any of their establishments they'd say, you've got to try this Australian stuff.'

When I moved to Australia later that year and started writing about wine, I got to experience the export boom up close. I saw hundreds of hectares of new vineyards being planted to satisfy booming demand. Saw the gleaming stainless-steel tanks and presses and refrigeration equipment being installed at wineries keen to expand production. As well as writing for *The Age*, I had a short-lived column in, of all things, the *Daily Commercial News*, a paper aimed at the shipping industry, writing about the latest export figures, interviewing people like Hazel Murphy, writing about the Flying Winemakers.

This is why, in 1996, I found myself sitting in a conference hall at the huge Wine Australia showcase exhibition at Darling Harbour in Sydney along with hundreds of winemakers in moleskins and marketing types in business suits, listening to chairman Len Evans announce the industry's Strategy 2025 vision: to achieve $4.5 billion in annual sales by the year 2025 and become 'the world's most influential and profitable supplier of branded wines, pioneering wine as a universal first choice lifestyle beverage'.

The boldness of the vision and the corporate-speak struck a chord. The export boom was well and truly on after that, reaching a peak in 2007 when 290 million litres of Australian wine were shipped to the UK. But by this time the value of shipments had started to fall. Where in the early 1990s the average price per litre of wine when it left the winery in Australia had been over $4, by the end of the 2000s it had dropped to around $2.50. The slide continued over the next decade: annual volumes to the UK have held relatively steady around the 250 million litre mark, but value per litre has dropped to around $1.50 and stubbornly remains there.

What these statistics show is that a whole generation of modern British drinkers has grown up seeing Australian wines as mostly inhabiting the cheap-and-cheerful end of the supermarket spectrum: wines shipped in bulk and bottled in market, bought less on quality and more on price. This is not accidental. It's exactly what some of the more powerful companies in the Australian industry wanted to happen back at the height of the boom.

In 2003 I interviewed Stephen Millar, then CEO of BRL Hardy (as it was known then, Accolade as it is today, owners of the Hardys brand), who was quite open in his ambition to make his company, and Australian wine in general, the Coca-Cola of the wine world. A couple of years later, at a major marketing conference in Adelaide, Hardys managing director David Woods told the audience that the future of Australian wine was in this 'popular premium segment' – that large FMCG ('fast-moving consumer goods') brands were 'as important to the wine industry as the wheel and combustion engine are to the motor vehicle industry'. Woods insisted that the key to ongoing success was to 'maintain a sense of fun, life and laughter', as exemplified by the new Hardys brand Four Emus – a response to the enormous success of the Casella family's Yellow Tail brand in the USA, featuring a vaguely Aboriginal design of a wallaby on the label. Yet more cheap wine marketed using Australian fauna.

Oz Clarke's old mate Andrew Pirie presented the opposing view at the conference, calling for Australia to unequivocally indulge in more aspirational marketing and head upmarket by producing more 'icon wines' like Grange, wines that 'can have a wonderful effect both on a company and a nation'. These contrasting views exposed the ongoing tension between the FMCG sector of the industry and the 'ultra-premium' sector – or, as a winery investor once defined them to me, the 'guzzle industry' and the 'sniff 'n' sip industry'.

What happened in the UK during the 2000s is that the guzzle industry won.

'That was the terrible sadness of the noughties,' says Oz. 'When the big boys stopped sending us the good stuff. We [the UK] still bring in more Australian wine than from anywhere else to this day, but so much of it now is second rate and has been for a long time because we won't pay the price. The big companies sell a lot more wine, but profitability goes out of it and so does pride and respect and all those other things.'

But history repeats. Just as the collapse of the export market in the 1950s and 60s helped expand Australians' interest in wine at home, so too did the bloated overemphasis on cheap-'n'-cheerful exports in the 2000s lead many Australian winemakers in the 2010s to focus instead on their own backyards, on making better, more interesting wines that would excite the local market. As a result, the last decade has seen an explosion of innovation, questioning and boundary-pushing that has re-energised the industry, bringing back a bright, burning excitement to the Australian wine scene – an excitement that can be seen from the other side of the world.

At the same time, a new export market for Australian wine has emerged, growing even more rapidly than the UK market did in its heyday of the late 1990s and early 2000s. Today, Australia has become less John Bull's vineyard and more the vineyard of the People's Republic of China.

———————————

It's autumn 2019 in the Yarra Valley, near Melbourne. Five wine-tasters stand behind some upturned barrels in a vineyard at TarraWarra Estate, sniffing and sipping chardonnay and pinot noir and talking about the wines. They're all speaking Mandarin.

The tasters are key opinion leaders flown over from China by giant online retailer Taobao: the group includes blind-tasting champion Adam Zhu and TV personality Tianfeng Yan. The event is being live-streamed to 600,000 people watching on their devices back in China: if they like what they see, viewers can order the wines through Taobao. And there in the middle of the group, glass of pinot in hand, is my 23-year-old daughter, Bridie, who has grown up surrounded by wine, learned Mandarin at school and university, and now sometimes works hosting events like this.

We've come a long way since the days of Oz and Jilly raving about Australian chardonnay on BBC2. This is how people are learning about Australian wines today in what has become Australia's biggest export market: a live broadcast and interactive shopping experience through their smartphone.

When I started writing about wine, many Australian producers told me China would one day become the greatest export market of all – despite very little evidence to back up their prediction. In 1995, the year Bridie was born, Australia shipped just 50,000 litres of wine to the People's Republic, worth about $100,000. This was less than one-tenth of 1 per cent of the amount shipped to the UK that year – a mere drop of wine that simply evaporated in a country as big as China. Exports grew in fits and starts through the late 90s and early 2000s as both the government bodies Austrade and Wine Australia and a growing number of Australian winemakers focused their efforts on China: shipments of 1 million litres in 2003 jumped to almost 4 million in 2005, then 20 million the following year. As remarkable as those figures are, though, it's the second half of the 2010s that was particularly breathtaking: in 2014 Australia shipped 40 million litres of wine worth $224 million to China; in 2019 we shipped around 150 million litres worth $1.2 billion. Australia became the largest supplier of wine by value in mainland China, and China is by far Australia's most important market.

As the livestreamed tasting demonstrates, and as my daughter has experienced for herself living in China at various times over the past few years, there are many reasons to be optimistic about the future prospects for Australian wine there. A vast and rapidly growing number of younger Chinese consumers are becoming genuinely interested in wine, and Australia's easily understood varietal labelling, fruit-driven styles and generally clean and green image all appeal to this demographic. Add to that the growing number of Chinese people who travel to Australia each year, either coming in as students or tourists, or to live and invest in the country, and you can see this cultural exchange deepening.

But there are also reasons to be cautious.

Despite the billion-dollar exports, despite the China–Australia Free Trade Agreement, despite the extraordinary success of Penfolds (by far the number-one Australian brand), the fact remains that Australia's – the world's – relationship with China has been and will continue to be volatile. Diplomatic relations are increasingly strained over Chinese human rights abuses, unlawful detention and interference in Australian domestic politics. The protests in Hong Kong tested global allegiances. The coronavirus pandemic sent economic shockwaves around the world, including through the Australian wine export industry. Who knows what the next five or ten years might hold?

And while the value of Australian wines into China is currently high, history tells us this could easily change: if the conditions are right, there is always the temptation for producers to dumb down, to sweeten up, to favour volume over quality. Look, for example, at Sweden: once an important destination for high-end Australian exports, now you can walk into a supermarket and buy 1-litre cartons of cheap shiraz labelled, believe it or not, Kangarouge.

'It never lasts,' says Oz Clarke. 'The pendulum is always swinging. In food and drink, something great is created and in our capitalist world people see a way to make more money. And the more you make of something, the less the quality.'

I press stop on my phone camera and Oz's grimace fades. He looks down at the sullen brown liquid in his glass. 'I have to say this wine hasn't actually got a single redeeming feature, except that it is what it is.'

He takes our glasses over to the sink and tips the Kanga Rouge down the drain, then holds each glass under running water for a little longer than is necessary, as though it needs extra rinsing.

'I've been looking at that bottle of wine for thirty years,' he says, bringing the clean glasses back to the table. 'Waiting for the right moment to open it. And now I have.'

'Well, I really, really appreciate you doing that.'

'Really? It's not often I give a man a really disgusting drink and he says he appreciates it.'

Oz puts the wineglasses down and picks up the corkscrew.

'Now. What shall we open next?'

Wine from native grapes?
Drinking in the future

The forest is thick on the New South Wales south coast. Tall eucalypts, knobbly banksias and straggly casuarinas crowd together in the sandy landscape. It's beautiful country. But I'm not here to admire the big gums and she-oaks. I'm here because of another plant that also thrives in this part of the world: a twirling vine with curving trunk and shiny green leaves that seems to be climbing up every other tree.

'This is Yuin country,' says Aboriginal Elder, educator and horticultural expert Noel Butler as we walk deep into the forest. 'Dad's family have always been here. We're Budawang people. Dad was born on a headland near Ulladulla. I was born here too, in 1949. Used to ride a horse into high school back when the place was all sawmills and dairy farms. We learned about the plants, what you could eat.'

Noel stops at a tree with a particularly abundant vine clinging to it, thick tendrils reaching for the upper branches. He puts down the bucket he's carrying and pulls out a small pair of secateurs. As his partner, Trish, and I watch, Noel reaches up into the green canopy and snips off a large bunch of what look like fat, glossy black grapes.

'There,' he says, handing me the bunch. 'Reckon they could make good wine?'

———

The first time I met Noel Butler was in late 2015, at the Rootstock wine and food festival in Sydney. The organisers of the festival had invited Noel and Trish to share their knowledge of Indigenous plants and food with the festivalgoers and the exhibiting wine-makers, brewers and distillers. *Dark Emu* author Bruce Pascoe was also a guest, and he introduced me to Noel. The first thing the Budawang Elder said to me was: 'Someone should make wine out of native grapes; they should come and visit me and I'll show them where to find them.'

I was stunned. I knew there were a couple of Australian forest fruits with the common name 'native grape'; I'd talked to a wine-maker in the past who'd toyed with the idea of fermenting these berries. But this was different. Here was an Indigenous man with knowledge of the native plants of his country with an invitation to collaborate.

The setting, Rootstock, was apt. The festival, then in its third year, had become a powerful magnet for the growing number of Australian drinks producers thinking differently about flavour, about their place in the country, about how best to eat and drink sustainably, and about building communities of other like-minded producers, consumers and communicators.

The brewers and distillers in that community had been turning to native ingredients for inspiration for a few years, using botanicals such as strawberry gum and pepperberry to flavour gin and vermouth, creating liqueurs from quandongs and riberries, using wattleseed in beer and whisky. This is one of the reasons why Bruce and Noel and Trish and other Aboriginal people had been invited to participate, to place Indigenous ingredients and culture at the heart of the conversation.

In contrast to the brewers and distillers, though, Australian winemakers have far fewer options when it comes to using Indigenous ingredients. According to the national research agency CSIRO, winemakers are restricted to using grape varieties imported from overseas because 'Australia has no native grape varieties suitable for winemaking'. Which made Noel's suggestion all the more startling: perhaps there *is* a species of 'native grape' out there that's suitable for winemaking – a species that researchers aren't aware of?

I wasn't the only one intrigued. Noel put the challenge out to other winemakers at Rootstock (proper, professional winemakers, as opposed to me, a backyard hobby fermenter), and Trish tells me when I visit her and Noel that they've had a lot of interest from people keen to explore the potential of native grapes in winemaking.

'But no-one's followed through,' she says, 'except you.'

———

After half an hour or so harvesting among the vines, the buckets Noel, Trish and I have brought with us are almost full of grapes. We've found plenty of ripe bunches within relative reach; there's lots more fruit high up in the branches.

It's an intriguing fruit. Yes, it looks like a black grape – cabernet, perhaps, or shiraz – but when you bite into it, it's mostly seed, surrounded by a thin layer of plum-like pulp, wrapped up in dark-purple skin – the most wine-grape-like bit – that stains your fingers a deep maroon. There's not a huge amount of flavour; it's slightly fruity, slightly vegetal, quite unfamiliar, tart, drying, astringent. No juice to speak of, either. And most berries leave a lingering, slightly acrid, peppery sensation on the tongue.

But the grapes that have been exposed to the sun and shrivelled a little taste quite different: the flesh is more dense, chewier, like dried goji berry, and has a deeper, richer, plum-like flavour. Still astringent, but less of the burn. When Noel talks of the old people walking through the bush and eating these grapes, he says it was probably these sun-exposed, slightly shrivelled berries they would have preferred. He suggests a good way of emulating the sun-dried effect would be to spread some of the grapes out on a baking tray and dehydrate them a bit in a low oven.

Noel emerges from behind a thick screen of vine leaves. 'This bloody plant needs controlling,' he says. 'Since they stopped burning the bush like my people used to, the place has been overrun with these vines. They're choking the bush.'

Finding a use for the fruit, then, is one way of bringing the native grape vine back into balance with its landscape – as well as being a potential commercial opportunity. Noel's deadly serious about this. 'I can see non-Aboriginal and Aboriginal people working together on this,' he says. 'It needs to be a joint thing: blackfellas and whitefellas working together.'

But he can also see the humour. 'Imagine blackfellas picking grapes in a national park and getting caught by a ranger,' he chuckles. '"We're making our own plonk now. Don't have to spend our pension on yours anymore!" Heh-heh. Aboriginals making their own grog. The wine industry will collapse …'

Suddenly, there's a loud crack from above and a branch comes crashing down through the canopy, aiming straight for Noel's head. He doesn't move – and the branch misses him. 'Ah,' says Noel, smiling. 'The creator's looking after me. The ancestors approve of what we're doing.'

Chemistry, on the other hand, is not on our side. When we get back to Noel and Trish's house in the bush, I pick a handful of berries off the stalk and crush them up in a jar. It's immediately apparent that, unlike shiraz or cabernet, these 'native grapes' don't release bountiful, readily fermentable juice when you squeeze them. Instead, they clump up into a squidgy, mucilaginous mass. Even if this gloopy, stubborn stuff did ferment, it probably wouldn't turn into something you could drink: no juice, no wine.

The answer to Noel's question, then – 'Reckon native grapes can make good wine?' – is no, probably not. Or, rather, not on their own. Not in the conventional winemaking sense, at least. But there are other ways they could perhaps be used to make other drinks.

———————

Turns out I'm not the first person to try to make wine from native grapes. In 1996, internationally renowned viticultural consultant Dr Richard Smart published a paper in the journal *Australian Grapegrower & Winemaker* outlining his experiments with the same species of vine, using fruit gathered in the bush next to the Mobbs family's Broken Bago vineyard near Port Macquarie, north of Sydney. Smart had come across mentions of various Australian species of vine distantly related to *Vitis vinifera*, the European wine grape, in the scientific literature, and was intrigued to see what opportunities these plants might offer to the Australian wine industry.

As soon as he started experimenting with the native grapes, he encountered the same problem I did – no juice – so he decided to make what's traditionally known as 'country wine'. In colder countries, such as England, where grapes are hard to ripen but other fruits such as blackberries and elderberries are abundant, people make country wine by mixing the berries with water, sugar and yeast. In his paper, Smart says he tried this technique, so the first thing I did when I got back to Melbourne with my buckets of native grapes was to use some of the fruit to make country wine.

I had no way of knowing what to expect, because Smart wrote his 1996 paper before the wine finished fermenting, and neither he nor winemaker Jim Mobbs can remember now what it tasted like. But when I called Jim to speak to him about the native grape experiment back in the 1990s, he recalled hearing about someone steeping the fruit in spirit. So, with the few kilos I had left, I did the same. At Noel's suggestion after we'd tasted the shrivelled berries off the vine, I dried some of the fruit out in a very low oven and then used both dried berries and fresh berries to make different batches of flavoured spirits: I steeped some in plain neutral-tasting vodka to see how the alcohol might extract the colour and flavour from them, and some in gin, with added sugar, in the tradition of English sloe gin, made using fruit foraged from hedgerows.

I also sent some of the grapes off to the Australian Wine Research Institute (AWRI). Noel was keen to have the fruit analysed: his practical and educational background in horticulture meant that he was curious about the chemical composition of the grapes. And the AWRI were keen to get involved. As Peter Godden, the institute's manager of industry engagement and application, told me, 'We have an important social licence to fulfil. There is an onus to get involved in projects like this.'

In 1996, Smart also sent some native grapes to the AWRI for testing. At the time, the person in charge of technical services at the institute was Peter Leske, the man who had handed me a taste of the briny *Salthouse* shipwreck champagne a couple of years before. Frustratingly, though, neither Smart nor Leske can remember what the results of those tests were, as both soon moved on to other projects.

It's not surprising, perhaps, that the native grape didn't pique the curiosity of anyone in the broader wine industry after Smart published his paper in 1996. As he wrote at the time, 'There is currently much written about "bush tucker" and its possibilities for commercial development [but] there is less consideration given to alcoholic beverages which might be made from Australian plants.'

———————

After arriving in Melbourne in 1992, I got the train into Flinders Street Station, the hub of the city, and walked up Swanston Street. One of the first shops I passed, a couple of doors along from the historic Young & Jackson hotel, was Nick's Wine Merchants, the CBD outpost of a business established in the late 1970s by Nick Chlebnikowski in his family's suburban supermarket.

Nick was an entrepreneur: he supported a lot of the boutique wineries emerging in Victoria in the 70s; sold high-end artisan foods in his shops; even set up an office in London to import fine Australian wines into England in the early 1980s (one of the bottles Oz Clarke opened after our disastrous Kanga Rouge experience in Putney was a delicious 1984 Yarra Yering cabernet Nick had imported). And when I walked past his Swanston Street store, there, on display in the window, were bottles of Nick's latest innovation:

Witjuti Bush Tucker liqueur, with labels sporting the 'genuine' signature of a mythical bush character, 'Boomerang Williams'.

'My father was interested in native foods in the early 1990s,' says Nick's son Yuri Chlebnikowski. 'I remember family Christmas one year, the business wasn't doing so well, we were looking for ways to diversify. Nick had been playing with witchetty grubs, making chocolates out of them, and one of my uncles said, why not put the grub in a bottle like the tequila producers do with the worm in the bottle? Everyone laughed and thought it was the stupidest idea ever. But the old man thought, why don't we give it a go?'

After a month or so of product testing and refinement, working out how to purge the grubs of their fat before steeping them in the right blend of sherry and brandy, Nick started selling the new product in his shops. There was a lot of interest in the city store, says Yuri, from passing tourists looking for Australian souvenirs: 'Billy Connolly came in and bought one. Somehow the Rolling Stones heard about it and ordered 100 of the bloody things. We were up all night, the whole family putting labels on bottles.'

The product lasted a little while longer but was deleted after the grubs became too hard to source. And while its kitsch value may have appealed to tourists, it failed to catch on with everyday Australian drinkers. I don't remember having the slightest desire to try it.

Almost twenty-five years later, Australian native fauna started appearing in bottles of booze again. Not witchetty grubs in sherry: green ants in gin. But this time, the product didn't feel like such a gimmick. It had been developed in a more thoughtful and respectful way. I was very keen to try it.

———————

The country around Darwin, in Australia's Northern Territory, is the traditional land of the Larrakia people. Daniel Motlop is a Larrakia man, former AFL star from a famous footy family, and general manager of Something Wild, an Adelaide-based Indigenous-owned food supply company. Daniel began to attract attention among the food media in 2015 when he and Something Wild business partner Richard Gunner took international superstar chef René Redzepi to the Top End and introduced him to magpie goose, edible green ants and other native ingredients that subsequently featured prominently on the menu at Redzepi's Noma pop-up restaurant in Sydney in 2016.

One of the drinks Noma had started serving a year or two before in Copenhagen was a gin distilled with ants. This inspired a handful of Australian distilleries to have a crack at making their own ant gin. One of them was the Adelaide Hills Distillery, which approached Something Wild to source green ants like the ones that had so excited Redzepi.

'But Richard (Gunner) asked me some simple questions that were a real eye-opener,' the distillery's Toby Kline told me when I interviewed him and Daniel for an article about the new gin in 2017. 'He said, "Are you doing the *right thing*? Are you sure that by using that traditional food, you aren't taking advantage of culture? Are you sure that you're contributing to the sustainability of that industry going forward?"'

To address these concerns a new joint-venture company, Something Wild Beverages, was formed to produce the gin, with Daniel and his family holding majority ownership, ensuring that control of the product, and profits from it, went back to the Aboriginal community from where and by whom the ants – *gulguk* in Larrakia language – were harvested.

'That's what it's about,' Daniel told me. 'A lot of people are selling Aboriginal ingredients and Aboriginal culture, but are they giving anything back? It's native Australian food. We think Aboriginal people should be reaping the rewards. My goal is to create jobs for Aboriginal people. I want to help Aboriginal people stay on their land and work, and to put money back into community.'

And the gin tasted extraordinary: when Daniel poured me a small glass and I took a sip – whack! – the formic acid from the green ants popped in the middle of my tongue like taut pearls of lime.

A few months later, I was sitting under a palm tree on the lawn in front of the Darwin Sailing Club, watching the sun go down over Fannie Bay. It's an early evening ritual for many Darwinites, and almost as popular with tourists as the nearby Mindil Beach Sunset Market. I was drinking a schooner of beer (of course I was) but not one of the big multinational-owned brands that dominate the taps in most Darwin bars. The golden fluid capturing the setting sun in my glass was the second product from Something Wild Beverages: a lager brewed using wattleseed. I posted a photo of this quintessentially Australian experience – drinking a beer incorporating native ingredients produced by a Larrakia-owned company on Larrakia country – on Instagram (of course I did) and Daniel Motlop, who was attending the Garma Indigenous Festival over in north-east Arnhem Land at the time, quickly replied, 'I need one.'

———

One of the reasons why drinks using Indigenous ingredients don't feel as exotic or gimmicky today as they did a generation ago is the now-widespread use of Indigenous ingredients in our food, particularly in high-end restaurants. Some of Australia's most famous chefs,

Jock Zonfrillo at Orana in Adelaide, Kylie Kwong in Sydney and Ben Shewry at Attica in Melbourne, have not only placed native flavours at the heart of their cooking, but have also gone out of their way to spend time with traditional owners, on country, learning about their food culture. Similarly, the best of the new wave of native-ingredient drinks, I think, are the ones that, like Something Wild's green ant gin and wattleseed lager, have a tangible connection to people and place.

On the east coast of Australia, in the Byron Bay hinterland, the Brook family have growing on their property many of the native botanicals they need to make their gins and liqueurs. As well as establishing a macadamia plantation in the late 1980s, the family revegetated 12 hectares of land with 35,000 subtropical rainforest trees. The forest is now home to many food plants, including native ginger and Davidson plum trees, which provide fruit for Brookie's Slow Gin, a tangy, spicy tribute to European sloe gin. And the macadamias, along with roasted wattleseed, are the hero ingredient in the distillery's newest product: a nutty, coffee-scented liqueur called Brookie's Mac. Trying this for the first time on the deck at the distillery, served straight over ice with a generous squeeze of lime, looking out over the macadamias and the rainforest and a sky painted orange with bushfire smoke, was an indelible Byron experience.

The Brook family's interest in native ingredients was cultivated by their friendship with local Indigenous chef Clayton Donovan, presenter of ABC TV's *Wild Kitchen* and founder of Byron Bay Wild Cider, a brand that features quandong and finger lime alongside apple and pear. During a visit to the farm in the late 2000s, Donovan went for a walk with Martin Brook and his son Eddie through their rainforest.

'I said to them: did you know you can eat that plant – and that one?' Clayton told me when I interviewed him in 2017. 'I gave them some insight into what I'd been taught, growing up around Nambucca Heads, walking through the bush with my aunties. I told them: it's not just a forest you've got here, it's a supermarket.'

In the tiny, remote central New South Wales town of Mendooran, forty-five minutes out of Dubbo, Brian Hollingworth of Black Gate Distillery also tapped into childhood memories to create one of the most remarkable native-ingredient drinks I've tasted. Black Gate is renowned for its powerful, rich single malt whiskies and rums: the barrels of new-make spirit are stacked up against the north-facing galvanised iron walls in the shed here so that the radiant heat creates what Brian calls 'a climate conducive to aggressive spirit maturation'. But Brian and his distiller partner, Genise, have also produced other drinks, including a liqueur and an eau de vie incorporating quandongs, or native peach – not because it was trendy, but because it just made sense.

'I grew up in Broken Hill,' Brian told me as he poured a glass of the liqueur in the cellar door at Black Gate. 'Born and bred. Worked in the mines, then as a tradie, then a machinist and then became a teacher, which is why I moved to Mendooran. Quandongs were a big thing in Broken Hill. Mum used to make quandong pies and quandong jam when I was growing up. There's heaps of them growing round here, so Genise and I decided to go and forage for them and make a liqueur with them.'

The liqueur is delicious, like a rich, raisiny, grown-up alcoholic Ribena. But the eau de vie, commissioned for René Redzepi's Noma pop-up in Sydney in 2016 and made by steeping quandong kernels in spirit, is even lovelier: delicate spice and candied-fruit aromatics, a lovely twist of bitter almond on the finish.

And in an old converted warehouse in the inner Sydney suburb of Marrickville, Texas-born brewer Topher Boehm is using a unique

Indigenous yeast culture to make some of his bold, barrel-aged Wildflower beers.

'I'd been wondering for a long time how brewers in the past got a good culture started before they could just go and buy whatever yeast they wanted,' Topher told me just before he launched his first beers in 2017. 'I knew that yeasts are everywhere in nature, on fruit on plants. So for the last couple of years I've gone out to various places around New South Wales with a few litres of wort and gathered cuttings of different plants – wattle, grevillea, blossoms – and put them into the wort to see if the wild yeasts and bacteria could give me a spontaneous fermentation.'

Most of these experimental wild brews produced beer that was not pleasant to drink: *too* feral, *too* sour. But a few turned out well – pretty funky, but within the bounds of good taste. So Topher took the yeast-rich slurry from those successful ferments, cultured it up and started using it in some of his brews, including one particularly vivid, fruity and refreshingly tart ale called Waratah, made from 100 per cent New South Wales ingredients: Riverina-grown barley and wheat, hops from Bemboka on the south coast, Indigenous yeast and souring bacteria foraged from wildflowers.

'Waratah epitomises our goals here at Wildflower,' said the brewer. 'The recipe was built on what was grown here, not on what we could order from international malthouses and hop fields. I mean, what does it really mean to be making beer in this country if you're not using all Australian ingredients?'

———————

Topher Boehm was inspired to use wildflowers to 'harvest' yeast because of similar techniques he'd seen other brewers using in the US. He wasn't aware when he started that there was also, as we've seen, a flower-ferment tradition in Aboriginal cultures, including the Noongar practice in Western Australia of steeping banksia flowers to produce mangaitch.

Nic Peterkin makes wine under the LAS Vino label in the Western Australian region of Margaret River. He has tried to make mangaitch, but it was unsuccessful – not enough nectar in the flowers, perhaps, or picked in the wrong season, or not the right species of banksia. But after tasting one of Topher's Wildflower beers and learning about his methods, he was encouraged to use similar yeast-harvesting techniques with wine.

During vintage in early autumn 2019, Nic took some freshly crushed pinot noir juice that had been given a short amount of skin contact, just enough to give the juice a faint rosé blush, and put it into two small fermenters. Into one he put white flowers gathered from trees in the bush near the vineyard; into the other red flowers, also gathered from the forest. The wines took longer to ferment than the 'control' – a standard pinot rosé fermented in barrel using wild yeasts on the grapes and in the vineyard and cellar – and produced quite different results: the white-flower ferment produced a more floral, citrusy, tangy wine with grapefruit-pith texture, while the red-flower wine was plumper, peachy, a bit oily, with a yeasty finish.

'An unintended yet beautiful consequence of fermenting with flowers', he says, 'is you start to notice them. You start noticing the different seasons and the bees. It makes you very aware of the environment around you.'

Nic's aunt is winemaker Vanya Cullen, whose parents, Kevin and Di, established one of Margaret River's first vineyards of the modern era, in 1971. Vanya isn't using Indigenous ingredients or techniques in her wines, but she is attempting to connect with Indigenous ways of thinking about land and belonging. And one of the ways she's doing that is by acknowledging the traditional owners on her wine labels.

As were her parents before her, Vanya is deeply concerned about the sustainability of her family's vineyard. She was instrumental in converting Cullen to certified organic and then biodynamic farming in the early 2000s, not just for environmental reasons, but also because she believes it is the best way to capture the taste of terroir in the wines made there.

The French concept of *terroir* – the idea that the flavour of something grown in a specific place can express the unique character of that place – has strong parallels with the Aboriginal notion of connection to country – the idea that people, plants, animals, land-scape and culture are all one. Coonawarra winemaker Sue Bell, who has Aboriginal heritage, explains that this concept of connection to country is easily grasped by the wine community.

'I think we have a strong spiritual connection to the places where we make wine,' she says. 'The health of the land and water is central to all our cultural activities: the land is your mother, you must care for it, you work with the land not on it, and every year when we make wine, it's a whole reflection of that. We already respect our sacred sites: think of how we talk about the beautiful soils of where I come from, in Coonawarra, or how we think of old vineyards like Hill of Grace. In the wine industry, we're already thinking and behaving in that way.'

She's not alone. A growing number of wine – and other drink – producers in Australia, like Vanya Cullen, have started acknowledging First Nations peoples not only on their labels but also whenever they tell the story of where they are and what they do. Winemaker Jeff Grosset in South Australia's Clare Valley was the first, in 2003, when he proposed using a word from the Kaurna people, traditional owners of much of the land around Adelaide, as a local alternative for terroir. The word he suggested was *pangkarra*. It describes a tribal band's defined territory that is passed on from father to son. Grosset mistakenly took the word to also mean the physical characteristics of a specific place, as terroir does, and although this wasn't quite correct, the idea was nonetheless revolutionary and is one that others, like Vanya Cullen, have subsequently taken up and developed further.

———————

In 2016, in Adelaide, the Australian Wine Industry Technical Conference, the country's largest regular gathering of the country's wine community, for the first time in its 48-year history began with an Aboriginal Welcome to Country. Kaurna man Michael O'Brien walked on stage at the Adelaide Convention Centre dressed in the traditional kangaroo skins of his people and, in front of more than 1100 delegates, spoke of his culture.

'We talk about a physical and spiritual connection to land,' he said. 'That when you walk this land it becomes a part of you and you become a part of it, and so therefore we share this land with you and you must share this land with us.'

O'Brien also talked Aboriginal fermentation, about how Kaurna people made tonics and alcoholic drinks by crushing and fermenting bitter quandong roots. His presence and his words set the tone for the first session of the conference, a discussion about terroir. Perhaps surprisingly, this was also the first time in the event's half-century history that the topic had been given such prominence.

'The time is right,' said winemaker Sue Bell as she introduced the session. 'It's been a pretty tough ten years in the Australian wine industry, and so we're seeking ways to validate our stories and sell ourselves better. We talk about this French word, terroir, on and on, and quite a few people have suggested we need an Australian [Aboriginal] word instead. But if you look at the original map of Aboriginal languages before colonisation, it's pretty hard to come up with one word.'

To demonstrate, Sue put up on the screen the Australian Institute of Aboriginal and Torres Strait Islander Studies map of Indigenous Australia: a patchwork of the hundreds of distinct language groups – such as Kaurna – that have existed before and since 1788.

'What this map shows is that different places in Australia had different practices in how they looked after the land or how they looked after themselves,' she said. 'If we want to harness this 40,000-plus years of human knowledge, perhaps we should think more about the concept of connection to country.'

One of those many different, well-defined places is Wonnarua country in the Hunter Valley. Former magazine art director Pete Windrim made a tree change and started working in the Hunter at his family's biodynamic vineyard, Krinklewood, in the early 2010s. The more time he spent in the vineyard, the more connected he felt to the spirit of the place.

'Biodynamics is all about trying to be in tune with your environment, reading the signs of the landscape, listening to it,' Pete told me for an article I wrote about the vineyard in 2017. 'I realised that the Aboriginal people around here, the Wonnarua, have been doing exactly that, on Wollombi Brook and the surrounding country, for thousands of years.'

Pete read *Dark Emu* and started discussing the history of the place with Elders. He was told that the hill above the river where the sun sets is the tail of the rainbow serpent; that the creator spirit, Baiame, is painted in a cave just over the ridge. So he made a new wine called River Blend, an unfiltered, cloudy, skins-fermented, apple-spicy blend of gewurztraminer and verdelho, grown on the bottom part of the vineyard, near Wollombi Brook. The back label reads: 'A toast to the Indigenous families that lived on this land before the Krinklewood family'.

When I sat down with Kaurna Elder Uncle Lewis O'Brien – Michael's father – in Adelaide, we talked about the parallels between the French concept of terroir and Aboriginal conception of country. I told him how winemakers, not just in France, but anywhere that grapes are grown and wine is made, soon learn to identify how different landscapes, and different parcels of land in each landscape, produce different flavours and qualities in the wine grown there. And how these subregions and vineyards and parts of vineyards would often have names given to them.

'That's what we do,' said Uncle Lewis. 'Everyone does it. It's a natural human thing to do when you're living on the land. You start to connect to it. It's that double possession: it possesses you, you possess it. And that's what we did, the same, every bit of country: you have to know that, that's what the secret is, you have to know all the places.'

So it makes sense, then, for Australian winegrowers to acknowledge the people who have been living in their country for countless generations?

'Yes, it does make sense. That's the interchange you want anyway. That's part of reconciliation and getting on with each other. I think we need to do that. It's important for country, how you build up mutual respect and use of country.'

———————

Winemakers, brewers and distillers aren't the only ones engaging with Indigenous culture. Scientists are also interested in finding out more about Aboriginal fermentation. The AWRI were keen to analyse the native grapes I harvested with Noel and Trish Butler, and when I visited the cider-gum trees in Tasmania to taste way-a-linah, I was tagging along with a group of three researchers who were there on a field trip.

Vladimir Jiranek is professor of oenology at the University of Adelaide and director of the Australian Research Council's Training Centre for Innovative Wine Production. He had read about way-a-linah and other examples of Aboriginal fermentation, and was curious about the microbiology involved in these processes. In 2016, after hearing Michael O'Brien talk about the Kaurna tradition of fermenting quandong roots, he initiated a research project into the subject. When Steve Cronin, the land management coordinator of the Tasmanian Aboriginal Centre, heard about the project, he invited Vlad and his group to sample some of the trees at *trawtha makuminya*. And when Vlad heard that I was writing about cider gums, he invited me along for the ride.

As we crisscrossed the frost plain at *trawtha makuminya*, moving from tree to tree, the researchers carefully held small sample tubes up to each trunk to capture some of the trickles; later, they took the samples back to Adelaide and analysed them. Since then, the team has gone on to take samples from cider-gum trees planted in other parts of Tasmania and in southern Victoria.

A year after the Tasmanian trip, I visited Vlad at the Wine Innovation Cluster building at the University of Adelaide's Waite campus and he took me through some of the preliminary results. The researchers had found that, as expected, the cider-gum sap contained sugars such as glucose, fructose and maltose, as well as organic acids and alcohol. Using DNA extraction and sequencing techniques, they had also discovered a very complex microbial population in the sap, including a number of as-yet-unidentified yeasts.

'We went to Tasmania hoping to find one perhaps one unknown yeast,' he said, 'and it looks like could end up finding loads, which is very exciting. This means there's a good chance we could find something useful for some sort of fermentation process. At the very least, it'll be great to report on a new species. I spoke about this at a scientific conference on yeast in Ireland recently and people were really excited about it, thought it was a fascinating topic.'

The key word there is 'useful'. As in *commercially* useful. Vlad has been careful to do the right thing with his research. At the beginning of the project, he said that his 'main interest is to reveal the huge scope and the wealth of accumulated knowledge of these [fermentation] processes ... that informed the Aboriginal people'. And in a later article he wrote that 'As our work progresses we will publish our findings and report back to the Aboriginal communities that have supported the study.'

But he also acknowledged there are commercial implications in his work, albeit limited in scope – certainly compared to the com-mercialisation of native plants in the pharmaceutical industry. For example, the cider-gum sap the researchers analysed contained almost no *Saccharomyces cerevisiae*, the yeast commonly used to ferment wine, beer and spirits around the world. But the non-*Saccharomyces* species in the sap did show 'interesting properties ...

including good growth at low temperatures – lower than is tolerated by non-*Saccharomyces* that are already sold for wine fermentation'. In other words, it might be possible to isolate and propagate a new, uniquely Australian yeast strain from way-a-linah that could then be sold to drinks producers.

And this is where it gets tricky.

Terri Janke is a highly respected Indigenous lawyer based in Sydney and a leading expert on the subject of Indigenous intellectual and cultural property. She has written extensively on how international and Australian laws intersect with customary Indigenous laws and traditional values, and how understanding this intersection can – and should – help Indigenous people both maintain ownership of and benefit from the non-Indigenous application of that knowledge.

In her paper 'From smokebush to spinifex: Towards recognition of Indigenous knowledge in the commercialisation of plants', Janke writes that 'plant knowledge [is] intrinsic to Indigenous identity and the legacy of tradition [but] the impact of sustained colonisation has meant that, as with the land, Indigenous people came to be seen as not owning their plant resources and plant knowledge', and that this has led to 'biopiracy, where Indigenous people's knowledge of plants has been taken without their consent'. As interest in Indigenous plants among researchers and companies grows, the need to protect Indigenous people's rights to resources and knowledge becomes more urgent. Currently, none of the existing environmental or intellectual property laws adequately or coherently affords that protection. There is an international agreement, the Nagoya Protocol, that provides a set of guidelines and standards in regard to traditional knowledge of genetic resources, but Australia has not yet signed up as a party to it. In response, Janke is calling for a national framework that empowers

Indigenous communities to license their cultural and intellectual property to third parties through well-defined consent, access and benefit-sharing agreements.

'Providing Indigenous people with the mechanisms to look after their own interests will enable self-determination,' she writes. 'As things stand, the current legal frameworks do not deliver self-determination.'

Which makes me wonder about my own 'research project' with Noel and Trish Butler, making drinks from native grapes. The whole adventure was initiated by Noel, an Indigenous man, but has proceeded on nothing more than mutual respect and a handshake: we haven't signed any formal agreement. This is partly because, from the beginning, I haven't been interested in any commercial outcomes. When it comes to making fermented drinks, I'm just an amateur, a backyard dabbler. I didn't do this because I want to sell wine made from native grapes. Or any kind of grapes for that matter. I've spent the last twenty-five years as a journalist believing it's a conflict of interest to profit from an industry you report on. When Noel threw down his original challenge, I responded solely out of curiosity, to see what a native grape drink might *taste* like and then write about the experience, not out of a desire to see how much money I could make from that drink.

But I'm not so naive to think that everyone's intentions are going to be equally respectful. I realise, and Noel and Trish realise, that there are people who might read these words and see dollar signs. Who might see native grapes as yet another Indigenous resource to be plundered.

I think I've been doing the right thing. But have I?

———

Now for the moment of truth. Eighteen months after our harvesting trip in the bush near Ulladulla, I sit down with Noel and Trish to taste the drinks I made using the fruit.

We try the country wine first. It's a pleasant, clear medium-pink colour in the glass. It looks like a rosé. It tastes like wine, too – although a lot of that is down to the fermentation esters and alcohol produced by the added sugar and yeast. It hasn't necessarily come from the fruit itself.

'That's nice,' says Noel, taking a sip. 'It tastes like a pinot … a pinot gris. I reckon that's agreeable. But not exciting.'

Surprising changes have happened to the wine over time. During and after fermentation, the texture was quite viscous and gloopy, like egg whites; Richard Smart also noted this viscosity in his experimental native-grape wine back in 1996. But after a year in bottle, it isn't viscous any more. What's more, as Trish points out, the peppery burn that characterises many of the fresh berries when you eat them is no longer present: the harsh sensation on the tongue when you bite into a native grape is caused by microscopic crystals in the fruit, and I suspect those crystals have fallen to the bottom of the liquid in the fermentation vessel.

Things get more interesting when I pour us all a small taste of the first flavoured spirit, made from fresh berries steeped in vodka. The liquid is a deep mulberry purple; the alcohol has sucked out all the colour from the berries. And where the spirit on its own smelled of not very much, the drink is now redolent of the flavour of the fruit – plummy, slightly vegetal, with an edge of tartness.

'Wow,' says Noel. 'You can taste the bloody grape all right. If you gave me a taste of that without telling me what it was first, I reckon I'd recognise the fruit straight away.'

The vodka flavoured with dried grapes is even better: a darker, denser purple with richer flavours less like the fruit itself and more like a liqueur, but with a character that's hard to describe because it's not quite like anything else.

'That's better than the one made with fresh grapes,' says Noel. 'It has more aroma.'

Trish's favourite, though, is the sloe-style spirit, made by steeping both fresh and dried grapes in gin: the predominant flavours are the botanicals used to make the gin, but the fruit has also given the drink a deep purple colour and a pleasant astringency to balance the sweetness.

'I like that,' she says. 'That's fabulous.'

Noel holds up his glass of deep purple liqueur and contemplates it.

'It's interesting that it's taken a stronger spirit to make it work,' he says. 'I reckon this has potential.'

So do I. And so does Peter Godden at the AWRI. The analysis of the grapes I sent him helped explain why the fruit struggled to ferment on its own: even if they had yielded more juice, the berries had relatively low levels of sugar and nutrient and very high levels of acidity. But he was fascinated by how the flavour of the berries lingered and evolved in his mouth after he'd tasted them. And he was excited about the anthocyanins in the fruit, the dark-pigment phenolics that give the grape skin – and the spirit in which the grapes steeped – its deep purple colour.

'It gives you a buzz, this research,' said Peter. 'I just think it's mind-blowing that we are creating new knowledge, and tasting flavours in drinks no-one has tasted before.'

It is mind-blowing. But the excitement of tasting these new flavours soon dissolves into a stream of questions about what happens next.

Noel threw down the challenge of making a drink from native grapes because he is passionate about non-Indigenous Australians embracing Indigenous food: 'We want Australian people to start using their own food. Today we use maybe a hundred varieties of different fruits and vegetables in Australia – and none of them originated in this continent. But there are *six thousand* edible plants in this country, which grow naturally, without any chemicals or fertilisers. We want people to start using *them* and growing *them*, for everybody's benefit.'

Two of the benefits, insists Noel, are financial and cultural: 'If everyone can buy native food from Aboriginal people as a first choice or provide some employment for Aboriginal people within the industry because of it, it's a great reconciliation process.'

To promote this, he and Trish have worked closely with chefs, including Ben Shewry from Attica, and have sold native ingredients to adventurous drinks producers such as Chris and Gab Moore of Sailors Grave Brewing in Orbost, East Gippsland. Topher Boehm of Wildflower brewing in Sydney is another keen collaborator. Noel and Trish also argue that encouraging Australians to embrace edible native plants is a way of acknowledging the countless generations of Aboriginal people who have nurtured those plants in the past.

'If they start eating the foods,' says Trish, 'they might start thinking more about the culture.'

'And the native grape is just another food,' says Noel.

True. But making *drinks* out of native grapes brings up particular issues. For a start, if the best use for this fruit is as a flavouring in strong spirits – rather than to make lower-alcohol wine – this could perhaps be seen as problematic.

'It's always been in the back of my mind,' says Trish, 'the whole alcohol thing. That it has ruined such a lot of Aboriginal lives – and here are Aboriginal people *making* alcohol. But, you know, someone is going to do it anyway. Why can't it be Aboriginal people? There are already other drinks being made using lemon myrtle and strawberry gum, and no Aboriginal person is getting any benefit from them.'

Daniel Motlop made a similar point when I interviewed him about his green ant gin. Was he concerned about the politics of using native ingredients to make alcoholic drinks? Did he see a problem in supporting Aboriginal communities by selling a product that has caused such harm in those communities?

'That's reinforcing a stereotype,' he told me. 'Everyone drinks, not just Aboriginal people. It's a stereotype if you say we *can't* make alcohol.'

Noel also points out that because we are using the native grapes in a non-traditional way, he's not revealing any sensitive traditional knowledge about the fruit.

'And anyway, these grapes came from my country,' he says. 'My knowledge about them is my intellectual copyright. And I want to share that knowledge and see what we can do with it. No-one has the right to tell me I can't teach or share whatever knowledge I have about something that's in my country.'

But he's also aware that by promoting the native grape, and by me collaborating with him and writing about that collaboration, he's potentially exposing yet another Indigenous resource to exploitation.

'Sure, a lot of people will want to just go and rip it off,' he says. 'When they read what you've written, they'll want to copy it. They'll say, "I'm into that. It's a product we can flog off and make money." But even if they did, even if someone else came up with a similar product, I would know that what *we* do is from *my* country. It's mine and that's on a cultural basis. And that is respected by all people with cultural value.'

Trish agrees: 'I believe that, because of the rise in cultural awareness now, people will want to buy Indigenous products from Indigenous people, I really do. They'll buy from others too, but there'll be a premium in something produced by Aboriginal people, from land that has been looked after the right way.'

Noel and Trish have thought about ways they can protect the intellectual property associated with a native grape drink. Noel suggests creating a name for it using existing Budawang language words – a new name for a new product that could then be protected by a trademark. And he and Trish talk about making the project part of Black Duck Foods, a company they are directors of, founded by Bruce Pascoe to help develop and commercialise Indigenous foods, as well as consulting with Elders, and lawyers like Terri Janke, about how to proceed.

Whatever happens with the project, though, Noel insists that he wants me to keep connected to it, in a joint venture. I'm the one who engaged with his original suggestion, he says, the one who made the trip to see him and Trish on country, the one who experimented with fermentation and maceration of the native grapes, the one who is now freely sharing the knowledge gained from that process. He'll make sure, he says, that I'm consulted.

It seems that I have crossed the line from observer to participant after all. And I don't quite know what that means. Or what happens next. But Noel does. He starts telling me about another kind of fruit that grows in the bush near him, with flavours that explode in your mouth. He reckons it could make an excellent liqueur.

'Could be equally as good as the native grape,' he says. 'Are you interesting in doing more experiments on other stuff, if we can get it to you?'

Maybe, I say, when I've finished writing this book.

'Okay, when you're ready,' says Noel. 'Because this is just the start. It could take another ten years to find the best thing to make the best drink. But what I think is if we get something that's really good there'll be a lot of interest, because it'll be different. And it'll be Australian.'

It's four years to the day, nearly, since Noel suggested that 'someone should make wine out of native grapes'. Three years since I stood under the canopy of a cider gum in Tasmania and tasted the light syrupy sap, glistening in the sunshine as it trickled from the tree. Over that time, I have learned so much about this country, about its fruits and flowers, about fermentation and drinking and history. But I can't help thinking this is just the beginning. That there is so much more to learn.

Postscript

A month after tasting the native grape drinks, the catastrophic bushfires that had been sweeping down Australia's eastern seaboard since spring 2019 reached the forests of southern New South Wales. Noel and Trish's place in the bush, where we'd gathered the grapes, was destroyed. They lost everything. Since then, helped by friends and family and many of the people who have collaborated with them over the years, they have begun the slow, difficult process of rebuilding and replanting. Once the forest starts bearing fruit again, we'll go back to making and sharing drinks.

All-Australian Negroni

Sydney, 2017

Just before Christmas 2015, Adelaide Hills winemakers and distillers Brendan and Laura Carter provided the final missing piece of a puzzle that had been consuming me for years.

Ever since the Australian craft gin renaissance kicked off in the early 2010s – followed by the release of the first modern Australian vermouths a couple of years later – I'd been hankering for someone to create a homegrown alternative to Campari so that I could start drinking an all-Australian version of that popular cocktail the Negroni: equal parts gin and red vermouth, and one part Campari. And the Carters' latest product, Okar, was exactly what I'd been waiting for: a bittersweet, dark-magenta *amaro* made using a bunch of native coastal rainforest botanicals including riberries, Davidson plum and strawberry gum.

I don't know why this had obsessed me so much. I'm not a big cocktail drinker, really. And I realise that yes, it would definitely be a greater achievement for someone to dream up and name a brand-new, truly Australian cocktail rather than one modelled on an international 'classic'. This is the endgame: a drink not-yet imagined, made using spirits, liqueurs, fruits and botanicals entirely sourced, fermented and distilled here, in this country, wrapped up in our cultural connections.

But with the arrival of Okar, I felt that, for now, being able to make a drink as famous as the Negroni without having to rely on ingredients produced overseas by multinational drinks companies was in itself still some kind of satisfying milestone – as well as a vote of confidence in the rapidly expanding and fast-maturing Australian winemaking, brewing and distilling community.

So when I was asked to speak about Indigenous fermentation and the new wave of interest in Indigenous ingredients at the Rootstock wine and food festival in Sydney in late 2017, I thought it would be a good idea to give everyone who came to the talk an All-Australian Negroni to sip while they listened to me prattle on.

It was – is – a pretty full-on cocktail. One part Something Wild Green Ant Gin, featuring citrus flavour explosions of gulguk and the richness of *boobiala*, native juniper. One part Maidenii Sweet Vermouth, blended by a French-born winemaker in central Victoria using herbal, savoury, earthy botanicals such as sea parsley, river mint and wattleseed. And one part Okar, with all its punchy, bitter, eucalypt-laced rainforest fruits.

The drink was *intense* – vivid, with layer upon layer of uniquely Australian flavours and tastes, from round and sweet to edgily astringent, menthol-pungent to citrus-sour, like a deep-purple psychedelic dream of flying through country, your senses heightened and alert to all the scents around you.

As I drained my glass, it struck me that this cocktail could not have been made even as recently as a decade ago: none of the three components existed then. I thought about how far we've come in such a short amount of time. And then I remembered a conversation I'd had with influential veteran Yalumba winemaker Peter Wall, and realised that this drink was, of course, just the latest development in a much, much longer Australian tradition.

I was talking with Peter about Yalumba's history of developing innovative products like Ver-Gin and Niblik back in the 1920s and 30s. I told him that one of the reasons I was writing this book was the growing interest among modern Australian drinkers in a much broader range of drinks than their parents drank, from cocktails to craft beer, from novel spirits to natural wines.

'And I think that's great,' he said. 'We're getting back to where we *were* in many ways. I'm not sure what happened in the meantime.'

Further reading

Abbott, E, *The English and Australian Cookery Book: Cookery for the Many, as Well as for the 'Upper Ten Thousand'*, Sampson Low, Son & Marston, London, 1864.

Allen, M, *The History of Australian Wine: Stories from the Vineyard to the Cellar Door*, Victory Books, Melbourne, 2012.

——'Not Forgetting Yous at All', in *Oil Paint and Ochre: The Incredible Story of William Barak and the de Purys*, Yarra Ranges Regional Museum, 2015, p. 29.

——'Vineyard of the Empire', *Tablet to Table*, 1(7), 2013, p. 315.

Beckett, J, '"I don't care who knows": The songs of Dougie Young', *Australian Aboriginal Studies*, 2, 1993, pp. 34–8.

Benwell, WS, *Journey to Wine in Victoria*, Pitman, Melbourne, 1978.

Bock, M, 'Inebriating beverages of the Indigenous Australasians', *Eleusis*, 6–7, 2002–03, pp. 127–40.

Brady, M, *First Taste: How Indigenous Australians Learned About Grog*, Alcohol Education & Rehabilitation Foundation, Canberra, 2008.

——*The Grog Book: Strengthening Indigenous Community Action on Alcohol*, Commonwealth Department of Health and Family Services, Canberra, 1998.

——*Teaching 'Proper' Drinking? Clubs and Pubs in Indigenous Australia*, ANU Press, Canberra, 2017.

Brady, M, & V McGrath, 'Making *tuba* in the Torres Strait Islands: The cultural diffusion and geographic mobility of an alcoholic drink', *Journal of Pacific History*, 45(3), 2010, pp. 315–30.

Caillard, A, *The Rewards of Patience*, Hardie Grant, Melbourne, 2013.

de Castella, H, *John Bull's Vineyard*, Sands & McDougall, Melbourne, 1886.

Clarke, O, *Webster's Wine Guide 1989*, Mitchell Beazley, London, 1988.

——*Red & White: An Unquenchable Thirst for Wine*, Little, Brown, London, 2018.

Deutsher, K, *The Breweries of Australia: A History*, Beer & Brewer Media, Sydney, 2012.

Dingle, A, '"The truly magnificent thirst": An historical survey of Australian drinking habits', *Historical Studies*, 19(75), 1980, p. 227–49.

Duncan-Kemp, A, *Our Sandhill Country*, Angus & Robertson, Sydney, 1934.

Dunstan, D, *Better than Pommard! A History of Wine in Victoria*, Australian Scholarly Publishing, Melbourne, 1994.

——'A sobering experience: From "Australian Burgundy" to "Kanga Rouge": Australian wine battles on the London market 1900 to 1981', *Journal of Australian Studies*, 17(2), 2002 (pub. 2004), pp. 179–210.

Dunstan, K, *The Amber Nectar: A Celebration of Beer and Brewing in Australia*, Penguin Books, Melbourne, 1987.

Evans, L, *Cellarmaster Says ...: A Revised Guide to Australian Wines*, The Bulletin, Sydney, 1968.

Fitzgerald, R, & T Jordan, *Under the Influence: A History of Alcohol in Australia*, HarperCollins, Sydney, 2009.

Flannery, T, (ed.), *The Birth of Sydney*, Text Publishing, Melbourne, 1999.

Gately, I, *Drink: A Cultural History of Alcohol*, Gotham Books, New York, 2008.

Gilling, T, *Grog: A Bottled History of Australia's First 30 Years*, Hachette, Sydney, 2016.

Halliday, J, *A History of the Australian Wine Industry 1949–1994*, Winetitles, Adelaide, 1994.

Humphries, G, *The Slab: 24 Stories of Beer in Australia*, Beer is Your Friend, Woonona, 2017.

Janke, K, 'From smokebush to spinifex: Towards recognition of Indigenous knowledge in the commercialisation of plants', *International Journal of Rural Law and Policy*, 2018:1, pp. 1–37.

Kelly, W, *Booze Built Australia*, Queensland Classic Books, Brisbane, 1994.

Laffer, H, *The Wine Industry in Australia*, Australian Wine Board, Adelaide, 1949.

Lake, M, *Cabernet: Notes of an Australian Wineman*, Rigby, Adelaide, 1977.

——*Classic Wines of Australia*, Jacaranda Press, Sydney, 1966.

——*Hunter Winemakers*, Jacaranda Press, Sydney, 1970.

——*Vine and Scalpel*, Jacaranda Press, Sydney, 1967.

Langton, M, 'Rum, seduction and death: "Aboriginality" and alcohol', *Oceania*, 63(3), 1993, pp. 195–206.

Linn, R, *Treading Out the Vintage: Oral History Project*, National Wine Centre, Adelaide, 2003.

McCarthy, L, *The Australian Spirits Guide*, Hardie Grant, Melbourne, 2016.

McGovern, P, *Ancient Brews: Rediscovered and Re-created*, WW Norton & Company, New York, 2017.

McIntyre, J, *First Vintage: Wine in Colonial New South Wales*, NewSouth Publishing, Sydney, 2012.

McIntyre, J, & J Germov, *Hunter Wine: A History*, NewSouth Publishing, Sydney, 2018.

McIntyre, J, M Brady & J Barnes, '"They are among the Best Workers, Learning the Ways of a Vineyard Quickly": Aboriginal People, Drinking, and Labor in the Early Australian Wine Industry', *Global Food History*, 5:1–2, 2019, pp. 45–66.

McKnight, D, *From Hunting to Drinking: The Devastating Effects of Alcohol on an Australian Aboriginal Community*, Routledge, London, 2002.

Nanni, G, & A James, *Coranderrk: We Will Show the Country*, Aboriginal Studies Press, Canberra, 2013.

Nash, M, 'The First House and the Hop Farm', *Locating Suburbia: Memory, Place, Creativity*, UTSe Press, Sydney, 2013, pp. 34–52.

Neill, R, 'Blackfella Wine', *The Weekend Australian Magazine*, 24 Aug, 2002, p. 10.

Norrie, P, *The History of Wine as a Medicine: From Its Beginnings in China to the Present Day*, Cambridge Scholars Publishing, Newcastle-Upon-Tyne, 2019.

Oliver, S, *Chateau Chunder: A Wine Revolution*, Electric Pictures, 2012.

Pascoe, B, *Dark Emu*, Magabala Books, Broome, 2014.

Pearce, H, *The Hop Industry in Australia*, Melbourne University Press, Melbourne, 1976.

Poliness, G, *Jimmy Watson's Wine Bar*, Grapevine Press, Melbourne, 1989.

Roach, A, *Tell Me Why: The Story of My Life and My Music*, Simon & Schuster, Sydney, 2019.

Roberts, I, & D Baglin, *Australian Wine Pilgrimage*, Horwitz Publications, Sydney, 1969.

Robin, L, C Dickman & M Martin, (eds), *Desert Channels: The Impulse to Conserve*, CSIRO Publishing, Melbourne, 2010.

Smith, K, M Langton, R Chenhall, P Smith & S Bawden, *The Alcohol Management Plan at Pormpuraaw, Queensland, Australia: An Ethnographic Community-based Study*, University of Melbourne & Foundation for Alcohol Research and Education, Melbourne, 2019.

Staniforth, M, 'The wreck of the *William Salthouse*, 1841: Early trade between Canada and Australia', *Urban History Review*, 28(2), 2000, pp. 19–32.

Strahan, F, (ed.), *The Core of the Apple: The Memoirs of George McGowan, Cider Maker, 1892–1982*, University of Melbourne, 1982.

Symons, M, *One Continuous Picnic: A Gastronomic History of Australia*, Melbourne University Press, Melbourne, 2007.

Walker, C, *Buried Country: The Story of Aboriginal Country Music*, Verse Chorus Press, Portland, 2014.

Wondrich, D, 'The Rebirth of an Essential Cocktail Ingredient', *The Daily Beast*, 6 Oct 2017, <https://www.thedailybeast.com/the-rebirth-of-an-essential-cocktail-ingredient>.

Wright, J, *The Generations of Men*, ETT Imprint, Sydney, 1999.

Acknowledgements

First of all, I'd like to thank Maggie Brady. If I hadn't read Maggie's work on Indigenous fermentation and been inspired to learn more about it, both through her writing and through conversations with her, this book simply wouldn't have taken shape.

I have been similarly encouraged along the way by Bruce Pascoe and Julie McIntyre: their contributions and help have been invaluable. Without Noel Butler and Trish Roberts and their boundless curiosity and enthusiasm, the book would have no final chapter: thank you. And to my publisher Sally Heath, editors Katie Purvis and Sam Palfreyman and the team at Thames & Hudson Australia: you have done a fantastic job, patiently and doggedly working to bring this at times stubborn project to fruition.

I'd like to thank my family, particularly Sophie, whose insight and guidance and editorial problem-solving has been invaluable, and Bridie and Riley, who've had to live through what ended up being a four-year saga, and who were there to provide support and consoling cocktails along the way. And to Jim, my father-in-law, whose gift of a case of wine to my mum more than thirty years ago planted the seed that has now grown into a full-blown obsession.

Huge thanks, too, to all the other people who have helped with historical information, poured delicious drinks, provided hospitality, shared insights and given advice over the last four years and more: Wondimu Alameo; Sue Bell; Mike Bennie, Giorgio de Maria,

James Hird and all the Rootstock crew; Topher Boehm; Jean Paul Bourguignon; Ross Brown; Justin Buckley and the gardeners at Rippon Lea Estate; Andrew Caillard; Georg Camorra; Oz Clarke; Richard Cornish; Seb Costello; Clive Crossley; Bryan Currie; the de Pury family of Yeringberg; David Dunstan; Jackie Dutton; Pearl Eatts; Peter Godden and Mark Krstic of the AWRI; Tom Griffiths; Tom Hearn of Bush TV; Euan Hills at Art Mob; Terri Janke and Charisma Cubillo of Terri Janke and Company, Lawyers and Consultants; Vladimir Jiranek; the Kinross Arts Centre; Matt Kirkegaard and Pete Mitcham of *BrewsNews*; Marcia Langton and her colleagues, Kristen Smith and Shane Bawden; Gilles Lapalus and Shaun Byrne of Maidenii Vermouth; Peter Leske; John Lewis; Iola Mathews at Glenfern Writers' Studios; Luke McCarthy; Hazel Murphy; Uncle Lewis O'Brien; Tracy O'Shaughnessy; Stephen Oliver; Rob Pelletier; Nic Peterkin; Richard Piper; Mick Quilliam; Sebastian Reaburn; Mary Ryan; Andry Sculthorpe; Bill Seppelt and Chad Elson at Seppeltsfield; Reid Sexton and Claude Nyaguy and the team at CUB; Ben Shewry; Dr Richard Smart; James Smith of the *Crafty Pint*; Gail Thomas; the Wandin family and Tony d'Abbs at Coranderrk.

Some of the stories and interviews in this book originally appeared in different form in various publications, including the *Australian Financial Review, Gourmet Traveller, Gourmet Traveller WINE, jancisrobinson.com* and *The Australian*.